MW00910215

HANDS-ON HYPERCARD™
Designing Your Own Applications

Mimi Jones
Dave Myers

WILEY

John Wiley & Sons, Inc.
New York • Chichester • Brisbane • Toronto • Singapore

For my mother and father—M.J.

For my kids—D.M.

RELATED TITLES OF INTEREST FROM WILEY

MASTERING HYPERTALK, Weiskamp and Shammas

PROGRAMMING WITH MACINTOSH TURBO PASCAL, Swan

DESKTOP PUBLISHING WITH PAGEMAKER FOR THE MACINTOSH, Bove and Rhodes

ASSEMBLY LANGUAGE PROGRAMMING FOR THE 68000, Skinner

Publisher: Stephen Kippur
Editor: Therese A. Zak
Managing Editor: Ruth Greif
Editing, Design, and Production: Publication Services

This publication is designed to provide accurate and authoritative information in regard to the subject matter covered. It is sold with the understanding that the publisher is not engaged in rendering legal, accounting, or other professional service. If legal advice or other expert assistance is required, the services of a competent professional person should be sought. FROM A DECLARATION OF PRINCIPLES JOINTLY ADOPTED BY A COMMITTEE OF THE AMERICAN BAR ASSOCIATION AND A COMMITTEE OF PUBLISHERS.
We have attempted to verify trademark information where possible or to print terms with proper capitalization and punctuation. Validity of trademark information can be obtained from the holder of the material.

Copyright © 1988 by John Wiley & Sons, Inc.

All rights reserved. Published simultaneously in Canada.

Reproduction or translation of any part of this work beyond that permitted by section 107 or 108 of the 1976 United States Copyright Act without the permission of the copyright owner is unlawful. Requests for permission or further information should be addressed to the Permission Department, John Wiley & Sons, Inc.

Library of Congress Cataloging-in-Publication Data

Jones, Mimi.
   Hands-on hypercard.

   Bibliography: p.
   1. Macintosh (Computer)—Programming. 2. HyperCard (Computer program) I. Myers, Dave. II. Title.
QA76.8.M3J66   1988   005.265   88-20464
ISBN 0-471-61513-7   (pbk.)

Printed in the United States of America

88 89 10 9 8 7 6 5 4 3 2

Contents

Foreword

In 1984, shortly after the introduction of the Macintosh, Bill Atkinson showed me a program he was working on, which he called "WildCard." It was sort of a super MacPaint program, but one that worked on a number of pages at a time like a deck of cards, rather than on just a single page. And it had text fields, like a database, so you could put text on each card and look it up later. Conceptually, the program was (at that point anyway) a cross between a Rolodex® and MacPaint.

But, of course, that was not nearly enough for Bill. He talked about all the other things he was going to do with WildCard—like give it the capability to go from any card to any other card by simply clicking a button, and playing music or dialing a phone, also with a single click on a button. But more importantly, Bill said, the information in a stack of cards could be vast. I realized then that he wasn't thinking about personal phone lists or calendars, he was thinking in terms of a card catalog of a city library or a complete encyclopedia, all with point-and-click access.

The next time I saw the program was nearly a year later, when I joined the WildCard team as its product manager. During the next two years a number of creative and enthusiastic people also became part of the team—writers, trainers, artists, programmers, testers, marketing people—all of whom helped shape HyperCard into what it is today. And throughout that whole period we had one clear thing in common: *We didn't know what we were making, but we knew it was going to be great.*

One of our guiding principles was that WildCard should be designed for people who didn't want to figure out how to make a computer work in order to make the program work for them (which, by the way, is the same principle that guided the development of the Macintosh). The Macintosh opened up computers to a whole new group of people through its intuitive graphic interface and consistent use of the desktop metaphor. That, in turn, started a mild revolution in information access because suddenly computers were no longer the tools of cloistered, intimidating "computer professionals." The Macintosh opened the world of information to anyone. Text, pictures, and sound in digital form could be displayed on the Macintosh screen, or played by its sound system. And here we were with WildCard, the program that would make getting to that information as easy as, well . . . , as easy as working with the Macintosh. There were so many ways to go, so many things we could apply Wild-Card to. In fact, the broad nature of WildCard's capabilities caused us a real dilemma: What should we call the program to reflect the different things it could do?

We tried a lot of different names. The way WildCard linked any piece of information to any other piece of information reminded us of Ted Nelson's Hypertext concepts, so for awhile we called it a hypermedia system. Not a very catchy name, so we looked for some particular capability to emphasize. Its rich mixing of text and graphics and sound made it a great multimedia education tool. The speed and capacity of its text storage and retrieval made it an ideal text database. Its powerful object-oriented programming language made it just right for developing applications or courseware, but the language was easy enough to learn that it was a superior user programming tool too. And the fact that we were giving it away free with every Macintosh made it an excellent universal information distribution delivery medium. Given all the things it could do, what could we call it?

We finally realized that it would be foolish to limit people's perceptions of the program because of a name, so going back to the concept of hypermedia, and information like a stack of cards, the name became HyperCard.

I look at HyperCard in two contexts: first, as what it can do for people, and second, how it fits into the evolving nature of computing in general. From the "people perspective" what makes HyperCard great is the same thing that makes personal computers great: They both put the power of information into the hands of ordinary people, and they both make that power usable.

But in its own way, HyperCard is also a whole new kind of computer. And that is the evolutionary context of HyperCard. When we brought out the Apple II in 1977, it changed the way people thought about computers and programs because the computers were at a personal scale and available on the consumer market. In 1983 and 1984, with the Lisa and Macintosh, we made computers and applications even more usable to more people through the use of a consistent and graphic user interface. And in 1987 with HyperCard, we brought the power of rich, interconnected media, the power of object-oriented programming, and the power of fast access to huge amounts of information to millions of Macintosh users.

I'm proud to have worked on all three projects. And as I look at what Apple is planning for the future, I see HyperCard breaking the ground for the structure of future computing because the volume of information available to us is only going to increase. As more information comes flooding into the office, school, and home, over cables and telephones and satellites, you'll absolutely have to have computers to help you navigate through large quantities of data to find the information you need. Furthermore, as the information moves beyond text and graphics into video, speech, and animation (and forms that we can't even envision yet), you'll need computers to create and manipulate those media. Finally, as the technology options themselves become daunting in their number and complexity, you will need computers simply to figure out the equipment you need to stay abreast of the tide of information. Where does Hyper-Card fit in all this? HyperCard is a good running start to stay in the race of information awareness.

That's why HyperCard is a program for both today and tomorrow, and why you need to learn it as a hands-on tool. Mimi Jones, a member of the HyperCard training team, has expanded the training she did here at Apple to give you your hands-on start with HyperCard. Her book, *Hands-On HyperCard*, takes you through HyperCard's richness step by step, making each feature useful and productive each step of the way. The approach is entertaining and enlightening, and it should help you get started using HyperCard to browse through other people's stacks and ultimately to customize or create your own. You'll find that this won't just make HyperCard more useful to you; it will make your Macintosh more valuable as well. What more could you ask for? Happy Stacking!

—Chris Espinosa

How to Use This Book

If you know how to point and click with your Macintosh and use pull-down menus, you'll have no trouble using this book to learn HyperCard.

The purpose of *Hands-On HyperCard* is to teach you how to create your own Macintosh applications, and to do so as quickly as possible without skipping over any important points that you can't live without.

Why this book? Doesn't the HyperCard manual teach you to use HyperCard? Well, yes and no. Although the HyperCard manual tells you how to use HyperCard, it doesn't tell you what you can do with it. That's this book's job. *Hands-On HyperCard* not only shows what you can do, it also teaches you how to develop practical applications. You'll learn some tricks, some good ways of working, and some secrets, but most of all you'll learn how to get some practical work out of this simple-to-use, yet complex, product. You'll learn using step-by-step instructions on real projects.

This book takes a "learn as you do" approach. Rather than telling you about every tool available from a menu, it tells you how to use a tool only when you need to use it. That way, you won't get bogged down trying to memorize how a tool is supposed to work before you even need it.

More importantly, this book is intended for the quick study or fast learner. It does not take up time giving you precious (but generally irrelevant) details about the intricacies of HyperCard. It's more of a workbook. By following the step-by-step instructions, you'll get up to speed in almost no time at all.

This book is divided into three parts: Beginner, Intermediate, and Advanced. Turn to the Beginner section if you are new to HyperCard and need to know how to navigate through stacks or become familiar with the basic principles. Turn to the second section, Intermediate Applications, if you are already familiar with HyperCard but need to know more about the paint, field, and button tools to get started creating your own applications. If you just want to learn about HyperCard programming, read the Advanced Applications section.

Each section includes its own step-by-step instructions for creating several different kinds of applications. You'll build on your knowledge of HyperCard as you complete the lessons.

An important note: Stacks created with HyperCard version 1.2 may not work with HyperCard version 1.0.1 or 1.1. If those stacks include any of the commands, abbreviations, or functions new in version 1.2, they will not run properly and you may get error messages. However, any stacks created with an earlier version of HyperCard will work just fine with version 1.2.

ACKNOWLEDGMENTS

Writing and producing any technical book, especially a computer book, usually involves a lot of people. *Hands-On HyperCard* is no exception. A number of people contributed to this book, supported us, and worked to make sure that this book is technically accurate and covers the right topics.

A special thanks to

—Chris Espinosa, the original HyperCard product manager at Apple, for his friendship and enthusiasm for HyperCard and this book.

—Susan Richardson and Maurilia Flores in Apple's Training Department, for the opportunity to work with HyperCard from the very beginning.

—Olivier Bouley in Apple's International Department of the thorough and enlightening technical review.

—Colette Kehoe, who under constant pressure managed somehow to test each instruction on each page of the entire manuscript.

To Danny Goodman, Craig Sheumaker, Janet Tokerud, Cynthia Kolnick, Elaine Winters, Monica Ertel, Peter Martin, Mike Westphal, and the good people at Activision: Thanks for sharing your HyperCard stacks and letting them be part of this project.

Several people answered questions, offered advice, and generally lent their support for this book, and to them, a heartfelt thank you: in particular, David Smith, David Leffler, James Redfern, Mike Holm, Dan Shafer, Sioux Lacy, Bryan Carter, Cathy Zier, and Steve Maller.

And finally, thank you to Teri Zak, the John Wiley editor for the book. Without her professionalism and ability to keep under control in the face of impossible schedules, this book would have never become a reality.

Introduction

WHAT IS HYPERCARD?

Let's get this out in the open right away. Apple describes HyperCard as a personal tool kit, a nondescript name if ever there was one. Apple created HyperCard for a good reason. HyperCard is *Apple's clever way of getting nonprogrammers to program the Macintosh.*

Uh-oh, you might say, programming (groan). WAIT! Don't jump to conclusions—the whole point of HyperCard is to take programming out of the hands of a select few and make it easy for the rest of us. You know those buttons, like OK and Cancel, that you click? Well, one feature of HyperCard shows how to create ones that will to do whatever you want. And those dialog boxes that appear? Another quick HyperCard feature shows how to create them as well.

In other words, with HyperCard you're no longer limited to buying Macintosh programs in the store. Now you can create your own without having to learn programming or spend long, sleepless nights writing programming code. You don't even have to wear horn-rimmed glasses. HyperCard finally opens up the Macintosh so us everyday folks can make it do what we want.

Sure, you don't actually have to know how to create stacks to use HyperCard. You can use it just to look at stacks of information that other people have made and to enter your own information into them. But once you see how easy HyperCard is to use, you won't be content just to sit on the sidelines using other people's stacks. You'll be in there with the rest of them, creating stacks to suit your needs.

HyperCard is best suited to create applications *for collecting and organizing information* such as client names, addresses, and phone numbers.

Okay, so HyperCard is for programming the Macintosh. Then what's all this about "stacks" and "cards" and "organizing information"? Those terms refer to HyperCard's data base features.

1

A HyperCard file is like a book (see Figure I.1). Each page has different words and pictures, yet together they have one purpose: to tell you a story, for example. But instead of reading pages, you read cards. A card is one screenful of information—no more, no less. And, instead of turning pages, you click on buttons to get from one card to the next.

The "books" you create with HyperCard are called **stacks**. A stack is a set of cards like index cards. Like books, stacks can provide information. But stacks can do much, much more. Among other things, they can play music, provide animation, and dial your telephone.

With HyperCard, you can do simple things like put names and addresses from your little black book into a stack. In fact, one of the many stacks that comes with HyperCard is an address book, or Rolodex® stack (see Figure I.2). It is like a form. You just type in the names and addresses, one name and address per card.

Each card is the size of a Macintosh Plus or SE screen. Text, fields, buttons, and graphics are all pieces of information on cards. You can create and assemble these pieces with tools available from HyperCard menus.

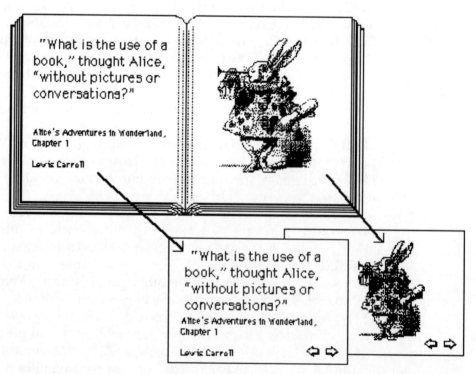

Figure I.1 A HyperCard file is like a book. Each page is equivalent to one card in HyperCard.

Figure I.2 A stack is a set of cards like a Rolodex® of names and addresses.

Fields are boxes in which you type text. They can be transparent or they can have plain or fancy borders (see Figure I.3).

Buttons are objects you click on to make something happen (see Figure I.4). For example, buttons can take you to another card or stack, play music, perform calculations, and sort cards.

Click on a paint tool to paint patterns on the screen, draw a line, or create other freehand artwork.

Once you know how to use these and other HyperCard tools, you can easily create useful applications.

What else makes HyperCard special? The ability to link one piece of information to another, from one card to another. This feature also lets you move quickly from one stack to another when searching for information (See Figure I.5).

And for those who want to program, HyperCard includes a programming language called HyperTalk. It is a high-level language with over 300 key words and phrases. Once you learn HyperTalk, you can add programs to objects such as buttons and fields.

How you store information in HyperCard is up to you. HyperCard gives you all the tools you need: a field tool for creating fields, a button tool for creating buttons, a paint palette for creating graphics, and a

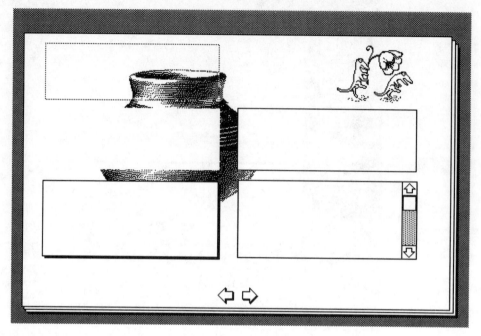

Figure I.3 Fields can have different styles but are always rectangular.

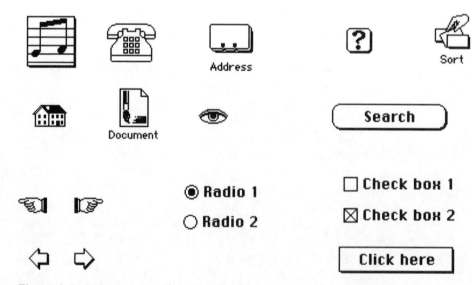

Figure I.4 Buttons can have different styles that include text and pictures.

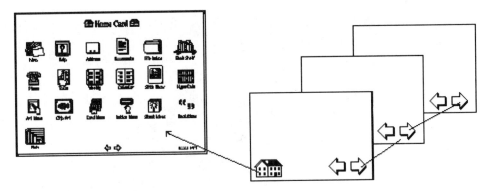

Figure I.5 Use buttons to link stacks together.

simple yet powerful programming language. You can learn how to use these tools at your own pace. And you can create stacks without even learning about HyperCard programming.

WHAT YOU CAN DO WITH HYPERCARD

HyperCard is useful for collecting and organizing large volumes of information in ways that make sense to you. For instance, most people will organize their address stacks by name, but you could just as easily organize yours by good clients, hot prospects, or heavy dates. Because you can organize information according to your own way of looking at it, you won't get bogged down sifting through hundreds of cards to locate specific information. HyperCard's **Find** command gives you fast access to any piece of information in any stack. What's more, you can link your cards in any way you like for faster retrieval.

The following stacks are samples of what you can do with HyperCard.

Electronic Atlas

You can have the world at your fingertips by creating an electronic atlas with HyperCard. (The stack pictured in Figure I.6 is called BusinessClass. It was created by Danny Goodman and is being distributed by Mediagenics (formerly Activision, Inc.). Beginning with a map of the world, you click on any country about which you need information.

Then you click on any one of a series of buttons listed along the bottom of the screen to see detailed information about that country (see Figure I.7).

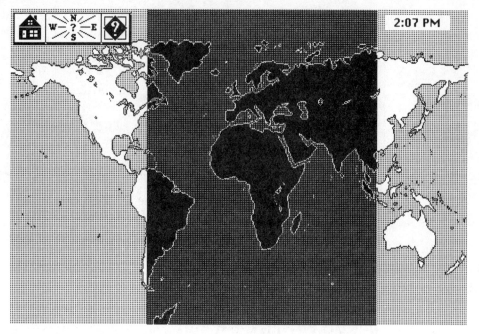

Figure I.6 BusinessClass startup screen. ©Danny Goodman.

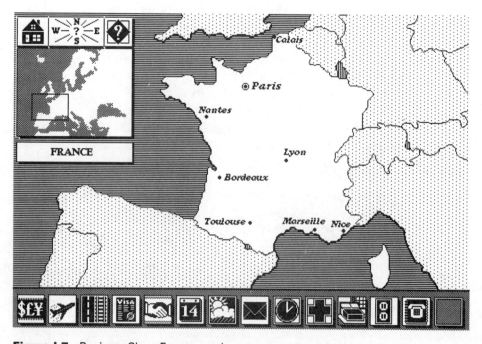

Figure I.7 BusinessClass France card.

For example, you click on the Airplane icon to see a list of airlines that travel to and from the country you chose. To make this list even more useful, the stack includes the phone numbers of those airlines. In fact, there is even a button that lists all the toll free numbers available.

Finding information is as simple as clicking on a button or typing the first few letters of the word you want to find.

Note Cards

HyperCard can help you keep information organized so that you can get to it when you really need it. For example, you can create note cards that contain information you've gathered for a research project. When you need information on a specific topic in that stack, use HyperCard's **Find** command for fast access to every card on that topic. In this book, you'll create an index file of HyperCard tips and tricks (see Figure I.8). It will explain how to create this kind of file in detail, step by step.

Organizer

Everyone can use the weekly planner stack that comes with HyperCard to keep track of appointments and other things to do (see Figure I.9).

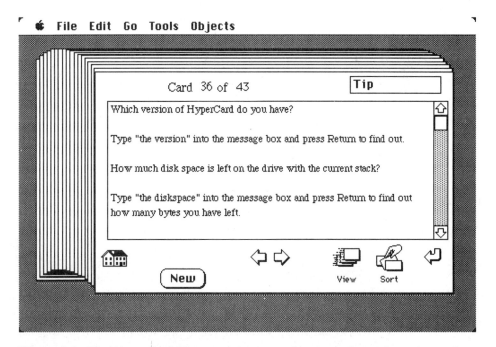

Figure I.8 The HyperCard Tips stack is a set of note cards, each card contains a HyperCard tip, trick, or shortcut.

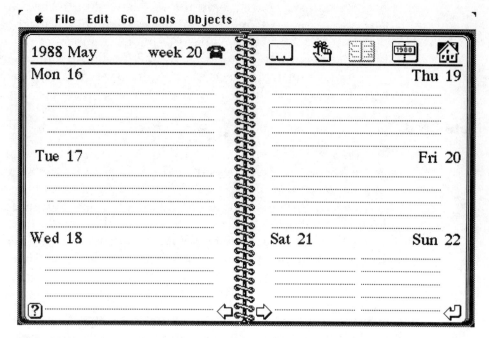

Figure I.9 HyperCard's Weekly stack helps you keep track of appointments. ©Apple Computer, Inc.

Reference Book

You can also create stacks that contain reference material that you access often. For example, if you are a technical writer, you could create a stack of cards that contains technical words and jargon used in your field along with a definition of each word. The Apple Glossary stack, created by Apple Computer, Inc., lists and defines technical words used in some Apple user manuals (see Figure I.10).

Personnel Records

If you work in personnel, you may want to create a stack that teaches new employees about company policies on benefits such as medical plans. Or you can create a stack that introduces new employees to your company and its products much as the short training films have done in the past (and probably still do). The difference is that the HyperCard stack can contain easily updated information such as who's who in the company, complete with a listing of each person in an organization chart. Apple developed a similar stack of a ficticious company called MegaCorp. That stack introduces new employees to the company (see Figure I.11).

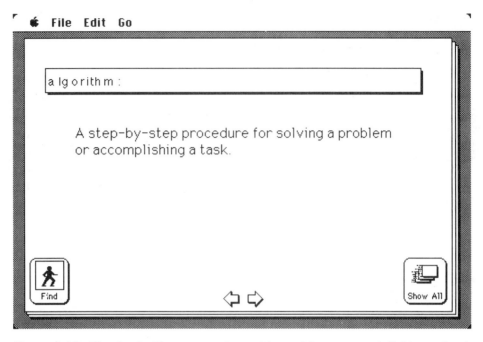

Figure I.10   The Apple Glossary stack provides quick access to definitions of technical words and acronyms. ©Apple Computer, Inc.

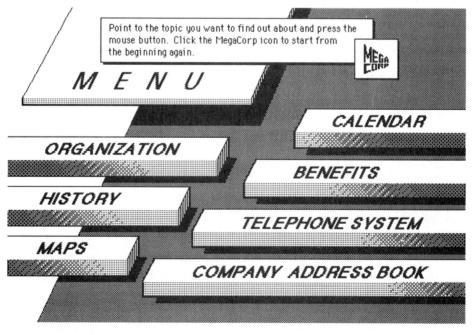

Figure I.11   The MegaCorp stack introduces new employees to MegaCorp. ©Apple Computer, Inc.

Invoices

If you own a small business, you can create a data base of your clients and tie that information to an invoice stack and a time card stack that keeps track of the hours you spend with each client (see Figures I.12A and B). This stack was created by Janet Tokerud, a Macintosh consultant to small businesses in San Francisco.

Tutorials

If you are an educator, you can create stacks that teach students about astronomy, chemistry, or any other topic, and include a multiple-choice quiz at the end! There are endless numbers of topics on which you can create lessons for students of any age (see Figure I.13).

Data Bases

Anyone who belongs to a club can create a stack that keeps track of its members. (The stack shown in Figure I.14 was created by Cynthia Kolnick, a writer in California. The stack is a data base containing infor-

8:34

(Print Invoice & Update)

JANET TOKERUD
322-30th Ave. #1
San Francisco, CA 94121

Occidental Express
4521 18th Street
San Francisco, CA 94114

1/13/88

End Date	Description	Hours	Mins	Rate	Total
9/3/87	Revised Ledger Sheets	2	30	30	85.00
12/9/87	Assist w/1099, Time & Cost Applications	1		30	40.00
12/18/87	Work on P&L Statement	2	10	30	75.00
1/4/88	phone consultation - damaged checks file		10	30	5.00

Amount Due   205.00

Figure I.12A An invoicing system. ©Janet Tokerud.

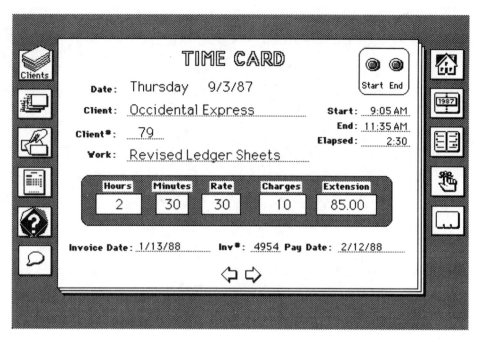

Figure I.12B A time card system. ©Janet Tokerud.

mation about the members of Writers Online, a freelance writers' collective.)

Sales Catalog

Create an electronic catalog of your products for customers to browse through (see Figure I.15). At the MacWorld trade show in January, 1988, some software companies were advertising their products on stacks. One company had a stack that demonstrated the features of one of its software products. Another company let you browse through a stack of clip art for sale. Exactly how to create a sales catalog stack is explained step by step later in this book.

About StackWare™

All the stacks shown above are applications created with HyperCard. You'll discover other categories of HyperCard applications that you can build yourself or buy from somebody else. The possibilities are endless— from building a small stack for private use in your home or office to building large interlinked stacks for commercial use. By hiding Hyper-

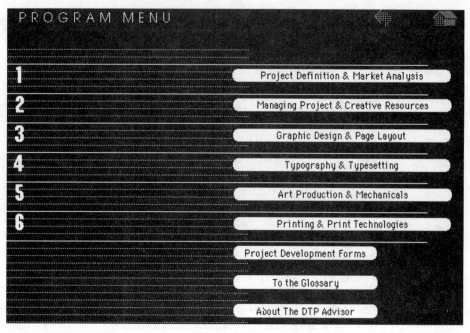

Figure I.13   Advice for desktop publishing. ©HyperSoft.

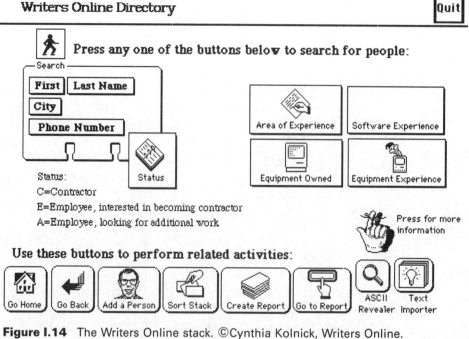

Figure I.14   The Writers Online stack. ©Cynthia Kolnick, Writers Online.

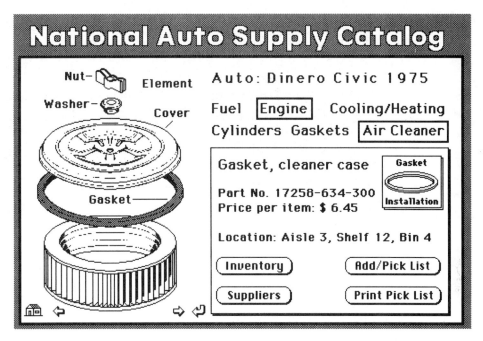

Figure I.15   A sales catalog from Stack Ideas. ©Apple Computer, Inc.

Card menus and replacing them with your own, you can create stacks that look almost like other Macintosh applications.

Apple has coined the word *StackWare* to refer to applications created with HyperCard and hopes to originate a whole StackWare industry.

The Versions of HyperCard

This book covers HyperCard versions 1.0.1, 1.1, and 1.2. The differences among the versions aren't terribly significant—just enough to throw you when you try to do something out of the ordinary. You'll see references throughout this book to features that apply to the different versions so you'll know which steps to follow. Boxes in the text identify any different steps needed for the same features.

By the way, in computer software development, new versions are always in the works. You can rest assured that HyperCard version 2.0 is now lurking in some programmer's mind even as you read this. Will what you learn in this book become obsolete? No, not at all. Once you've got the hang of HyperCard, later versions will only add to your repertoire. Perhaps there will be a color HyperCard since Apple now has a color Macintosh. Whatever version 2.0 (and later) brings, what you learn here will still apply.

A Very Short Commercial

There's an order form at the end of this book. If you want to purchase a disk that contains all the stacks in this book, plus other useful stacks, send the form and a check. If someone else has used the form, then a 3 by 5 card or the back of an old envelope will be just fine.

SECTION ONE FOR ABSOLUTE BEGINNERS

SYSTEM AND MEMORY REQUIREMENTS

Before you get your heart set on using HyperCard, there are a couple of requirements you must know about. For one, HyperCard works only on Macintosh Plus, Macintosh SE, and Macintosh II computers.

HyperCard does not work on Macintosh 512K's or 512Ke's because they do not contain enough RAM memory. You must have at least 1 megabyte of RAM to use HyperCard on your Macintosh. HyperCard 1.0.1 and 1.1 use about 750K of RAM. Version 1.2 uses about 700K.

You also need either a hard disk or two 800K disk drives, System 3.2 or higher and Finder 5.3 or higher. To print stacks on the LaserWriter, use LaserWriter 4.0 or higher.

For faster HyperCard performance, set the RAM cache in the Control Panel to Off. HyperCard has its own way of caching information in and out of memory, so turning off the Macintosh RAM cache speeds up HyperCard. To turn off the RAM cache, choose **Control Panel** from the menu. Click the Off button next to the RAM Cache.

HyperCard with MultiFinder

If you're using HyperCard with Apple's MultiFinder program, your computer should have at least 2 megabytes of RAM. You should also set the memory size for HyperCard to at least 750K. To do that, start at the desktop screen and click on the HyperCard icon so it's selected (black). Choose **Get Info** from the File menu. Click in the box labeled Application Memory Size at the bottom of the Get Info box, erase the number in the box, and type **750**. To get top HyperCard performance, type **1000** instead of 750. This sets the HyperCard memory to 1 megabyte.

1 Exploring Hypercard

In this chapter, you'll learn what stacks and cards are made of, how to open HyperCard, how to browse through some stacks, and how to find specific information in those stacks. The lessons in this chapter (1) explain how HyperCard is put together and (2) show how to

- Open HyperCard
- Click on buttons
- Set or change skill levels
- Use the Home card to access stacks
- Find specific information
- Get back to the Home card from any stack

THE ELEMENTS OF HYPERCARD

As you learned in the Introduction to this book, HyperCard stacks are made up of a series of cards. Each card contains related information, for example, a set of notes, a list of contacts, even a group of images or sounds.

Stacks

- A **stack** is a set of cards on the same topic just as a book is a set of pages about the same topic.

Cards

- A **card** is one screenful of information.

A card is the size of a Macintosh Plus or Macintosh SE screen, which is 7.11 inches (horizontal) by 4.75 inches (vertical). In computer jargon, that size works out to 512 by 342 in pixels. A pixel (short for "picture element") is one dot on a Macintosh screen.

So if you're using a Macintosh Plus or Macintosh SE, the card fills the screen (see Figure 1.1). But if you're using a Macintosh II or a large screen monitor, the card does not fill the screen. Is there any way to change the size of a card to match the screen? Not yet.

Each card has a front and a back, referred to as a *foreground* and a *background* (see Figure 1.2). A foreground is a set of visual elements such as pictures, buttons, and fields that appear on only one card in the stack. What you put on the background appears on every card in the stack. The foreground is also referred to as the card or card level.

Backgrounds

- A **background** is a set of visual elements such as pictures, buttons, and fields shared by several cards in a stack. By sharing a background, the cards in a stack look consistent which makes it easier to navigate through and use that stack.

Designing a background is like designing a form to be filled out. In addition to fields, you can add buttons and artwork to a background.

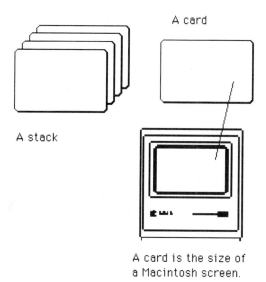

A card

A stack

A card is the size of
a Macintosh screen.

Figure 1.1 A stack is a group of cards, each the size of the original Macintosh screen.

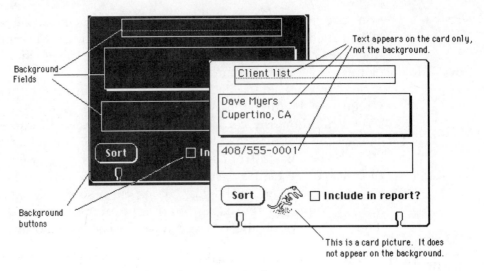

Figure 1.2 Each card has a front and a back.

Stacks generally have one common background that all the cards share. But stacks can have more than one background. The purpose of the background is to save time and disk space. You only have to draw the template (or form) once. Having several cards share the same background graphics saves disk space.

Stacks, cards, and backgrounds are only three of the basic elements in a HyperCard application. The other two are fields and buttons.

Fields

- A **field** is an area on a card that contains text. You type and edit text in fields. You can choose from any type style or font in your System file for the field text. Whether the field is created on a background or on a card, text is always typed at the card level (foreground). That is, the text typed into a background field is not shared with other cards.

Buttons

- A **button** is something you click on to initiate an action. Sometimes buttons can be invisible, but most of the time they are represented by an icon. An icon is a picture that represents an object such as a button, stack, document, or program. In the Finder, for example, a MacWrite document icon looks like a piece of paper with lines on it.

Buttons contain little programs that tell HyperCard what to do when you click on them. For example, the right arrow button on the Home card contains a program that tells HyperCard to go to the next card.

You'll learn how to program these buttons in Sections 2 and 3 of this book.

How These Elements Work Together

When you create a new stack, the background is the first thing you design. Although you can leave the background blank (white), more often you'll use a combination of background buttons, background fields, and background pictures. Each time you create a new card, it is added on top of the background but remains transparent so you can see the background elements. You can then add some foreground elements such as card buttons, card fields, and card pictures to a particular card. The elements you add will appear on that card only.

Lesson 1:   STARTING HYPERCARD

1. Turn on your Macintosh.

2. If you have a hard disk, create a new folder on it. Name that folder HyperCard (see Figure 1.3).

3. Copy the files and folders on your HyperCard disks into the folder named HyperCard.

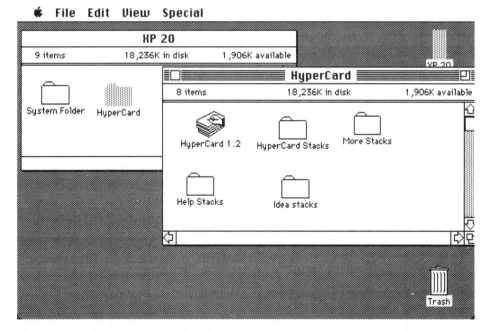

Figure 1.3 Copy all HyperCard files and folders into a folder named HyperCard.

If you don't have a hard disk, you can use floppy disks in the normal manner. However, you'll face a lot of disk swapping and other delays. It's better to use HyperCard on a hard disk drive than two floppy drives. Always make copies of your disks and use the copies, not the originals.

Okay, now you're organized and ready to go.

HyperCard 1.2

4. Double-click on the HyperCard icon to start HyperCard.

The Home Card—There's No Place Like Home

The Home card is the first card you see when you start HyperCard (see Figure 1.4). The icons on the Home card represent stacks. Clicking on an icon takes you to that particular stack. When you're finished working with that stack, you can either go from there to another stack or return to the familiar Home card. The Home card acts as your Home base. You'll look at the stacks included with HyperCard in a moment.

HyperCard initially has one Home card and four other cards that together form the Home stack. You can add other cards to this stack later, but for now you'll learn about these five cards.

Figure 1.4 The Home card.

Tip: Some stacks that you buy contain an installation program that puts an icon for that stack on the Home card. If the Home card is full, just add a new card for storing the other icons.

The Home Stack and the Cards within It

The Home stack contains five cards (see Figure 1.5). The first card is, of course, the Home card. It's the card you'll use most often. HyperCard uses the next three cards to find other stacks, programs, and documents. And the last card is the most important card of all: User Preferences. That's the card you'll use to tell HyperCard which menus and features you want to use.

To see the other cards in the Home stack, you'll click on the buttons that look like arrows at the bottom of the Home card.

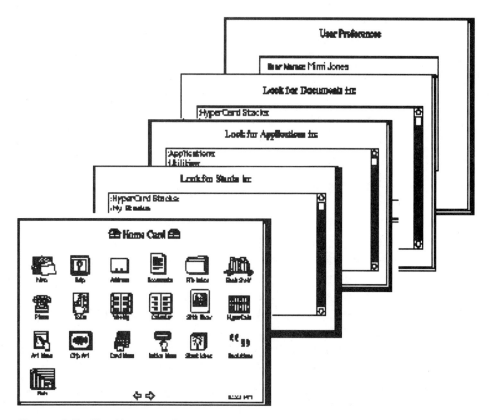

Figure 1.5 The Home stack.

Lesson 2:   CLICKING ON BUTTONS

To move backward to the previous card, click on the Left Arrow button. You move forward to the next card by clicking on the Right Arrow button (see Figure 1.6).

1. Move the mouse pointer to the Right Arrow button. Click once on that button to go to the next card.

The second card in the Home stack, Look for Stacks in:, lists the names of all folders and disks holding HyperCard stacks.

The Look for Stacks in: Card

This card helps HyperCard find stacks quickly. At first that may not sound like a big deal, but, as you add more stacks to your hard disk, you'll begin to appreciate the usefulness of this card. Without this card, every time you wanted to open a stack, HyperCard would first ask you to locate that stack in the Finder.

The list of folders on this card are called **pathnames**. HyperCard uses pathnames to find stacks that you want it to open.

Look at the pathnames listed on the Look for Stacks in: card (see Figure 1.7). Do not erase these pathnames. Without these names, Hyper-Card won't be able to find the stacks that were packaged with it. All folders are preceded by a colon to indicate the name of a folder. The names of floppy or hard disks are not preceded by a colon. You can type pathnames on this card or let HyperCard do it for you. If you type them, put a colon before a folder name only.

Here's what happens behind the scenes when you click on a stack icon on the Home card: HyperCard looks through all the folders listed on the Look for Stacks in: card until it finds the stack you clicked on. When HyperCard finds the stack, it opens that stack.

If the pathname for a stack you want to open is not listed on this card, HyperCard displays a dialog box asking you where that stack is located (in which folder). This will appear as the standard Macintosh dialog box (see Figure 1.8).

In response, you would open the folder that contains the stack you want to use and then double-click on the name of the stack to open it.

Figure 1.6 The Right and Left Arrow buttons.

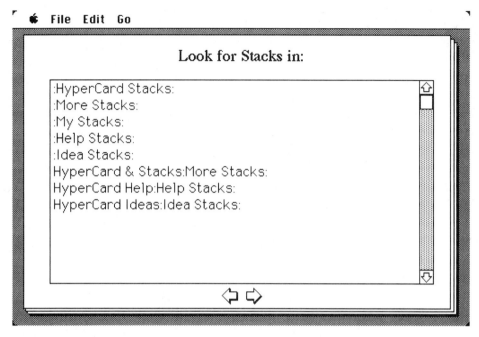

Figure 1.7 This card lists the names of disks and folders that contain stacks.

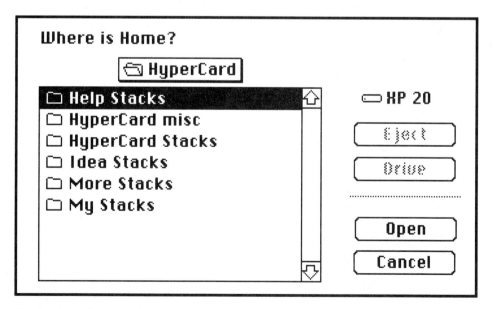

Figure 1.8 The standard Macintosh dialog box appears when HyperCard can't find a stack.

HyperCard then adds the pathname to the Look for Stacks in: card once it has found the stack you chose to open. So, the next time you click on that stack icon, HyperCard won't ask you where that stack is. (Of course, if you moved a stack to another folder after telling HyperCard where it was, HyperCard will ask you again where that stack is located.)

2. Click once on the Right Arrow button to go to the next card.

The Look for Applications in: Card

Yes, you can open other applications from within HyperCard. But you have to tell HyperCard where those applications are located on your disk. That's the purpose of this card—to help HyperCard find applications quickly (see Figure 1.9). So, when you tell HyperCard to open MacWrite, for example, it automatically knows where to find MacWrite.

Another great HyperCard feature is that you can open applications from within any HyperCard stack. And what's even better, when you open an application from within a stack, HyperCard brings you right back to the opened stack *after you've quit the application*. That means that

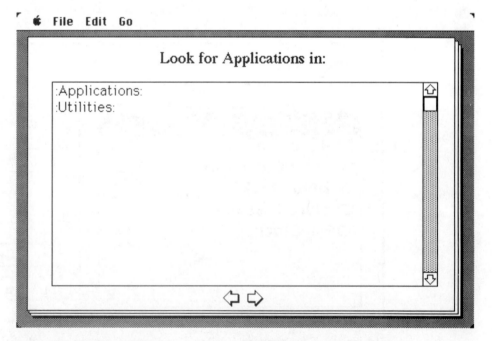

Figure 1.9 This card lists the names of disks and folders that contain applications such as HyperCard, MacPaint, and other programs.

you don't have to quit HyperCard, start the application from the Finder, quit the application, and then open HyperCard from the Finder again. To open an application from within HyperCard, you'll use a special HyperCard command. You'll learn more about opening applications from within HyperCard later.

3. Click once on the Right Arrow button to go to the next card.

The Look for Documents in: Card

This card shows HyperCard where files created by other Macintosh applications are stored, for example, spreadsheets created with MicroSoft Excel or paint files created with MacPaint (see Figure 1.10). HyperCard needs to know where these documents are stored if you want to open specific files from within HyperCard.

Not only can you open other applications from within HyperCard, but you can also open a specific file using a specific application. For example, you can tell HyperCard to open a memo with MacWrite.

4. Click once again on the Right Arrow button.

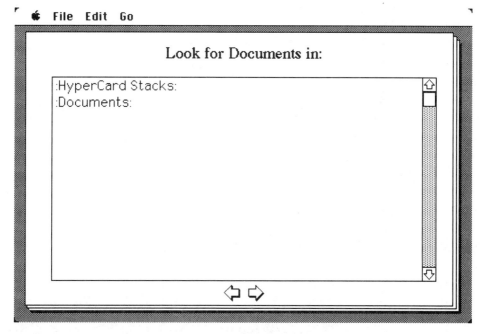

Figure 1.10 This card lists the names of disks and folders that contain documents created with applications such as MacWrite or MacPaint.

The User Preferences Card

This card is the last card in the Home stack. Unlike the previous three cards in the Home stack, the User Preferences card is not used by Hyper-Card for finding files. Instead, you use this card to set or change the HyperCard skill level to the one with which you feel most comfortable.

Because the User Preferences card is so important, it deserves a lesson of its own.

Lesson 3:   SETTING THE SKILL LEVEL THAT'S RIGHT FOR YOU

The User Preferences card lists the five skill levels (called **user levels**) available in HyperCard (see Figure 1.11):

- Browsing: Find and view information
- Typing: Add and change information
                                     in fields
- Painting: Create graphics

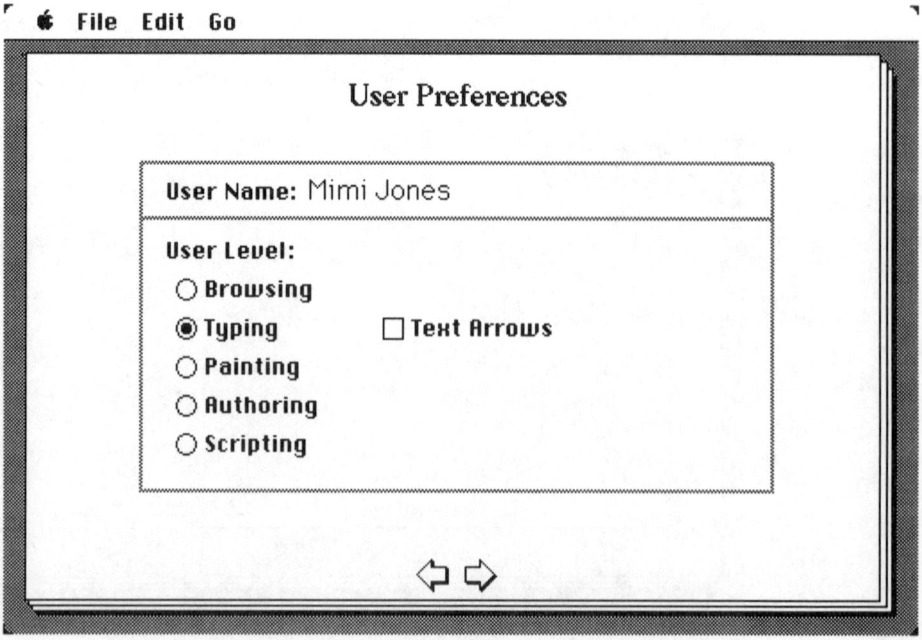

Figure 1.11 Choose your skill level on the User Preferences card.

- Authoring: Create buttons and fields
- Scripting: Create HyperTalk programs
                                      (**scripts**)

HyperCard user levels are similar to the skill level settings you find in most Macintosh video games. With game programs, you usually have your choice of three settings: beginner, intermediate, and advanced. When you desire more challenge or more features in the game than the current setting allows, you switch to the next highest setting. You change HyperCard user levels in much the same way. In this book, you'll go from one level to the next as you go through the lessons, beginning with the Typing level. When you first start HyperCard, it is automatically set at the Typing level.

Browsing is the most elementary level, and Scripting (programming) is the most advanced. The skill levels are cumulative. That is, when you choose one further down the list, it gives you the features that preceded it as well as new features. For instance, if you choose Painting, you also get all features available with the Typing and Browsing skill levels as well.

Browsing

At the Browsing level, you can look at cards in the stacks either by clicking a button or pressing the Right or Left Arrow keys on the keyboard. You can also find information quickly with the **Find** command. However, at this level you can't add or change text, graphics, or anything else on the cards.

Browsing, as its name implies, is like being in a library and flipping through books to see what's there. (In fact, some libraries—particularly at universities—refer to their rows of books as stacks.)

Later on, when you're creating your own stacks and want to prevent others from intentionally or accidentally changing or deleting information in a stack, you can limit the user level by setting it to Browsing.

So far, although the user level is set for Typing, you've only used the functions available at the Browsing level: viewing cards and finding information.

Typing

At the Typing level, you can enter and change text in fields. A **field** is an area on a card that holds text or numbers. For instance, a field can contain the title of a card or the results of some calculation.

Chapter 2 explains more about fields and shows what you can do at the Typing level.

Painting

At the Painting level, you can draw pictures on the cards. HyperCard has a set of painting tools available at the Painting level. You can also copy or cut and paste cards at this level and import graphics from other paint programs onto cards.

Section Two in this book shows what you can do at the Painting level.

Authoring

At the Authoring level, you can create fields and buttons. The buttons range from the familiar OK and Cancel to others with widely different functions. You can also link cards with buttons so that clicking on a button takes you to a new card.

Section Two shows what you can do at the Authoring level.

Scripting

At the Scripting level, you can do it all. Scripting is another name for programming. HyperCard includes a complete programming language called HyperTalk. You can add programs, or **scripts**, to buttons, fields, cards, backgrounds, and stacks.

Section Three in this book shows what you can do at the scripting level.

Setting User Preferences to Typing

Because you're going to start some later lessons at the Typing level, go ahead and set the User Preferences card to Typing now if you haven't already.

*1. If your User Preferences card is not set at the Typing level, click in the circle next to **Typing** to set it for typing.*

2. Click in the Text Arrows box so an X appears.

The Text Arrows option, when checked, lets you use the arrow keys to move the insertion bar inside of fields: left, right, up, and down. To move from card to card, hold down the Option key while you press the Right Arrow key. If you don't check Text Arrows, the Right and Left Arrow keys move you to the next and previous cards.

3. Click on the Right Arrow button to go to the next card.

You're home!

Lesson 4:   LEAVING HOME

When you're ready to leave home and explore other HyperCard stacks, all you have to do is click once on one of the stacks pictured on the Home card. You'll do that next.

What You See Is What You Get

HyperCard includes several stacks that are ready to use. The following pages give you a brief description of each stack on the Home card for easy reference.

Intro

Introduction to HyperCard stack icon. This stack is for users new to HyperCard. It introduces the user to HyperCard. And it does a good job of explaining the elements of HyperCard.

Help

Help stack icon. Complete with glossary and index, this stack gives you online help quickly and concisely.

Address

Address stack icon. Keep all your important names, addresses, and phone numbers in this stack.

Documents

Documents stack icon. A stack of cards with information about the files in the folders listed on the Look for Documents card in the Home stack.

File Index

File Index stack icon. A set of file cards for filing notes about a subject.

Book Shelf

Book Shelf stack icon. A card that you can copy and modify to use as a sort of directory to other stacks. Includes buttons linked to other stacks: Clip Art, Help, Home, and Chemistry.

Phone

Phone stack icon. A card that dials your telephone. Click on Area Codes to access all area codes in the U.S.A and Canada. Click on the question mark for instructions on how to use this card. (You'll need a modem.)

To Do

To Do stack icon. A daily to-do list. Use it to organize and remind you of daily tasks.

Weekly

Weekly stack icon. A weekly appointment book. Use it to keep track of meetings and appointments. Each card displays a different week.

Calendar

Calendar stack icon. Yearly calendar listing all 12 months. Click on any week in the year to go directly to the Weekly stack.

Slide Show

Slide Show stack icon. Contains a few scanned images. Click anywhere to see the next card.

HyperCalc

HyperCalc stack icon. A calculator of sorts. Calculates the number you enter on line 2 of either column by the equation you enter in line 3 of either column. Click anywhere outside of the fields to begin the calculation.

Art Ideas

Art Ideas stack icon. Lots of clip art for you to copy and paste on the cards you create or modify. The art is free. You don't have to get Apple's permission to use it anywhere.

Clip Art

Clip Art stack icon. A few cards of HyperCard clip art, plus some animated sequences. The art in this stack is also free.

Card Ideas

Card Ideas stack icon. Several cards designed to give you ideas for creating cards for your own stacks. You can copy cards from this stack and paste them in other stacks. You're free to use these designs when creating stacks for personal use. However, if you want to use one of these card ideas to create a stack to sell, be sure to check with Apple Computer for permission. Some of these Card Ideas are copyrighted.

Button Ideas

Button Ideas stack icon. Several buttons that you can copy and use in other stacks. Many of these buttons are preprogrammed with useful scripts.

Stack Ideas

Stack Ideas stack icon. Several cards designed as templates for creating your own stacks. You're free to use these designs when creating stacks for personal use. However, if you want to use one of these stack ideas to create a stack to sell, be sure to check with Apple Computer for permission. Some of the Stack Ideas are copyrighted.

Quotations

Quotations stack icon. Interesting quotations from famous people. Read a quotation, then click on the Who Says? button for the name of the person quoted.

Plots

Plots stack icon. Use this card to create bar, coin, and pie charts. Change the numbers in the column on the right of the card. Then click on the Bar, Coin, or Pie button to make the chart. Copy the finished chart onto a card in another stack if you like.

> *Tip:* Sometimes the buttons on a card are not clearly visible.
> Press the Option and ⌘ key at the same time to reveal where the
> buttons are. An outline appears around every button on the card.
> In HyperCard version 1.2, holding down the **Shift** key as well as
> the **Option** and ⌘ keys outlines all fields as well as buttons.

Is it starting to click? Then you're ready to click on a stack pictured
on the Home card.

Your Magic Rolodex

Here's an example of how to use one of HyperCard's standard stacks.

1. Click on the Address button.

The Address stack contains several cards that all look alike.
Each card in this stack lists the name, address, and phone number for
one person (see Figure 1.12).

Figure 1.12 The Address stack includes several buttons that are linked to other
stacks. (The number to the left of each button corresponds to a number in the list
below. These numbers don't appear on the card.)

2. Click on the Right Arrow button to go to the next card.

You can turn this stack into your own personal address book by deleting the information that is not useful to you and adding the names and addresses of people you know instead. You'll do that in Chapter 2.

The pictures on the left of each card are buttons you click on to perform tasks for you.

1. The first button is the Home button. Click on it to go Home.
2. The next button takes you to the Calendar stack.
3. The third button takes you to the weekly appointment book.
4. The fourth button takes you to a to-do list.
5. The fifth button flips through the cards like a slide show.
6. The last button is a Sort button. Click on it to sort the cards alphabetically by first or last name.

You can add more buttons like these to your Address cards. You'll learn how to do that in later chapters.

A menu bar should appear at the top of the screen. If there isn't one, press the ⌘ key and Spacebar at the same time to display it.

Tip: Some stacks include commands that hide the menu bar. Pressing the ⌘ and Spacebar keys at the same time makes the menu bar appear if it's hidden. Pressing those two keys again makes the menu bar disappear if it's showing.

Lesson 5:   FINDING SPECIFIC INFORMATION

HyperCard has an extremely fast search feature. In fact, HyperCard can search a stack of 500 cards in less than one second.

*1. Choose **Find** from the Go menu. A box appears at the bottom of your screen. Inside the box is the word Find followed by quotation marks.*

*2. Type **Ka** between the quotation marks (see Figure 1.13).*

3. Press the Return key to begin the search.

HyperCard finds and displays the first card with the letters *Ka* in *any* field on any card in this stack (see Figure 1.14).

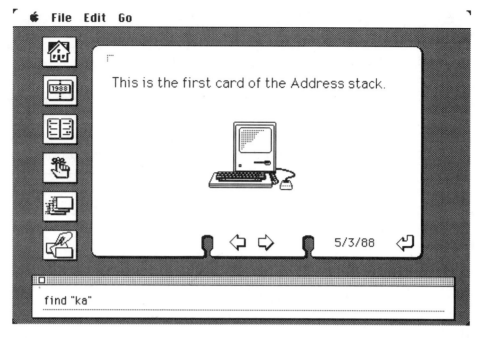

Figure 1.13 To use the **Find** command, type the word you want to search for between the quotation marks.

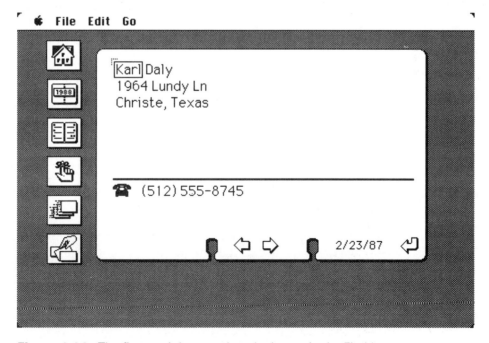

Figure 1.14 The first card that matches the letters in the Find box appears.

4. Press Return again to find the next card with Ka in it.

That's all there is to finding text in HyperCard. Now you're ready to go home.

Shortcut: Press ⌘-F to find a word. It's the same as choosing **Find** from the Go menu. Keyboard shortcuts, when available, are listed to the right of menu choices in the pull-down menus.

Lesson 6:   GOING HOME

Home is where you live in HyperCard. The Home card provides a familiar reference point from which to go forward and seek out other stacks. No matter where you are in HyperCard, you can always go Home. In fact, most cards contain a button that takes you back to the Home card.

The Home button looks like a little house (see Figure 1.15).

1. Find the Home button on the Address card. Click on it to return to the Home card.
2. Click on the Slide Show stack icon. This stack does not have a Home button. If you can't find a Home button, you can always choose **Home** from the **Go** menu.

Shortcut: Press the ⌘ and H keys from any card to return to the Home card.

SUMMARY

HyperCard has five user levels: Browsing, Typing, Painting, Authoring, and Scripting. To change the level, go to the last card in the Home

Figure 1.15 A typical **Home** button looks like this.

stack and click in the circle next to the level you want. In this chapter, you've been using commands available at the Browsing level. All these commands and more are available from the other levels.

A **stack** is a set of cards with similar information. A **card** is one screenful of information (the size of a Macintosh Plus or Macintosh SE screen). Each card has a front and a back, referred to as a **foreground** and a **background**. What you put on the background appears on every card in the stack. What you put on the foreground appears on only that card in the stack. Cards also have fields, buttons, and graphics. You can put these objects on the foreground, background, or both.

Home is where the heart is in HyperCard. All the stacks included with HyperCard are listed on the Home card. To get from one card to another in the same stack, click on the Right and Left Arrow buttons. Or use the **Find** command to search the fields on a card for a specific word.

In the next chapter, you'll learn how to navigate through HyperCard stacks.

2 Navigation

In this chapter, you'll learn how to get around in HyperCard by using some of the stacks provided with HyperCard. The lessons in this chapter show how to

- Open stacks
- Move within stacks
- Move between stacks
- Use the Message box
- Get Help

Lesson 7: OPENING STACKS

You can open a stack in one of three ways:

- Double-click on a stack from the Finder as you did the HyperCard program.
- Click once on a special button such as those that appear on the Home card.
- Choose **Open Stack** from the File menu. Then choose the name of the stack to open.

You've already opened stacks the first two ways. Now open a stack by using the File menu choice **Open Stack**.

1. Choose **Open Stack** from the File menu.
2. In the window that appears, pull down the HyperCard Stacks folder and choose the folder that contains the stack you want to open. For now, choose the HyperCard folder (see Figure 2.1).

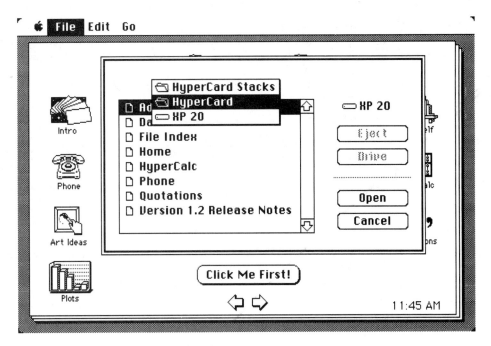

Figure 2.1 Choose the HyperCard folder.

Next you'll open the stack named Card Ideas which is in the Idea Stacks folder.

3. Double-click on the Idea Stacks folder to open it. Double-click on Card Ideas to open the stack of card ideas (see Figure 2.2).
4. Go to a card by clicking on the miniature picture that represents it.
5. Use the commands on the **Go** menu to navigate through the card ideas.
6. Go to the Home card when you're through looking at the card ideas.

Using the Find File Desk Accessory to Find a Stack

This desk accessory is available with System 4.1 or higher. Pull down the menu to see if **Find File** appears in that menu. Use **Find File** if you're not sure where the stack you need to open is located. In the Find File dialog box, type the name of the stack you want to find and press Return. Find File lists all the folders you must open to get to a particular stack.

Figure 2.3 shows what Find File would display if you told it to find the Home stack.

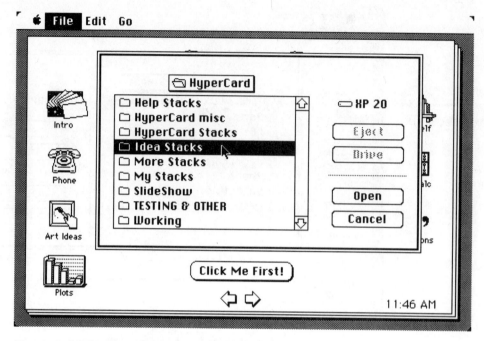

Figure 2.2 Double-click on the Idea Stacks folder.

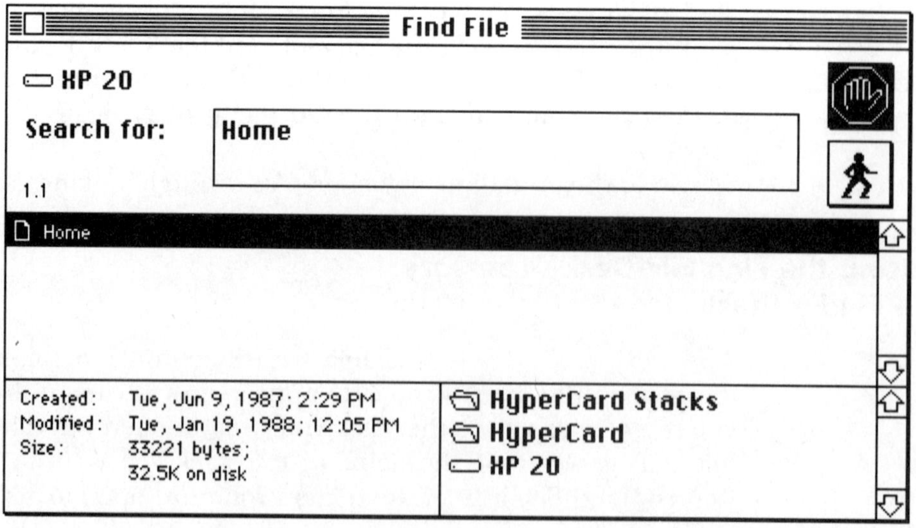

```
████▌      Find File    ▐████
⌐ XP 20                                      🖐
Search for:    Home
1.1                                          🚶
📄 Home                                              ⇧

                                                     ⇩
Created:    Tue, Jun 9, 1987; 2:29 PM      🗁 HyperCard Stacks   ⇧
Modified:   Tue, Jan 19, 1988; 12:05 PM    🗁 HyperCard
Size:       33221 bytes;                    ⌐ XP 20
            32.5K on disk                                          ⇩
```

Figure 2.3 The Find File desk accessory.

XP 20:HyperCard: HyperCard Stacks   is the pathname for the Home stack in this example. In other words, the Home stack is in the folder named HyperCard Stacks, which is in the folder named HyperCard on the hard disk named XP 20.

Lesson 8:   MOVING WITHIN STACKS

You used the Right and Left Arrow buttons on the Home stack to go back and forth between cards. Not all stacks have buttons like that. They might have buttons similar to arrows such as pointing hands. If not, don't worry. HyperCard has many ways to move between cards. This lesson shows you some of those ways.

Using the Arrow Keys on the Keyboard

Pressing the Right Arrow key on your keyboard takes you to the next card in the stack if you didn't check the Text Arrows box on the User Preferences card. Likewise, pressing the Left Arrow key takes you to the previous card.

If you checked the Text Arrows option, hold down the Option key when pressing the Right and Left Arrow keys to go to the next and previous cards.

About the Go Menu

You can always use the **Go** menu to navigate among the stacks on your disk. The **Go** menu lists commands for going to the previous and next cards.

1. Choose **Next** from the **Go** menu (or press ⌘3) to go to the next card in the Card Ideas stack.
2. Choose **Prev** from the **Go** menu (or press ⌘4) to return to the previous card.

In addition, the **Go** menu has other useful navigational commands. **First** takes you to the first card in the stack. **Last** takes you to the last card in the stack. Every stack has a beginning and an ending card—these two commands just help you get there faster.

The **Back** command on the **Go** menu takes you to the previous card displayed whether it was in the same stack or in a different stack.

Another way to move quickly within a stack is to use the **Find** command to find a card with information on a particular topic.

Lesson 9:   MOVING BETWEEN STACKS

Some buttons go from one stack to another when you click on them, a feature that lets you move between stacks. But you can't always count on a card's having buttons to take you to other stacks. One thing you can count on is the **Open Stack** command from the **File** menu. But there are a couple more ways to jump to other stacks. This lesson shows two more ways to do that.

Retracing Your Steps with the Tilde (~) Key

When you've already opened two or more stacks, you can jump quickly from one to the other by pressing the Tilde key (~). Some keyboards have an ESC key instead of a Tilde key. Use either the Tilde key (~) or ESC key to retrace your steps, displaying the cards in the sequence in which you viewed them, not necessarily in the order in which cards are arranged in the stack.

Pressing the Tilde or ESC key is the same as choosing **Back** from the **Go** menu.

Press the Tilde or ESC key now to go back to the last card you looked at.

The Recent Card

The Recent card displays the last 42 cards you've looked at. If you've looked at a card more than once, it won't appear twice on the Recent card. Recent displays only the last 42 unique cards. To jump to one of the cards displayed in miniature, just click on the little picture. (The card you looked at last appears with a white frame around it.)

Use the Recent card to jump quickly from one card or stack to another (see Figure 2.4).

1. Choose **Recent** from the **Go** menu.
2. Click on the picture of the card that you want to return to. In this case, click on the picture of the Home card.

> *Shortcut:* Press ⌘-R to display the Recent card.

So what's the difference between the Tilde or ESC key and the Recent card? Pressing the Tilde key retraces your steps one card at a time. So,

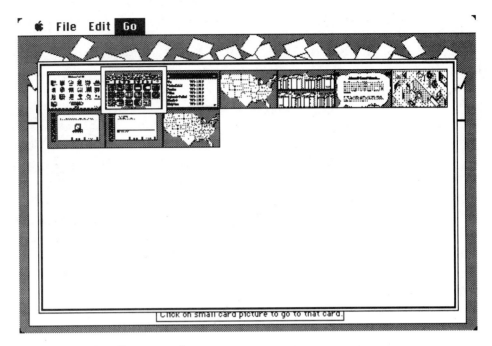

Figure 2.4 The Recent card

to go back to the tenth card, you'd have to press the Tilde key 10 times. With Recent, however, you'd only have to click once on a specific card in the Recent card to go directly to that card. Instead of backtracking, use the Recent card to go quickly to a card. You'll use the Tilde key when you need to backtrack through your cards, for example, when you're testing a stack you've created.

Lesson 10:   GET HELP

The fastest way to open the HyperCard Help stack is by pressing the ⌘ and ? keys at the same time. Of course, you can also see the Help stack by choosing **Help** from the Go menu, or by clicking on the Help icon on the Home card.

1. Press ⌘ and ? at the same time. You don't have to hold down the Shift key while you press the ? key to go to the Help stack (see Figure 2.5).

2. Click on the Browse tab (see Figure 2.6).

3. Click on Navigating in the list on the card.

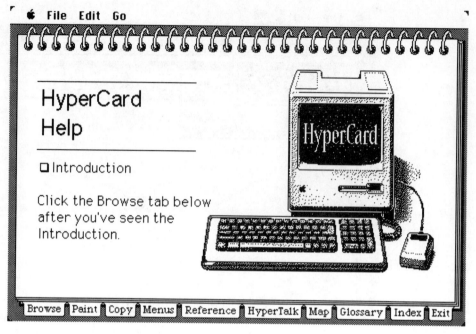

Figure 2.5 The Help stack.

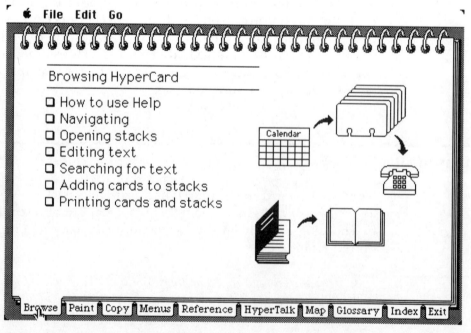

Figure 2.6 First card to appear after clicking on the Browse tab.

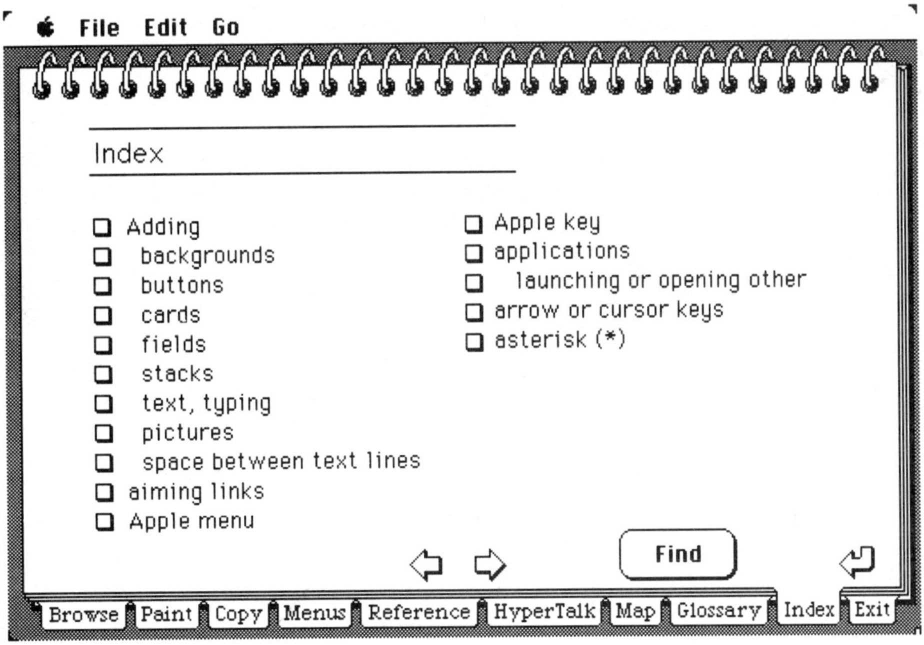

Figure 2.7 The Help index.

4. Click on the Index tab. The cards in the Help index list topics in alphabetical order (see Figure 2.7).

To find information on a specific topic in the Help index, click on the Find button and type the name of the topic. You can also click the Right Arrow button until the topic appears, but the Find button is faster. (The bent arrow in the lower right corner of the Help index is referred to as a Return button because clicking on it returns you to the previous card.)

5. Click once on the Find button.

*6. Type **menu** between the quotation marks. Press Return.*

7. The word menu appears on the list. Press Return again for the next occurence of the word menu. Click on Edit menu for information about the Edit menu.

8. Click on the Exit tab to go back to the Home card.

Lesson 11: TALKING TO HYPERCARD WITH THE MESSAGE BOX

HyperCard understands over 300 key words and phrases. *Go, put, dial, find, get,* and *sort* are among the most common key words you'll use in the

Message box. These words are called **commands**. Commands are action verbs that you use to give instructions or orders to HyperCard.

The Message box is like a communicator device. It is a box in which you type instructions that tell HyperCard what to do. Use it to talk directly to HyperCard, bypassing menu and keyboard commands.

To see the Message box, you can either choose **Message** from the **Go** menu, or press ⌘M. You can type only one line at a time into the Message box.

HyperCard understands plain English, so the words you type will be in plain English. For example, typing **go to stack help** into the Message box and then pressing Return tells HyperCard to open the stack named Help. Pretty simple stuff.

Shortcut: Type **go help** for the same result.

In this lesson, you'll learn how to use some of the words that control HyperCard. First, you'll use the Message box to tell HyperCard where to go.

*1. Choose **Message** from the Go menu. The Message box appears at the bottom of the screen (see Figure 2.8).*

Once the Message box is displayed, you can move it anywhere on the screen so it doesn't cover up important text. To move the Message box, click on its top gray bar and drag it to the new location.

2. Click on the top bar of the Message box and drag it to another position on the screen (see Figure 2.9).

3. If the insertion point is within a field, click inside the Message box to move the insertion point inside of it. Drag the insertion point through the words in the box to select them. Press the Backspace key.

Tip: When the insertion point is not in a field, you don't have to erase the words in the Message box. Just begin typing and the old words automatically disappear.

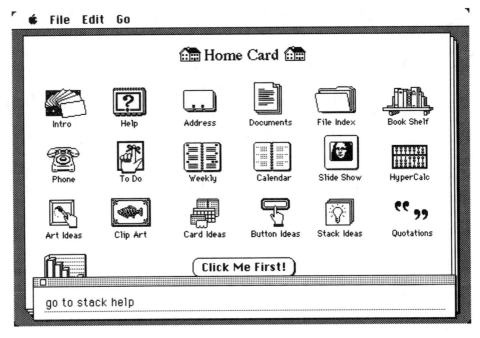

Figure 2.8   The Message box.

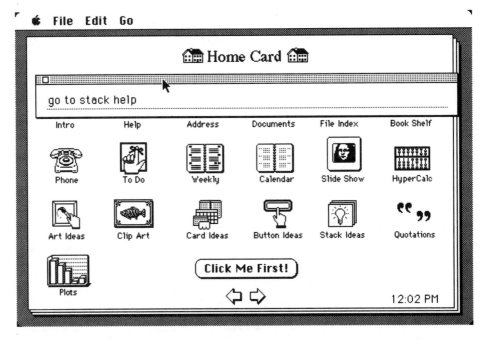

Figure 2.9   Click on the top bar of the Message box and drag to move it.

4. Type **go Quotations** *into the Message box and press Return to go to the stack of famous quotations.*

The Message box stays on the screen until you click in its close box, or press ⌘-M again (see Figure 2.10).

To send a new message, choose **Message box** from the Go menu again. Then type your new message. To erase the words in the Message box, hold down the mouse button and drag the insertion point over the words: then press the Backspace key. You can then type a new message if you like. Next, you'll ask HyperCard to display a desk accessory for you. To do this, you'll use the key word "doMenu." It chooses the named menu item for you.

5. Type **doMenu Calculator** *into the Message box and press Return. (Be sure to type* **doMenu** *as one word.) HyperCard looks in all the menus for calculator. When it finds calculator, in the* 🍎 *menu, it puts the calculator on the screen.*

Requesting Information

You can also use the Message box to display the time and date. Some HyperCard words and phrases don't require a command word like **go** or **doMenu** to know what to do. These HyperCard words are known as **functions**. Functions always begin with the word *the* and enable you to request specific information from HyperCard. For example, typing **the date** into the Message box and pressing Return displays the current date as known by the internal clock in your Macintosh (see Figure 2.11).

Practice using the Message box by typing some of the functions in the chart below. Press Return after typing the message to see the results. The results will appear in the Message box (see Figure 2.12).

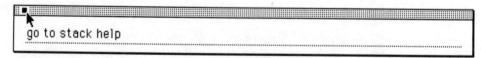

```
go to stack help
```

Figure 2.10 Clicking in the close box puts the Message box away.

```
the date
```

Figure 2.11 Type a function into the Message box and press Return.

```
┌─────────────────────────────────────────────────────────┐
│▒□▒░░░░░░░░░░░░░░░░░░░░░░░░░░░░░░░░░░░░░░░░░░░░░░░░░░░░░░░░░│
│ ┌─────────────────────────────────────────────────────┐ │
│ │ 5/5/88                                              │ │
│ └─────────────────────────────────────────────────────┘ │
└─────────────────────────────────────────────────────────┘
```

Figure 2.12 HyperCard displays the requested information in the Message box.

What You Type	*What You See*
the date	today's date in this form: 2/27/88
the long date	today's date in this form: Wednesday, July 27, 1988
the time	the time in this form: 8:00 AM
the long time	the seconds as well: 8:00:44 AM
the version	the version of HyperCard you are using: v 1.2
the diskspace	the number of bytes left on the disk that contains the stack you are using at the moment: 297472

For further information about sending messages to HyperCard, go to the Help stack.

1. Press ⌘? to go to the Help stack if it isn't already displayed.
2. Click on the Index tab.
3. At the Help index, click on the Find button and type **searching** into the Message box. Press Return.
4. Click on Message box or one of the subentries beneath it (**searching** and **with HyperCard**) for more information.

By the way, these messages you've been using are HyperTalk commands and functions. HyperTalk is a programming language built into HyperCard. You'll learn how to add HyperTalk commands and functions to cards, buttons, and other objects later in this book. The Help stack also offers information about HyperTalk. To see a list of the all the HyperTalk commands that HyperCard understands, follow these steps:

1. If you haven't opened the Help stack yet, press ⌘? to do so.
2. Click on the HyperTalk tab.
3. Click on the word *Commands* in the list on the card that appears. You'll see a list of command words (see Figure 2.13).

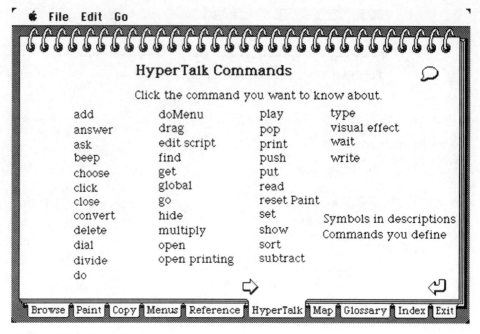

Figure 2.13 HyperTalk command words.

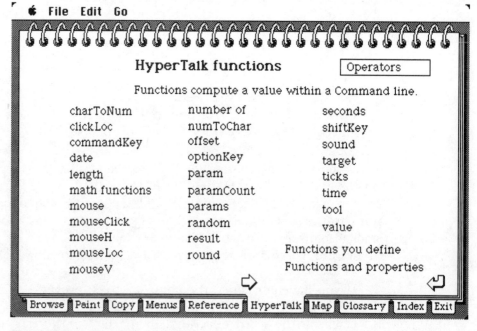

Figure 2.14 HyperTalk functions.

4. Browse around by clicking on a specific command word or on different buttons.

5. Click on the HyperTalk tab again to go back to the first card about HyperTalk. Then click on the word *Functions* to see a list of Hyper-Talk functions (see Figure 2.14).

6. Press ⌘-H to go back to the Home card.

The Find Box and the Message Box— Which Is Which?

You've probably noticed that the Find and Message boxes look similar. Actually, there is only one difference between the two: the Find box displays the Message box with the **Find** command and quotation marks already in it. All you have to do is type a word between the quotation marks that appear in the Message box. The Message box is either empty or contains the previous Message typed into it. If you recently used the Find command, it will appear in the Message box when you display the Message box.

KEYBOARD EQUIVALENTS

The commands on the Go menu help you navigate through stacks. Instead of choosing these commands from the Go menu, you can press certain keys on your keyboard to do the same thing. Table 2.1 contains all the keyboard command equivalents to the choices on the Go menu. These keyboard commands appear to the right of each choice on the

Keyboard Command	Equivalents on the Go Menu
⌘ - ~ or ~	Go to the last card shown
⌘-H	Go to the Home card
⌘-?	Go to the Help index
⌘-R	Go to the Recent card
⌘-1	Go to first card in stack
⌘-2	Go to previous card in stack
⌘-3	Go to next card in stack
⌘-4	Go to last card in stack
⌘-F	Go to a card with a specific word
⌘-M	Go to the Message box

Table 2.1 Keyboard equivalents on the Go menu.

Go menu. Not all choices on other menus have keyboard command equivalents. Many keyboard shortcuts appear in boxes throughout this book.

Appendix C lists all the keyboard shortcuts in HyperCard. Use Appendix C as a quick reference to keyboard shortcuts.

SUMMARY

In HyperCard, there's usually more than one way to do something such as navigate between cards and stacks. You choose the one that is most suited for what you want to do. If you like using the mouse to pull down menus, all the commands you need are listed in the menus. If you're a touch typist, you'll find the keyboard commands quicker to use. In some cases, it's easier to talk directly to HyperCard with the Message box.

What's more, you never have to worry about getting stuck because HyperCard's complete on-line Help system is only a click away.

3 Using What You've Got

In this chapter, you'll learn how to make practical use of the stacks packaged with HyperCard—the ones that are pictured on the Home card. Four of these stacks (Address, Weekly, Calendar, and To Do List) include buttons that connect them to each other. You'll use these stacks as you would a daily organizer: to keep notes, schedule appointments, maintain an address book, and organize your other day-to-day tasks. Another stack dials your telephone for you. And another creates charts from numbers you enter.

The lessons in this chapter show how to

- Add cards to a stack
- Enter information onto cards
- Delete cards from a stack
- Save and undo changes you make
- Sort cards
- Dial a phone number using the auto-dialer button
- Use the plots stack to create Bar, Coin, and Pie charts

Lesson 12: ADDING CARDS TO THE ADDRESS STACK

Before going on, make sure you are at the Typing level; that is, you've chosen **Typing** from the User Preferences card. If you are at the Browsing level, you won't be able to complete the lessons in this chapter. To change the level to Typing, follow these steps:

1. Press ⌘-H to go to the Home card.
2. Choose **Last** from the Go menu.
3. Click on Typing. Check Text Arrows by clicking in the box if no **x** appears.
4. Press ⌘-M to see the Message box.
5. Type **go address** into the Message box and press Return.

Opening the Address Stack

1. If you're not at the Address stack, press ⌘-M to see the Message box, type **go address** and press Return.
2. Press the Right Arrow button once to go to the next card.

Adding a New Card to This Stack

Follow the steps below to add your name, address, and phone number to this stack.

1. Choose **New Card** from the Edit menu. Type your name. Press Return. Type your address (see Figure 3.1).

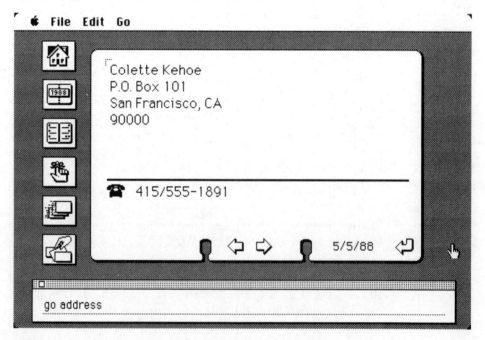

Figure 3.1 Enter your name and address.

2. Press the Tab key to move from one field to the next. The insertion point moves to the next field where you enter a phone number. To go back to the previous field, hold down the Shift key and press Tab.
3. Type your phone number.
4. Press Tab again. The insertion point moves into the last field on this card, which contains today's date. HyperCard automatically puts today's date on a card whenever you add or update a card in this stack.
5. Choose **New Card** from the Edit menu again or press ⌘N to add another card to the address stack.

Saving Changes

HyperCard saves a little differently from other Macintosh programs. For instance, in most programs you choose **Save** or **Save as** to save changes to a file before quitting an application. But, in HyperCard, a change is saved as soon as you make it. For example, the new card you added was saved as soon as you added it. And the words you typed into a field were saved as soon as you pressed either the Tab or Return key.

Changes you make in HyperCard are saved as soon as you do any one of the following:

- Press the Return or Tab key
- Choose a command or tool from any menu (or use its keyboard equivalent)
- Click the mouse outside of the text field
- Go to another card

But what if you don't want to save the change you just made? Then use HyperCard's **Undo** command, which is explained in the next lesson.

Lesson 13: UNDOING AND DELETING

Cards, pictures, or text that you deleted can be brought back with the **Undo** command if you use it before doing anything else.

The Undo Command

To undo your last action, choose **Undo** from the Edit menu or press the ⌘ and Z keys at the same time.

The **Undo** command undoes, or reverses, the last thing you did.

Whether you deleted a group of words, a card, or a picture, the **Undo** command will bring it back. But this command works only for the last thing you did. If you deleted a card and then deleted a group of words, using **Undo** will bring back that group of words but *not* the card you deleted previously.

Undo not only brings back something you deleted, it also undoes something you did, such as drawing an object with one of the paint tools or typing text into a field.

Fields and buttons that have been deleted cannot be brought back. However, if you resize a field or button, choosing **Undo** puts that object back the way it was.

Deleting Buttons and Fields

To delete buttons and fields, the user level must be set to Authoring or Scripting. To delete graphics, the user level must be set to Painting or higher. You'll learn how to delete these objects later in this book.

Deleting Characters

You can delete characters in a field by backspacing over them with the Backspace key, just as you do in any other Macintosh program. Move the insertion point after the character to be deleted and press the Backspace key.

Deleting One or More Words

To delete a word in a field, double-click anywhere on the word to select it and then press the Backspace key or type a word to replace it. When you select a word, it appears inverted. In this book, selected words are sometimes referred to as *highlighted*.

To delete more than one word, select the group of words to be deleted and press Backspace or type something (see Figure 3.2). The selected words will disappear in any case.

1. Erase your phone number in the Address stack by dragging the insertion point through the phone number and then pressing the Backspace key.
2. Press ⌘-Z to undo the deleted word.

Deleting the Contents of a Field

Instead of selecting the entire contents of a field, you can use the Message box to tell HyperCard to empty its contents for you. To tell Hyper-

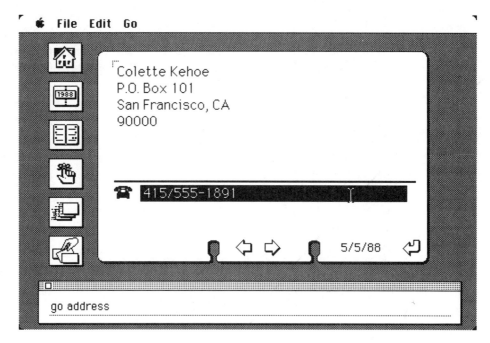

Figure 3.2 Delete selected words.

Card which field you want it to empty, you must refer to that field by either its name or number.

Fields are automatically numbered in the order in which they are created, beginning with 1. So the first field created would be Field 1. You can't see the field numbers at this level, but you can rest assured that if there are four fields on a card, then there is a field 1, field 2, field 3, and field 4. And, most likely, the number corresponds to a field's position on the card (from top to bottom and left to right), the topmost field being Field 1. See Figure 3.3 for an example of fields and their order numbers.

You'll learn more about fields in Section Two where you'll change the user level to Authoring. From that level, you'll have access to all the information about a field, including its field number. And you'll be able to assign a name to each field if you like. As for now, assume the fields are numbered in the order in which they appear on the card, from left to right. So the first field has an order number of 1.

1. Press ⌘-M to see the Message box if it isn't displayed. Otherwise, delete any words inside of it now.
2. Type **put empty into field 1**. Press Return.

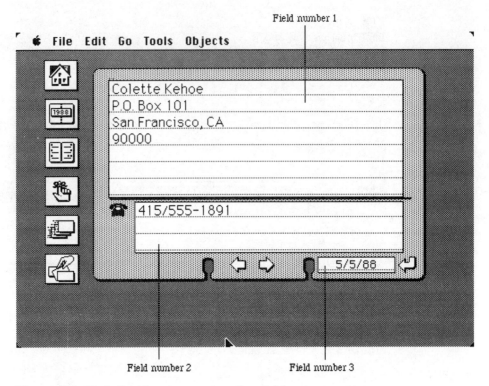

Figure 3.3 Each field has a corresponding field order number.

The field is emptied. To empty another field such as field 2, just change the 1 to a 2 (in the Message box) and press Return again. Text removed from a field with the Put Empty into Field command will not reappear when you use Undo. Why not? Because the Put Empty into Field message clears the field text without first copying it to the Clipboard. For the same reason, erasing text with the **Clear** command can't be undone.

You can also use the **Delete** command to delete text from a field. The chart below contains examples for using the **Delete** command.

What You Type	*What Happens*
delete last word of field 1	The last word in Field 1 disappears.
delete line 1 of field 1	The text in the first line of Field 1 disappears.

Delete a Card

To delete one card, display the card to be deleted and then choose **Delete Card** from the Edit menu. Instead of choosing **Delete Card** from the menu, you can press the ⌘ and Backspace keys at the same time to delete the card. (If you accidentally delete a card, choose **Undo** from the Edit menu before you do anything else.)

Delete Several Cards

The **Delete Card** command on the Edit menu can be tedious if you have several cards to delete. A quicker way to delete several cards is by using the Message box.

1. If the Message box is already on the screen, click inside of it to position the insertion point in it and select all the words inside. If the Message box is not on the screen, press ⌘-M to display it. The insertion point automatically moves into it.
2. Display a card you want to delete on the screen.
3. Type **doMenu delete card** and press **Return**.

The card that was on the screen disappears. To delete another card, go to that card and press Return again. The Message box stays on the screen until you either click in its close box or press ⌘-M again.

The only time you *can't* delete a card is when that card is the only one left in the stack. In that case, you might as well delete the stack. No **Delete Stack** choice? This choice appears in the File menu when you move up to the Painting level.

Lesson 14: BROWSE CARDS

Many stacks like the Address stack have a Browse button (see Figure 3.4).

Click on this button to flip through cards in this stack. HyperCard shows you the cards in the order in which they appear in the stack.

1. Click on the Browse button to begin browsing.
2. Click anywhere on the card to stop browsing.

Figure 3.4 The Browse button.

Tip: If you don't have a Browse button, type **show all cards** into the Message box to display all the cards, one at a time.

Lesson 15: SORT CARDS

Click on the Sort button to sort the cards in this stack (see Figure 3.5).

HyperCard gives you three choices: you can sort by first name, last name, or date.

1. Click on the Sort button.
2. Click in the Last Name button to sort the cards alphabetically by last name.

This particular Sort button has already been programmed to sort by one of three fields. In Section Three, you'll learn how to change the program in this Sort button to make it sort by any field you choose.

Lesson 16: FOUR STACKS IN ONE

Four stacks that were meant to work together as an organizer are named Weekly, Calendar, Address, and To Do. These stacks are pictured as icons on the Home card.

Click on the stack named Weekly on the Home card. Each card in this stack contains a different week of each, month like a weekly appointment book.

HyperCard automatically shows you the card for the current week. How did it know what today was? HyperCard cleverly looks at the setting on your Macintosh internal clock and then displays the card with the date that corresponds to that setting.

Figure 3.5 The Sort button.

But what if you wanted to see what you've scheduled for a particular week in July? You could click through the cards in this stack one at a time, or you could use the Find command. But there's an even quicker way.

Look at the buttons on the top of this card (see Figure 3.6). When clicked on, these buttons take you to other stacks: Address, To Do, Calendar, and, of course, Home.

1. Click on the Calendar button at the top of this card to go to the yearly calendar. A box appears around this week. Each six months is on a card of its own. If July is not on the calendar now, click the Right Arrow button to see the other half of the calendar.
2. Click on the week of July 18. HyperCard opens the Weekly stack to the card with the week that includes July 18.

    Next you want to see if you have listed anything on your To Do list for that week.
3. Click on the To Do button (it looks like a finger with a string around it).

Suppose you had a meeting with Karl at 4:00, and you wanted to

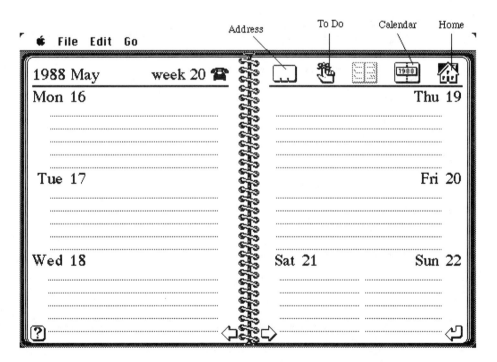

Figure 3.6 Buttons on each card in the Weekly stack.

call him to reschedule it. If you had his number in your Address stack, you could just select his name in the To-Do list and then click on the Address button. HyperCard would take you right to the card with his phone number. And, from that card, you could dial his number.

Follow these steps to recreate the above scenario:

1. Press the Tab key to position the insertion point in the first field of the To Do list.
2. Type **Meet with Karl at 4:00** in your To Do list.
3. Select **Karl** and click on the Address button (see Figure 3.7). HyperCard takes you to the first card in the Address stack that matches the selected word.
4. Select Karl's phone number on the Address card, lift the receiver of your telephone, wait for the dial tone, and then click on the Phone button (see Figure 3.8).

Note: If you have a rotary-dial phone, click on the Phone button before lifting the receiver. The next lesson explains how to make changes to

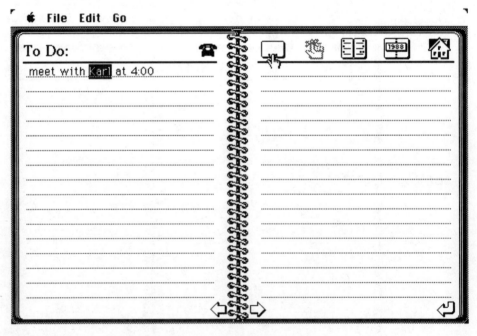

Figure 3.7 Select **Karl** and click on the Address button.

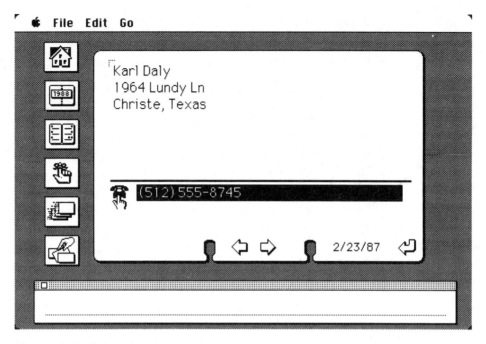

Figure 3.8 Select the phone number and click on the Phone button.

the Phone card so the settings match your particular telephone or audio device.

Sure, HyperCard can dial phone numbers for you. All you have to do is select the number to be dialed and click on the button that looks like a telephone. But *don't forget* that, before HyperCard can do all that, your Macintosh must be hooked up to your phone with a modem or other audio device that can send tones over a telephone line.

Lesson 17: USING THE PHONE CARD

The Phone card you saw briefly in the previous lesson is the same one you can access from the Home card. Let's look at the usefulness of the Phone card.

1. Press ⌘-H to go to the Home card. Then click on the Phone button.

The Phone card has several fields and buttons (see Figure 3.9). You can get help with these fields and buttons in two ways. The first way is to click on the Question Mark button.

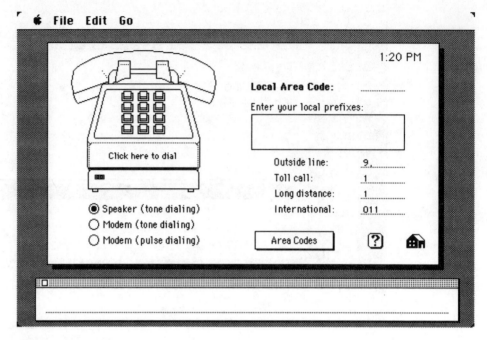

Figure 3.9 Phone card.

2. Click on the question mark in the bottom right corner of the card. It gives you general instructions on how to use the Phone card. After reading the instructions, click on them to put them away.

The second way to get help is by clicking on a word on the Phone card for which you need more information.

3. Click on any word for more information about a word; for example, click on **Toll call** *to see information about placing toll calls. After reading the message, click on it to put it away.*

Okay, now let's fill in the blanks. The first field contains the area code of the number you wish to dial.

The Area Code

4. Press the Tab key to move the insertion point into the first field. Type your local area code in the first field. Press the Tab key to go to the second field.

Free Calls within the Area Code

5. Enter the first three digits of the phone numbers within your local area code that you can call without paying extra. The first three digits of a phone number

> *Tip:* If you're in some strange and distant city, you might not know the area code offhand. If this city happens to be either in the U.S. or Canada, you are in luck. Just click on the button labeled Area Codes. The insertion point appears between the quotation marks inside the Find box. Type the name of the city (or nearest large city if you're in someplace most people never heard of) in the Find box and press Return. When you've found what you were looking for, click on the Phone button to get back to the Phone card.

tell HyperCard if this is a toll call or a free (nontoll) call within your area code.

The next field contains the number you must dial before dialing an outside line. For example, in a hotel, you usually need to dial 9 first before calling a number outside the hotel.

Outside Line

6. Clear the outside line field if you don't need to dial 9 for an outside line. To clear this field, select it and then press the Backspace key.

Toll Call

*7. Type a **1** into the toll call field if the number you are calling is within your area code but is not a free call. (Some areas require that you dial a 1 before a phone number for which you are charged by the minute, even if it's in your area code.)*

Long Distance

8. You can skip the long distance field. HyperCard automatically dials a 1 before the phone number if this call is outside your area code.

Speaker or Modem

The three buttons on the left of the card tell HyperCard whether your Macintosh is connected to a telephone with an audio device or a modem and what kind of phone you are using.

Audio device   If the Macintosh is connected to an audio device instead of a modem, click on the Speaker button.

Modem   If you have a push-button phone, click on the **Modem** (tone dialing) button.

If you have a rotary phone, the kind with the wheel you rotate to dial a number, click on the **Modem** (pulse dialing) button.

The Phone card works with any Hayes-compatible modem.

9. Click in the button to the left of the kind of phone connection you're using: Speaker, Modem (tone dialing), or Modem (pulse dialing).

10. If you chose either Speaker or Modem (tone dialing), lift the handset of your phone before dialing just as you would to manually dial the phone. Make sure you hear the dial tone. Then click once on the picture of the phone where it says, "Click here to dial." A dialog box appears for you to enter a phone number.

If you chose Modem (pulse dialing), don't pick up the phone before dialing. Dial the number and then pick up the phone.

11. Type a seven-digit local phone number or include the area code if it isn't a local call. Don't use hyphens. Press RETURN.

*12. If the first three digits of the number you dial don't match any of the numbers in the second field, a dialog box appears asking you **Is this a local (nontoll) call?***

If it is a local number for which you are not being charged extra to call, then click in the Yes button. If you must pay extra for this call, then click in the No button. If it is not a toll call, HyperCard will add the first three digits of this number to the second field.

If you use hyphens (for example, 555-1212) you must surround the number with quotation marks, like this: "555-1212." If you use hyphens without quotation marks, HyperCard will subtract these numbers from each other and dial the result.

To make this card more useful, add the Phone button to cards in other stacks. Then, as you're using those other stacks and want to make a call, all you have to do is click on the Phone button. This button contains instructions to get the Phone card so you can make a call. Section Two in this book shows how to copy buttons from one card to another.

13. Click on the Home button in the bottom right corner of the Phone card to return to the Home card.

Now that you've set up the Phone card to work properly for your situation, do the following practice exercise.

Dial-a-Card for Practice

Assuming your phone, Macintosh, and modem are all connected properly and you have opened the Address stack, you are ready to dial a number using the Phone button.

1. Go to the Address stack. From any card in the Address stack, use the **Find** command to find the card with the name of the person you want to call. Choose **Find** from the Go menu.
2. Type the name of the person to call; for example, type **Liz**. Press Return.
3. Pick up the telephone receiver. Listen for the dial tone.
4. Select the phone number on the Address card displayed and then click on the Phone button next to the phone number (see Figure 3.10). Usually there is a slight delay (one or two seconds) before you actually hear the phone ring.

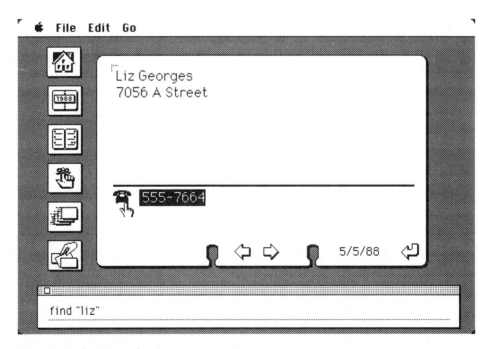

Figure 3.10 Dial-a-Card.

HyperCard dials the number. Someone answers. You talk. When you're done, hang up. That's it. In the future, using a computer to dial a telephone, just as you did now, will probably be standard practice.

Lesson 18: USING THE PLOTS STACK

Use this stack to create Bar, Pie, or Coin charts. All you have to do is type the numbers for the chart into the rightmost column on this card and then click on the kind of chart you want HyperCard to create. Next you'll practice using this stack.

1. Go to the Home card. Click on the Plots button.

2. Press the Tab key to move the insertion point into the first field. Type any number into the first field, for example, 50. Press Return to go to the next line in the column. Type another number. Press RETURN.

3. Continue entering any numbers you like, pressing Return to go to the next line.

4. Click on one of these three buttons along the bottom: Bar, Coin, or Pie (see Figures 3.11–3.13). Watch as HyperCard creates a chart using the numbers you provided.

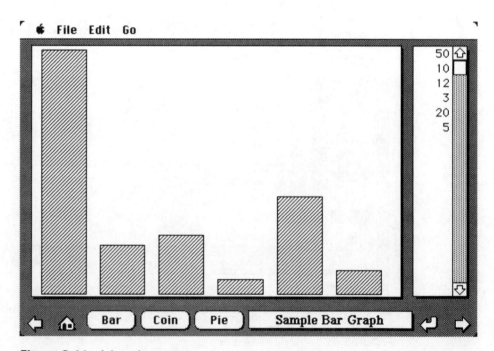

Figure 3.11 A bar chart.

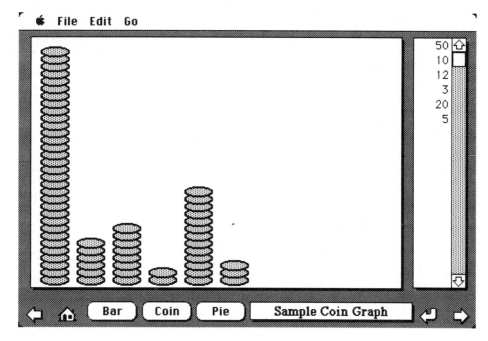

Figure 3.12 A coin chart.

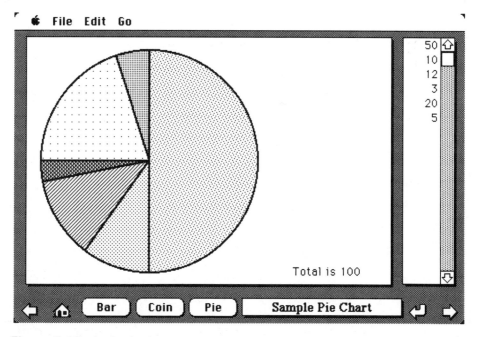

Figure 3.13 A pie chart.

Once you switch to a higher level (Painting, Authoring, or Scripting), you can copy the charts you create onto cards in other stacks. You can also use the **Export Paint** command (available at the Painting level) to copy the chart into a file readable by MacPaint and other paint programs.

5. For now, go Home.

SUMMARY

HyperCard's Address, Weekly, Calendar, and To Do List stacks are linked in ways not possible with papers and books. Those stacks are included with HyperCard to help you keep track of appointments, addresses, phone numbers, and other notes.

In this chapter you practiced adding and deleting cards as well as the information on them. So now you can change and update stacks like the Address and Datebook with your own information. And, since HyperCard automatically saves the changes you make, you don't have to use a **Save** command—in fact, there is no **save** command in HyperCard. But there is an **Undo** command that brings back a word or card you've deleted.

The Phone card can dial phone numbers for you at the click of a button once you've initially set up the fields and connected your Macintosh to a modem or other audio device. And the Plots stack will draw charts for you based on the figures you enter.

In the next chapter, you'll learn all about HyperCard's printing functions. Then you're ready for Section Two, where you'll graduate to the Painting and Authoring levels as you learn how to create your own stacks.

4 Printing Everything and Anything

In this chapter, you'll learn about HyperCard's printing options. But, even better, you'll learn a few secrets for printing just the cards you want. The File menu limits you to three printing choices: **Print Card**, **Print Stack**, and **Print Report**. But the tips and tricks in this chapter help you print beyond those limits.

The lessons in this chapter show how to

- Set up the page for printing
- Print one card
- Print one stack
- Print a select group of cards
- Print reports
- Print mailing labels
- Print files from other programs

HyperCard gives you several printing choices. With the appropriate print command from the File menu, you can print one card or all the cards in a stack.

Before using a **print** *command, remember to turn on your printer.*

Lesson 19: SETTING UP THE PAGES FOR PRINTING

Before printing a card, a stack, or anything else, first use the Chooser to select the kind of printer you are using.

69

Choosing a Printer

1. Pull down the menu and select **Chooser**.
2. Click on the ImageWriter or LaserWriter icon, depending on which you are using.
3. Click in the close box to close the Chooser window.

Using the Page Setup Command

Choose **Page Setup** from the File menu.

Most likely, you are familiar with the Page Setup dialog box since it is a standard feature in most Macintosh applications. The choices are self-explanatory if you have an ImageWriter. You just choose the kind of paper you have, whether you want the pages printed vertically or horizontally, and which, if any, special effects you'd like (see Figure 4.1).

You get a few more page setup choices when printing with a Laser-Writer because it is capable of higher resolution (a sharper, clearer print-out) than the ImageWriter (see Figure 4.2).

Size of page   The **Reduce** and **Enlarge** features do not work for Hyper-Card stacks. These features are standard Macintosh printing features that work with other applications.

Type of fonts   Click in **Font Substitution** if you used or plan to use nonlaser fonts such as Los Angeles or some other ImageWriter font on your cards. HyperCard will substitute the nonlaser font with the closest laser font it has.

Smooth graphics   Click in **Smoothing** to print graphic images with the best quality a LaserWriter can produce.

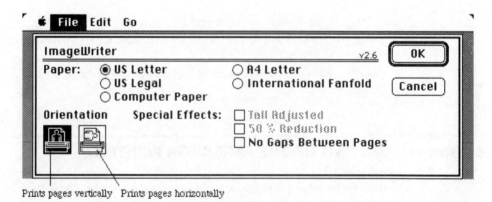

Prints pages vertically   Prints pages horizontally

Figure 4.1   Page setup screen for ImageWriter.

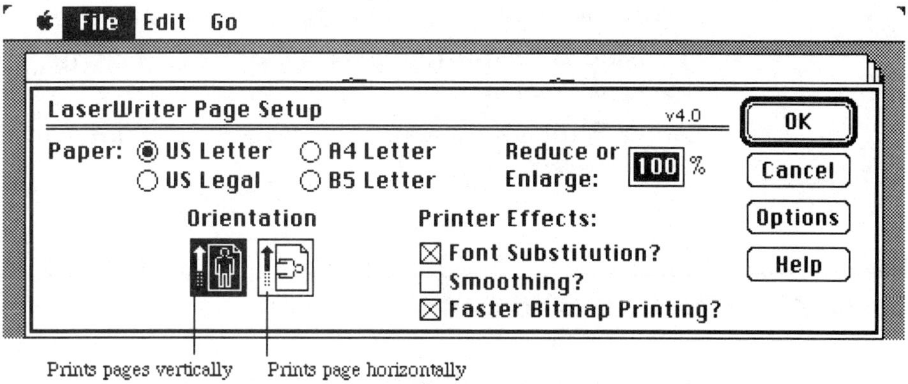

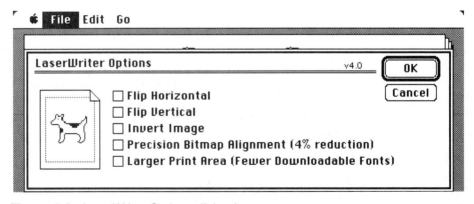

Figure 4.2 Page setup screen for LaserWriter.

Faster printing Click in **Faster Bitmap Printing** if you have a LaserWriter. This choice prints pages as fast as possible. The only time you wouldn't use this option is if you're using a printer that uses a slower speed. In that case, the printer manual will tell you not to use the **Faster Bitmap Printing** choice.

More printing options Click on the **Options** button to see what other choices you have (see Figure 4.3).

> **Flip Horizontal** flips the image so it's facing the opposite way. Click on this option and watch what happens to the dog in the picture in the Options dialog box.
>
> **Flip Vertical** flips the image so it's upside down. Click on this option and see what happens to the dog again.

Figure 4.3 LaserWriter Options dialog box.

Invert Image prints white as black and black as white.

Precision Bitmap Alignment helps the LaserWriter print graphics as clearly as possible.

Larger Print Area prints text and graphics closer to the edges of the printer paper.

Lesson 20: PRINTING ONE CARD

Computers are great organizers and reminders. But there are times when a computer just can't compete against a piece of paper, such as when you're running errands. Suppose you typed a list of errands on your To Do list in HyperCard. Instead of lugging your Macintosh around with you and searching for a place to plug it in, you could save yourself the trouble and use the **Print Card** menu choice.

The instructions for printing one card are simple:

1. Find and display the card you want to print.
2. Choose **Print Card** from the File menu (or press ⌘-P).

HyperCard immediately begins printing the card currently on the screen, using the settings in Page Setup (in the File menu). If necessary, change those settings before printing.

Lesson 21: PRINTING ONE STACK

Print a whole stack? When you want to see all the cards in a stack, choose **Print Stack** from the File menu. Often you may print a stack just to see how someone else put it together (how many cards were used and what appears on each card). HyperCard prints all the cards as they appear on the screen, complete with their background information.

More likely, you'll print the stacks that you create. Having a printout of each card in your own stack helps you with the process of designing and editing it.

To print all the cards in a stack:

1. Open the stack you want to print.
2. Choose **Print Stack** from the File menu.

The Print Stack dialog box appears with several options to choose from, such as how many cards you want printed per page and how you want it formatted (see Figure 4.4).

Table 4.1 lists the print options in the Print Stack dialog box.

3. Select the print options you want in the Print Stack dialog box. Refer to Table 4.1 for information about each option.

Lesson 22: PRINTING 10 CARDS IN A ROW

The Message box comes to the rescue once again. You can use it to tell HyperCard how many cards to print, beginning with the card on the screen.

1. Go to the first card to be printed.
2. Make sure the cards are in the order you wish to print them. You can use the Sort button to reorder these cards. For example, to print the first 10 cards in the Address stack in alphabetical order by last

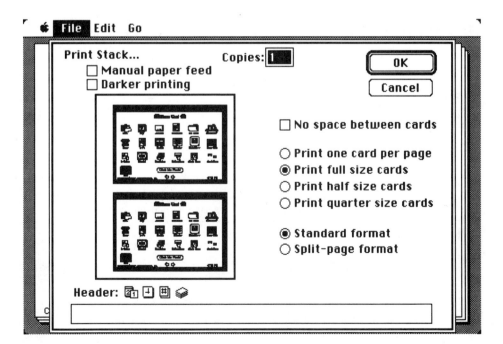

Figure 4.4 Print Stack dialog box.

Manual paper feed	Check this to print individual sheets of paper. After printing one sheet of paper, HyperCard pauses printing until you add the next sheet.
Darker printing	Check this if you want the ink on the pages to print darker.
Fast laser printing	Check this if you have a LaserWriter.
No space between cards	Check this if you do not want any white space between the cards on each page.
Cards printed per page	Print one card per page
	Print full-size cards (2 per page)
	Print half-size cards (8 per page)
	Print quarter-size cards (32 per page)
Standard format	Prints cards evenly spaced on the page. This option leaves enough room on the left edge for binder holes.
Split-page format	Prints cards with enough space between them to fold the paper without creasing the cards. You'll also have enough room for binder holes.
Header	From left to right, the header icons are *date*, *time*, *page number*, and *stack name*. Choose one or more of the header icons by clicking on the ones you want to appear in the header (see Fig. 4.5). Then type any text that you want to appear at the top of each printed page into the Header field. Text and icons that you put into the Header field will be printed at the top of each page.

Table 4.1 Options in the Print Stack dialog box.

name, click the Sort button. Then choose Last name in the dialog box.

3. Press ⌘-M to display the Message box.
4. Type **print 10 cards** into the Message box, and then press RETURN.

HyperCard prints the first 10 cards, beginning with the one shown on the screen.

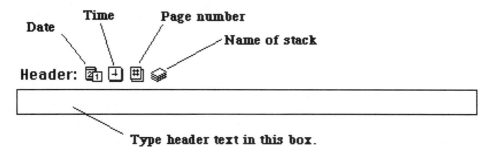

Figure 4.5 Header icons.

Lesson 23: PRINTING A SELECT GROUP OF CARDS

Sorry to say but there is **no menu choice** to print a subset of cards in a stack such as all cards in the Address stack that have 11/07/88 in the Date field. But that doesn't mean it can't be done. To print a selected group of cards, you need to tell HyperCard three things:

- when to start selecting cards to be printed
- which cards to select
- when to stop printing

You can do this by typing these special commands into the Message box:

open printing with dialog
print card
close printing

For practice, follow these steps:

1. Go to the Address stack.

2. Press ⌘-M to show the Message box.

*3. Type **open printing with dialog** and press* RETURN *(see Figure 4.6).*

*4. Choose **Print Full-Size Cards** for the print format if it isn't already selected. This prints two cards per page.*

*5. Click OK. **Now preparing to print . . .** appears on your screen. Make sure the printer is on. Nothing will print until you've selected enough cards to fill one page—in this case, two cards.*

Meanwhile, HyperCard puts these cards into a queue. (If you chose eight cards per page, HyperCard wouldn't start printing until you'd selected eight cards.)

*6. Go to the first card to be printed. Type **print card** into the Message box. Press RETURN. **Now preparing page 1 . . .** appears on the screen. Nothing will print yet until you choose another card to print.*

*7. Go to another card to be printed. Again, type **print card** into the box and press RETURN.*

*8. Type **close printing** and press RETURN.*

The **Close Printing** command tells HyperCard to stop putting cards in the queue because you're done selecting cards to print.

Tip: You can skip the Print Stack dialog box by typing **open printing** in the Message box. Then choose cards to print, typing **print card** in the Message box each time. Type **close printing** when through.

Once you know how to write programs (or scripts) in HyperTalk, there

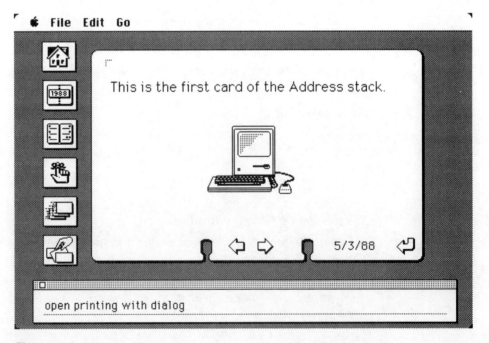

Figure 4.6 Use the Message box to print selected cards.

are many other ways for you to print a select group of cards. There is even a way to print reports that list information from the fields in two or more stacks. You'll learn about HyperTalk commands in Section Three.

Lesson 24: PRINTING REPORTS

A report is a list of text that appears in one or more fields of a stack. HyperCard reports cannot include any graphics or buttons, just text. And unfortunately, you cannot change the font that HyperCard uses in printed reports. However, you can print reports in different formats and HyperCard makes printing them simple.

See Figure 4.7 for a sample HyperCard report.

The printed list can be limited to certain fields or you can print text from every field. You can print a report in one of three formats:

- labels
- columns
- rows

In the practice exercises that follow, you'll print reports in each of these formats.

Printing a Report in Column Format

In this exercise, you'll print a report on the information stored in the File Index stack.

The File Index stack, included with HyperCard, is a group of cards that look like index cards and are used to file information about different subjects much as paper file index cards are used. The File Index stack has just two fields for entering information: an index number and a description. Printing a report on this stack would list the index number and description on every card in this stack.

1. Go to the Home card and click on File Index.

*2. Choose **Print Report** from the File menu now (see Figure 4.8).*

Manual Paper Feed

Before choosing a report format, first tell HyperCard what kind of paper you're using—computer paper with holes or single sheets of paper like letterhead or typing paper.

To print reports on individual sheets of paper, click in the Manual paper feed box so that an **X** appears. After printing one sheet of

Card Name	Name and Address	Phone Number	Date
first	This is the first card of the Address stack.		7/26/87
Card 2		1591.549431 Some demo, huh? You said it!	1/11/88
Card 3	Roger Benrey 9541 Mount Vernon Dr	555-3005	2/23/87
Card 4	Loween Blank 6686 Martin Ave Prairie, Texas	(214) 555-5456	2/23/87
Card 5	Richard Boyd 6686 Black Mountain Rd	555-6080	2/23/87
Card 6	The quick brown fox jumps over the lazy dog!!!		1/11/88
Card 7	Shannon Browne 7814 Olive Ave	555-1765	2/23/87
Card 8	Chris Caldwell 8689 24th Street	555-0879	2/23/87
Card 9	Emmett Cardenas 1919 Short Street	555-8487	2/23/87
Card 10	Joshua Carlson 6291 Elliot Street	555-3109	2/23/87
Card 11	Karl Daly 1964 Lundy Ln Christe, Texas	(512) 555-8745	2/23/87
Card 12	Annette Darling 400 Ohio Ave Bristol, Pennsylvania	(215) 555-0696	2/23/87
Card 13	Maria Deguara 7745 Foxborough Drive	555-1622	2/23/87
Card 14	Bill Diamond 6999 Brewster Way	555-9909	2/23/87
Card 15	Dean Diffie 1346 48th Avenue	555-5816	2/23/87
Card 16	Kris Everly 2938 Maple Ln	555-4431	2/23/87
Card 18	Randy Fiscus 7670 Stambaugh St	555-2027	2/23/87
Card 19	Rebecca Gadja 9338 Bayshore Rd Ashland, Kentucky	(606) 555-8460	2/23/87
Card 20	Liz Georges 7056 A Street	555-7664	2/23/87
Card 21	Gary Grant 8698 66th Street	555-9320	2/23/87

Figure 4.7 Sample HyperCard Report.

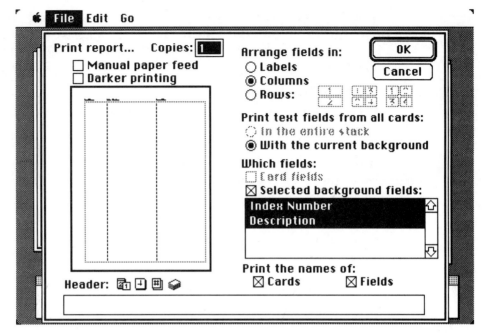

Figure 4.8 Print report dialog box.

paper, HyperCard pauses printing until you add the next sheet. To print reports on computer paper, uncheck this box by clicking in it so the **X** disappears.

Now take a closer look at the report formats you can choose. Each is described below.

Label Format

Choosing **Labels** prints card information as it would appear on an envelope. The standard format is for three-across mailing labels. You can adjust the size of the labels by clicking on the lower right corner of the top left label and then dragging it up, down, left, or right. As you drag, the dimensions of the label appear at the bottom of the dialog box. Let go of the mouse when you see the correct dimensions.

Column Format

Choosing **Columns** prints each field in a separate column:

Card Name:	Description:	Index Number:
Card 1	Contents of my lateral file.	1000
Card 2	Report on stress resistance.	1001

Column width is at first determined by the number of fields in the stack. For example, if you have 10 fields, a column report will have 10 columns, each of the same width. You can change this width by dragging the lines in the dialog box to the left or right. Some columns can be wide, some narrow.

Row Format

Choosing **Rows** prints each field of text on its own line, one under the other:

Card Name: Card 1
Description: Contents of my lateral file.
Index Number: 1000

Card Name: Card 2
Description: Report on stress resistance.
Index Number: 1001

You can choose rows of text to be printed in one or two columns by clicking on the appropriate diagram to the right of the Rows button.

- (1) Selecting the first diagram prints the contents of each field on a separate line or row.
- (2) Selecting the second diagram prints fields in the same way except in two columns instead of one. It prints cards down one column until it reaches the end of the page; then it prints down a second column on the same page.
- (3) Selecting the third diagram prints fields in two columns but back and forth from left to right instead of down one and then the other (see Figure 4.9).

The other print report options are explained as you follow the steps in the following examples.

3. Click the Columns button to tell HyperCard to print each field in its own column.

All fields on a card are usually created on a background that is shared by several cards. But stacks can have more than one background, so when printing a report, you need to tell HyperCard which fields to print: the ones on a specific background or text from all backgrounds.

In the Entire Stack

Prints text in fields on each background in the stack. For example, if a stack has two backgrounds and the first background has two fields but

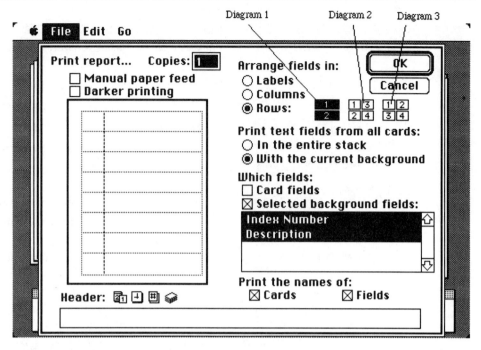

Figure 4.9 Diagrams 1, 2, and 3 for Row format options.

the second has six fields, HyperCard prints the text in the two fields AND the text in the six fields, for a total of eight fields.

With the Current Background
If a stack has two backgrounds, HyperCard prints only the text on the cards with the background currently shown on the screen.

4. To choose it if it isn't already chosen, click the button for With the Current Background.

You can also narrow down exactly which fields to print. You can choose from among card fields and background fields.

Card Fields
Check this box to see a list of all fields that appear on the card currently on the screen. This choice is gray because there are no card fields on individual cards in this stack. If there were, those fields would appear in the scroll box, and you'd click on each field you wanted in the report. (The fields you click on are then highlighted.)

Selected Background Fields
Check this box to see a list of all fields that appear on the background currently on the screen. In the scroll box, select the fields to be printed.

5. Click in Selected Background Fields if it isn't checked. All fields in this stack were created on the same background, so this is the only option you have right now.

6. In the scroll box, select (by dragging on them) the fields labeled Index Number and Description if they aren't selected.

Printing the Names of Cards and Fields

Next you'll choose if you want the names of cards or fields also to appear on the report. These options are described below.

Cards   Checking this box adds a column that lists the names of cards.

Fields   Prints field names as headings above each column.

*7. If they aren't checked, click in the boxes for **Print the names of** cards and fields to include the names of each card and field in this stack. In the printed report, **Card Name** appears underlined as the title above the first column. The names of all cards are then listed in this column. If a card doesn't have a name, its card number is printed instead, for example, Card 1. The words **Description** and **Index Number** (the names of the two fields in this stack) appear underlined above the second and third columns of this report.*

Adding a Header to the Report

You can create a header to appear on each page of this report by following these instructions:

8. Click on a header icon to select it. You can choose one or more of the four header icons. They are, from left to right, Date, Time, Page Number, Stack Name. Choose the Date icon by clicking on it once.

9. Press the space bar a few times to add space between the header icon and header text. Type header text into the Header field, such as your name and title of the report.

Whatever you put in the Header field appears at the top of each page that is printed.

Now you're ready to print this report.

10. Click the OK button in the upper right corner of the screen. After a moment, the report begins printing. It should look similar to Figure 4.10.

If you need to design and print more complicated reports, for example, ones that include information from several stacks, or reports that

6/23/88	Ginger Jones	File Index Report

Card Name	Index Number	Description
Card 1	1000	Contents of my Lateral file, items organized in numerical order. Use the Find command in the Go menu to search for an item like "sprocket" or "form".
Card 2	1001	Report on stress-resistance in new metals
Card 3	1002	Company cafeteria menus through August
Card 4	1003	Form W-4 that I filed last year
Card 5	1004	Memo to Thompson about product strategy for '87. No reply.
Card 6	1005	Newspaper clippings about recent sales meeting. Police investigations attached.
Card 7	1006	Award from National Institute of Sprockets for outstanding gear tooth design
Card 8	1007	Article clipped from Pinions on Parade about recent reorganization
Card 9	1008	Healthco claim forms and receipts
Card 10	1009	My résumé, updated July
Card 11	1010	GlobeTrotter Airlines frequent flyer plan rules, regulations, and stubs
Card 12	1011	New Product request forms
Card 13	1012	Call for Papers of 15th annual convention of sprocket designers, Baltimore, Mass.

Figure 4.10 Printed Report.

include graphics, then you need a stack named "Reports!" This stack was created by Michael Long of Nine to Five Software and is published by Mediagenics (formerly Activision, Inc.). With this stack, you can design your own report layouts, adding fields with different fonts, graphics, and more.

Lesson 25: PRINTING MAILING LABELS

No program that manages information would be complete without a choice for printing mailing labels. This choice appears in the Print Report dialog box. To print names and addresses on mailing labels, first open the stack that has the information you want to print.

1. Choose **Open Stack** *from the File menu. Find and choose the Address stack.*

2. Choose **Print Report** *from the File menu.*

> *Tip:* Click to put an **X** in the box for Manual Paper Feed. Then you can test if the labels are aligned correctly in the printer. If the printing isn't just right on the first sheet of labels, adjust the label paper in the printer, and print again. Once everything is aligned, turn off the Manual Paper Feed to print the labels continuously.

3. Click on the Labels button.

The standard format is for three-across mailing labels (see Figure 4.11). Notice that the top left label has a small black square in its lower right corner. Click on that square and drag up, down, left or right to shrink or enlarge the size of the labels. As you drag, the label dimensions change (see the bottom of the dialog box).

4. Change the label size to two across instead of three across (see Figure 4.12). Drag the black square until you see two columns of labels instead of three. Let go of the mouse when you see the correct dimensions.

5. Click OK to begin printing.

Lesson 26: PRINTING FILES FROM OTHER PROGRAMS

Suppose you are a sales manager. Last week you used Microsoft Excel to create a new budget for your department, but you can't remember what all those figures were. You have been browsing a HyperCard stack that contains last quarter's budget information. You decide to update it. Instead of quitting HyperCard, printing the budget file, and then starting HyperCard again, you can use HyperCard's Message box to tell HyperCard to print that file now.

Assuming the budget is in a file named Budget for Q3 and the name of the Microsoft Excel icon (as it appears beneath the icon in the Finder) is Excel, here's how you'd print that file:

1. Press ⌘-M to show the Message box.

*2. Type **Print "Budget for Q3" with "Excel"** and then press RETURN.*

Be sure to include the quotation marks around both the name of the file to print and the application used to print it. Type the name of the application exactly as it appears beneath its icon in the Finder.

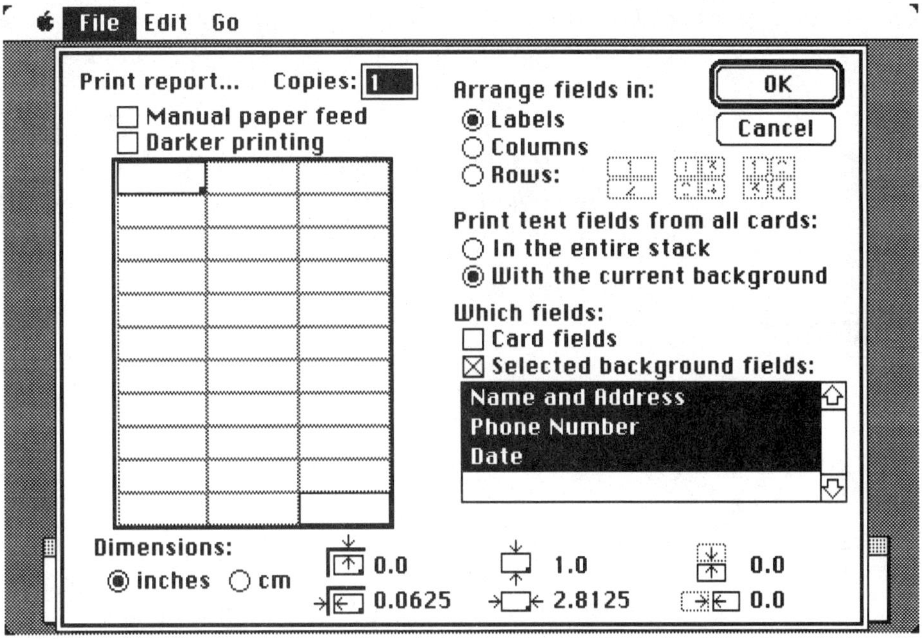

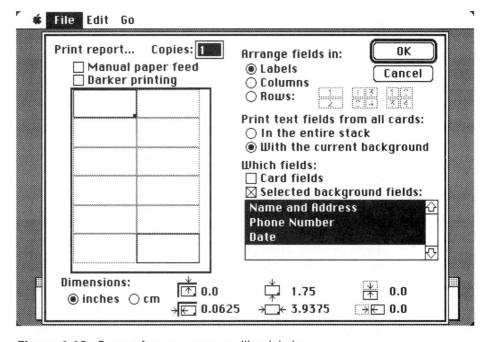

Figure 4.11 Mailing label format.

Figure 4.12 Format for two-across mailing labels.

3. HyperCard presents the dialog box that asks you where Budget for Q3 is. You would then find and double-click on this file in the dialog box.

4. As soon as HyperCard has located both the file to be printed and the application with which to print it, you'll see the Excel print dialog box. Click OK to begin printing. Once this file is printed, HyperCard closes the file and application and brings you back to the same card in the stack that was on your screen when you gave the **Print** *command.*

SUMMARY

HyperCard gives you menu choices to print

- a card
- a stack
- a report

When printing a stack, you can choose to print

- one card per page
- full-size cards (2 per page)
- half-size cards (8 per page)
- quarter-size cards (32 per page)

When printing a report, you can choose which fields to print. **Print Report** also gives you three report formats: labels, rows, and columns.

You can print a select group of cards by entering three special printing commands into the Message box in this order: **Open Printing**, **Print Card**, **Close Printing**.

You can also use the Message box to print files created with other applications like Microsoft Excel or MacWrite, for example.

Congratulations! You're No Longer a Beginner!!!

Now you really know all you need to know to use HyperCard stacks. However, if you're like most people, you won't be content just to use stacks that others have made. You'll want to make the most use out of HyperCard by creating stacks that are useful to you.

So go on to Section Two—Intermediate Applications. There you'll learn how to create some fun and simple stacks as well as more complicated but practical ones.

SECTION TWO INTERMEDIATE APPLICATIONS

You create stacks in one of two ways:

- Copying and modifying existing stacks
- Building new stacks from scratch

This section shows both ways as you change the user level from Typing to Painting to Authoring. Each new level gives you more tools and menus for creating HyperCard applications.

Chapters 5 through 8 show how to create stacks the easy way: *by modifying existing ones*. Chapters 9 through 12 show how to create stacks from a blank screen. Chapter 13 shows how to create a second Home card with buttons linked to the stacks you created in this book. You'll also see how easy it is to create buttons that will open other Macintosh applications at the same time you're working with HyperCard.

Here are the applications you'll learn how to create, step by step, in the chapters of this section:

- An organization chart
- An index file of HyperCard tips
- A resume
- A stack of imported pictures
- A catalog of products
- An application launcher

In Section Three you'll learn how to enhance some of these stacks with sound, animation, visual effects, and dialog boxes.

5 Quick Stacks

In this chapter you'll create two stacks: an organization chart for your company and an index file for filing notes about HyperCard. By copying and making changes to stacks that already exist, you'll be able to create these new stacks rather quickly.

Lesson 27: CREATING AN ORG CHART

Already part of the standard HyperCard stacks, the Idea stacks—Stack Ideas, Card Ideas, Button Ideas, and Art Ideas—provide model cards and tools for creating your own stacks. **Stack Ideas** contains several cards to use as backgrounds when creating a stack similar in form. **Card Ideas** provides several cards to copy and paste into stacks. **Button Ideas** is virtually a toolbox of buttons that you can copy, with their underlying programs as well! And **Art Ideas** contains loads of clip art for various occasions.

The model cards in Stack Ideas are referred to as *templates* or *skeletons* because they provide an outline for the contents of the stack. In other words, a **template** is like a form that you fill out.

Using the Stack Ideas

Follow these steps to create a new stack from one of the Stack Ideas cards:

1. Press ⌘-H to go to the Home card.

2. Click on the Stack Ideas icon. In the Stack Ideas Index that appears, you can click on any stack pictured to go to that stack.

3. Click on the hand in the lower right corner of the screen to see the next index card. Find and click on the picture labeled Org Chart (see Figure 5.1).

88

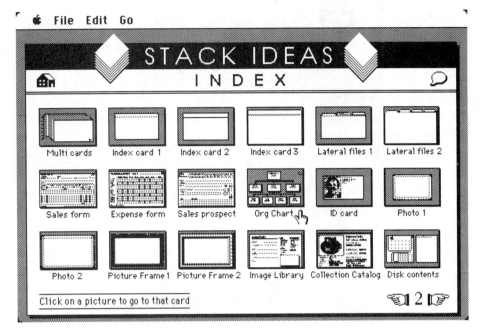

Figure 5.1 The second card in the Stack Ideas index includes a button that takes you to a ready-made organization chart.

*4. After the org chart appears on the screen, choose **New Stack** from the File menu. A dialog box appears for you to enter a name for the new stack (see Figure 5.2).*

*5. Type **My Org Chart** as the name of this stack.*

See the **X** in the box next to **Copy current background**? Leaving the **X** in that box tells HyperCard to save a copy of this card's background. Leave the **X** in the box.

Before saving the new stack, choose where you want to save it. You'll save this stack in the HyperCard folder instead of the Idea Stacks folder (see Figure 5.3).

6. Pull down the Idea Stacks folder and choose the folder named HyperCard.

Note: The Drive button won't work unless you have a disk in one of your floppy drives. Click on the Drive button before clicking on the New button if you want the new stack to be copied to another disk.

7. Click on the New button to save a copy of this card as the background for your new stack. It should look like Figure 5.4.

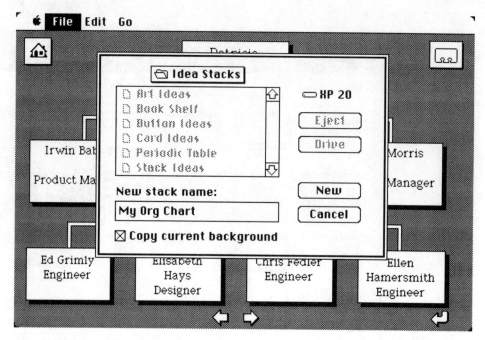

Figure 5.2   The New Stack dialog box.

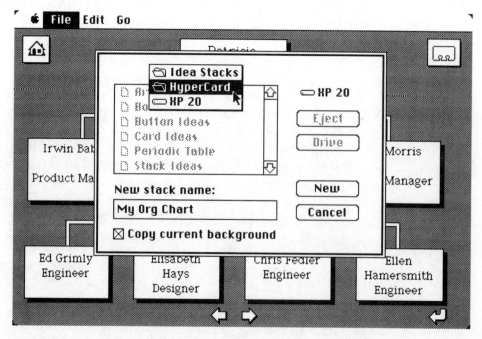

Figure 5.3   Save your new stack in the folder named HyperCard.

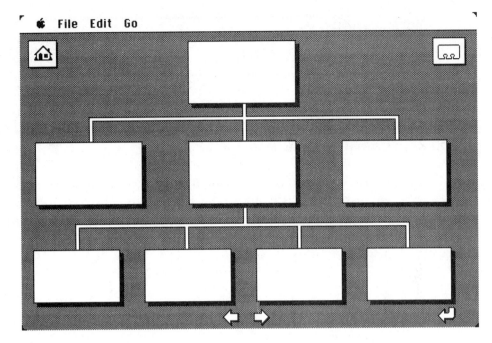

Figure 5.4 Your new org chart.

8. Press the Tab key to move the insertion point into the first field. Type the names and titles of people in your organization into the fields, pressing the Tab key to move from one field to the next.

Tip: Hold down the Shift key while you press Tab to move back into the previous field.

---

*9. To add more people to the org chart, you can add a new card for their names. Choose **New Card** from the Edit menu to add a new card to this stack.*

Shortcut: Press ⌘-N to add a new card to the stack.

Congratulations—you've just created your first stack! Following the procedures in steps 1 through 9 above is the simplest way to create a stack.

You can modify your stack in lots of different ways once you move to a higher skill level, which you'll do in the next lesson.

Tip: While your org chart is on the screen, press ⌘-P to print it now.

Lesson 28: CREATING AN INDEX FILE

You aren't limited to copying a card from the Stack Ideas. You can copy any card that exists and then modify it to suit your needs.

In the previous lesson, you created an org chart by copying a card from one stack to use as the background of your new stack. The background became the *template* for the new Org Chart stack. (A template is like a form to be filled out.) What you put on a background appears on all cards in the stack. What you put on a particular card appears on that card only. For example, the boxes on the org chart appear on every new card you add to this stack, but text typed into the fields of one card appear on that card only.

In this lesson, you'll copy the background of the File Index stack to create a template for a new stack. The File Index stack is a group of cards that look like index cards and are used to file information about different subjects. You can get to this stack from the Home card.

To create the new stack, first display a card whose background you want to copy. In this case, display any card in the File Index stack since they all share the same background.

1. *Press ⌘-H to go to the Home card.*
2. *Click on the File Index button to open that stack (see Figure 5.5).*
3. *Choose **New Stack** from the File menu.*

All cards in the File Index stack share the same background. To copy this background for the new stack, leave the **X** checked in the box next to **Copy current background**.

4. *Pull down the HyperCard Stacks folder and choose the folder named HyperCard. That's where you'll save the new stack (see Figure 5.6).*

You'll use this new stack for filing information about HyperCard shortcuts, tips, and tricks.

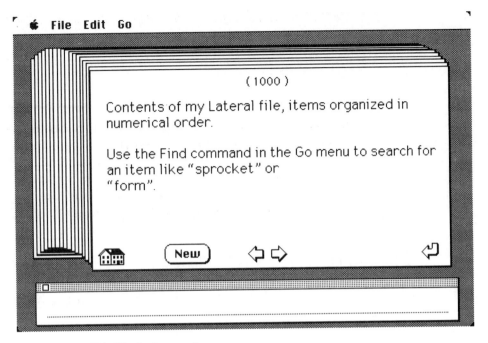

Figure 5.5 The File Index stack.

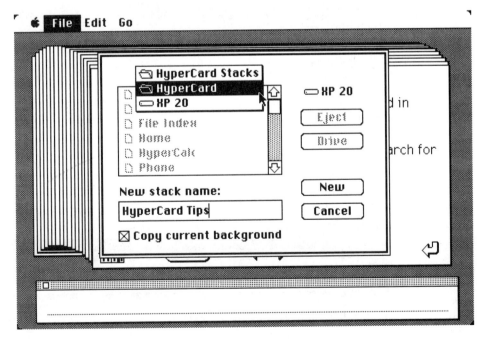

Figure 5.6 Dialog box for creating new index file.

*5. Type **HyperCard Tips** for the name of this stack. (You'll customize this stack in the next three chapters.)*

6. Click on the New button to create the new stack.

Shortcut: Instead of clicking on the New button after typing the stack name, you can press Return to create the new stack.

HyperCard copies the current background and presents you with the first card to be filled out. Notice that the text wasn't copied from the File Index card. Text within fields appear only on the foreground of each card, not on the background.

You're finished. Now you have a new file called HyperCard Tips (see Figure 5.7). In the next chapter, you'll learn how to use some paint tools to customize the pictures and other graphics on the background of this stack.

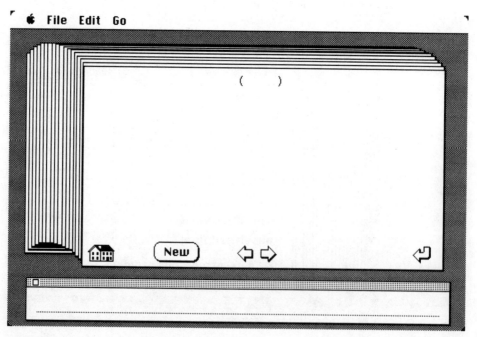

Figure 5.7 Your HyperCard Tips stack.

SUMMARY

Who said you couldn't learn how to create a HyperCard stack in a few easy steps? Well, you did it. Of course, creating a stack can take more than a few steps depending on how many changes you want to make.

In this chapter you learned how to create quick stacks by copying the background of an existing stack. That card became the background (or template) for your new stack. You can use that template as is or you can customize it by adding or changing graphics, fields, and buttons to suit your needs. You'll learn how to customize stacks in the chapters that follow.

Once again, here are the steps you follow to create a quick stack:

1. Display a card to be used as the template for your new stack.
2. Choose **New Stack** from the File menu. Make sure the box with Copy current background? is checked.
3. Choose the folder in which to save this stack.
4. Type the stack name and either click on the New button or press Return.
5. Add new cards by choosing **New Card** from the Edit menu.

6 Customizing Your Stack

In this chapter you'll learn how to customize the HyperCard Tips stack that you created in the previous chapter. And once you've modified the pictures on the background, you'll change the first card into a Title card.

The lessons in this chapter show how to

- Use HyperCard paint tools
- Modify background pictures
- Create new pictures and designs
- Erase pictures or painting mistakes
- Create a Title card
- Type with paint text

Before you get started, open the stack named HyperCard Tips that you created in Chapter 5. To open it, choose **Open Stack** from the File menu. Pull down the HyperCard Stacks folder and double-click on the folder named HyperCard. (Remember, you saved HyperCard Tips in this folder earlier.) Find and double-click on the stack named HyperCard Tips.

Lesson 29: CHANGING THE USER LEVEL TO PAINTING

The pictures you see on cards in stacks were created using HyperCard painting tools. These tools are not available from the Browsing or Typing levels, so you can't modify pictures at either of those levels. And there's no choice on the menus for viewing the background. So you can't really tell which pictures are on the background and which ones are on individual cards, except by browsing through all cards to see which objects are common to all. To get the menus and tools you need for looking at backgrounds and modifying pictures, you'll choose the next level on the User Preferences Card—Painting.

You can change the user level in one of two ways. You already know one way to do this: go to the last card (User Preferences) in the Home stack and click in the circle next to **Painting**. A quicker way to change the user level is by using the Message box, which you'll do next.

Use the Message Box to Change the User Level

With the Message box, you can change the user level from any card or stack. You can also see the user level that HyperCard is set for now (see Figure 6.1).

Tip: To see which user level you are currently using, type **the userlevel** into the Message box and press **RETURN**. The number that corresponds to the current level appears in the Message box.

Follow these steps to change the setting to **Painting** (see Figure 6.2):

1. If the Message box is not shown on the screen, press ⌘-M to show it.
2. Type **set userlevel to 3** into the Message box. Be sure to type **userlevel** as one word. (You can also type **set the userlevel to 3**.)
3. Press **RETURN**.

You can set the user level to any of the five levels on the User Preferences card by typing **set userlevel to** followed by the number (1 to 5) of the level you need. (Each user level has a number associated with it.) The numbers correspond to the five levels on the User Preferences card, from top to bottom:

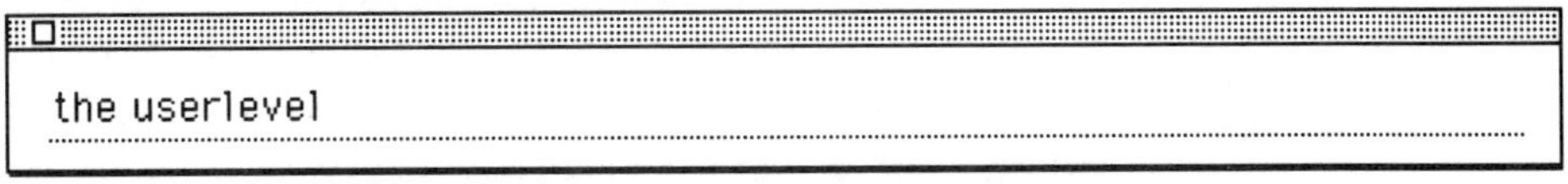

---
the userlevel

Figure 6.1 Use the Message box to verify the user level.

```
set the userlevel to 3
```

Figure 6.2 Use the Message box to change the user level.

Browsing	userlevel 1
Typing	userlevel 2
Painting	**userlevel 3**
Authoring	userlevel 4
Scripting	userlevel 5

The User Preferences card is now set for Painting. The Painting level gives you a new menu: the Tools menu (see Figure 6.3).

By the way, the phrase **set userlevel to** is in fact an example of scripting (programming) using the HyperTalk language. Easy, wasn't it? And straightforward, too. After all, HyperCard is Apple's way of easing you into programming the Macintosh. So here Apple already has you programming without your even realizing it.

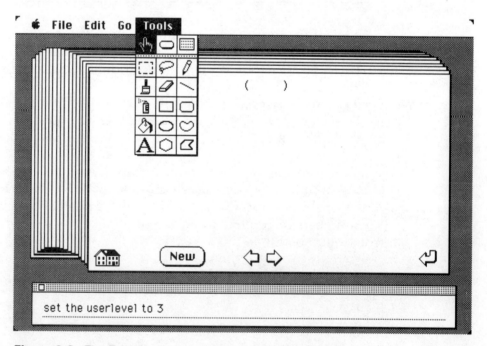

Figure 6.3 The Tools menu now appears in the menubar.

Lesson 30: ABOUT THE TOOLS MENU

The Tools menu shows the tools you can use to create and modify pictures on cards. For example, there is a brush tool you can use like a paint brush to "paint" pictures on a card. You can even choose the width of the brush stroke. And there are tools for erasing pictures or parts of pictures that don't turn out the way you had planned.

Since you often use more than one tool when creating artwork for your stack, HyperCard provides what's known as a "tear-off menu." You can "tear off" the Tools menu and put it anywhere on the screen. That way, the tools will be more easily accessible, and they won't obscure your artwork.

Tear Off the Tools Menu

To tear it off the menu bar, pull down the Tools menu and, keeping the mouse button pressed down, drag the menu off the menu bar. The outline moves with the pointer as you drag the mouse outside of the tools menu. Before you release the mouse button, you should see a faint outline of the Tools menu (see Figure 6.4).

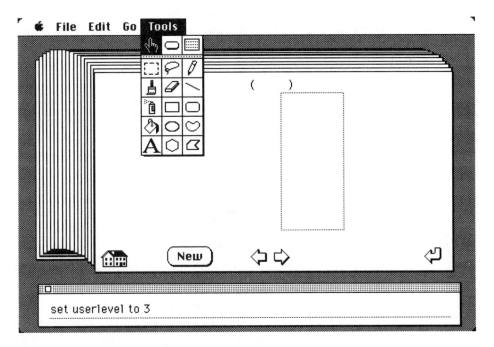

Figure 6.4 Tear off the Tools menu.

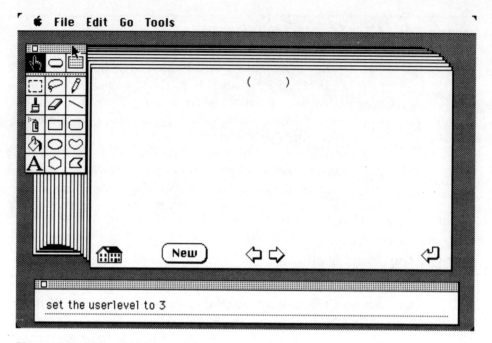

Figure 6.5 Move the menu to the upper left corner of the card for easy access.

A good place for this menu is the upper left corner of the screen where it won't cover up any fields on the cards. To move the menu, click in the gray area along the top of the menu and drag it to its new location (see Figure 6.5).

Shortcut: To put the Tools menu away, click in its **close** box or press the OPTION and TAB keys at the same time. Press the OPTION and TAB keys again to put the Tools menu back on the screen.

The Browse, Button, and Field Tools

The three tools on the first line of the Tools menu are unique to HyperCard. They are, in order from left to right, the Browse tool, the Button tool, and the Field tool (see Figure 6.6).

Choose the Browse tool to enter text in fields and to use navigation commands. The Button and Field tools, although on the Tools menu, are not functional at the Painting level. You'll need to change the user

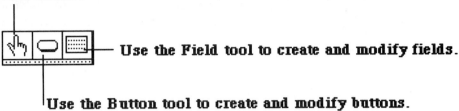

Figure 6.6 Unique HyperCard Tools

level to Authoring before you can use these tools to create buttons and fields. (You'll learn how to create buttons and fields later.)

The Paint Tools

All the tools below the first line in this menu are called **paint** tools. These tools enable you to create circles, lines, squares and other graphics, just like you do in MacPaint and in other kinds of painting programs (see Figure 6.7).

Lesson 31: PAINTING ON A SPECIFIC CARD

In this lesson, you'll learn how to use paint tools in the HyperCard Tools menu to customize one card in the HyperCard Tips stack. Then you'll look at the difference between painting a line or picture on a background and painting it on an individual card.

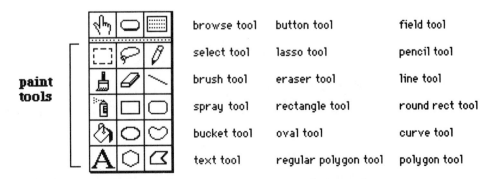

Figure 6.7 The tools on the Tools menu named in order from left to right.

Making a Mess and Cleaning It Up

To choose a paint tool on the Tools menu, just click on it; then the mouse pointer turns into the chosen tool. For practice, follow these steps to spray paint on a card and then erase it:

*1. Click on the **Spray** tool in the Tools menu. Now put the pointer anywhere on the card (see Figure 6.8).*

2. To spray paint, click the mouse. Each time you click, a spot of spray paint appears. If you hold down the mouse and drag, you can paint graffiti all over your screen just like kids do on buildings and in subways (see Figure 6.9).

> *Tip:* While your work of art is on the screen, choose the Browse tool, and then press ⌘-P to print it. (The **Print** command is available only when you are not using a paint tool.)

Now for some soap and water.

*3. Click on the **Eraser** tool. The pointer turns into a square eraser (see Figure 6.10).*

4. While holding the mouse button down, drag the Eraser over the sprayed area to erase the paint.

You just used the Spray tool to paint on a card. The background,

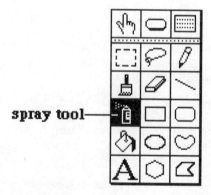

spray tool

Figure 6.8 The Spray tool can add texture to graphics.

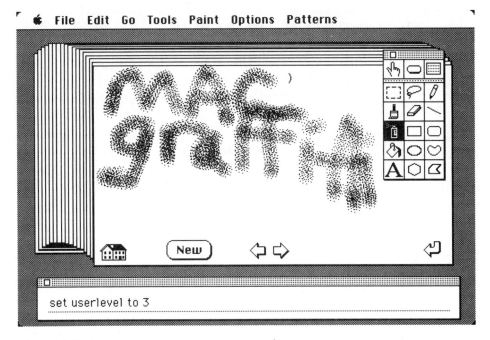

Figure 6.9 Is this art?

however, is where the picture of the index cards was created. That's why when you erased the spray marks, nothing else was erased.

Tip: Double-clicking on the **Eraser** tool erases all paint text and graphics on the card or background currently displayed.

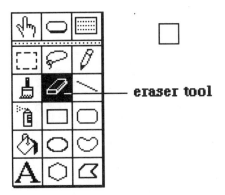

— eraser tool

Figure 6.10 The Eraser tool erases pictures created with any of the paint tools.

Lesson 32:   PAINTING ON A BACKGROUND

In this lesson, you'll use some of the paint tools to customize the background for your HyperCard Tips stack. By making changes to the background, you are modifying the template common to all cards in this stack.

Now You See It, Now You Don't.

1. To see the background for the card currently displayed on the screen, choose **Background** *from the Edit menu. This choice appears on the Edit menu only when the user level is set for Painting, Authoring, or Scripting.*

When you're looking at a background, buttons and graphics that were put on a particular card do not show. Neither does text typed into fields. In fact, they seem to disappear. But they are only temporarily gone; when you choose **Background** *again, field text, graphics and buttons on a particular card will show again.*

2. Choose **Background** *from the Edit menu again to return to the card.*

Shortcut: Press ⌘-B to see the background; press ⌘-B again to see the card.

Think of the **Background** command as an on/off switch. You turn it on to see just the background of the card. You turn it off to see both the card and its background. What you put on a background appears on all cards you add to this stack when any card with that background is displayed (see Figure 6.11). What you put on a card itself appears on that card only.

As mentioned, stacks can have more than one background. But so far you've been working with stacks that have only one background.

If your stack has more than one background, you have to be a little careful when adding new cards to the stack. Have the proper background on the screen before adding a new card, because that's the background the new card will get. You'll learn when and how to create other backgrounds later in this section.

To learn how to customize a stack template, you'll modify the background of your HyperCard Tips stack.

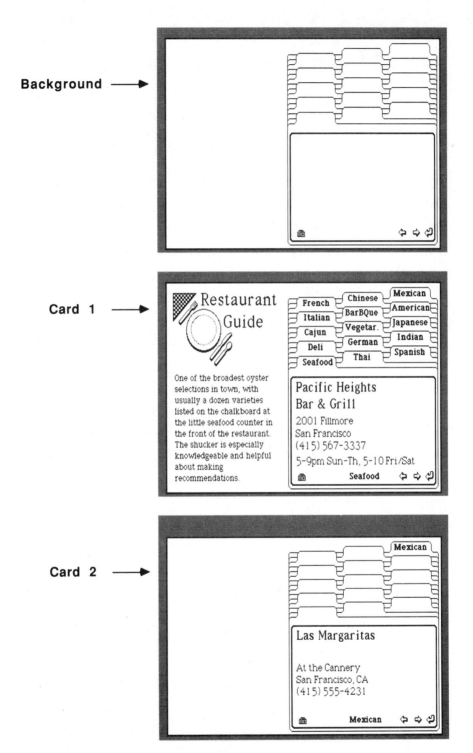

Figure 6.11 Background pictures are shared by cards.

USE THE SELECT TOOL TO MODIFY PICTURES
ON CARDS

Suppose you want to make all the index cards a little longer to fit more text. You can use the Select tool and some special keys to do so. To make the white area of the index card bigger, first you'll go to the background, and then you'll select the bottom part of the index card. Then you'll drag the selected area while holding down some special keys to make it larger.

Here's a quick way to do this:

1. Open the HyperCard Tips stack if it isn't already on the screen. Tear off the Tools menu and drag it to the upper left corner of the screen.

*2. Click on the **Select tool** in the Tools menu. The pointer turns into a crossbar (see Figure 6.12).*

*3. Choose **Background** from the Edit menu to see only the background. You can always tell when you're editing a background because diagonal lines appear on the menubar (see Figure 6.13).*

*4. Get the Message box out of the way by clicking in its **close** box. You can put away the Tools menu in the same way. Choose Grid from the Options menu. This menu choice helps you keep graphics aligned as you move them.*

5. Now use the Select tool to draw a box around the bottom portion of the index card. Move the crossbar to the lower-middle left side of the card and press the mouse button. Then drag the crossbar to the right and down so you've selected the bottom half of the index card as shown in Figure 6.14. Release the mouse button.

A moving dotted line appears around the selected area.

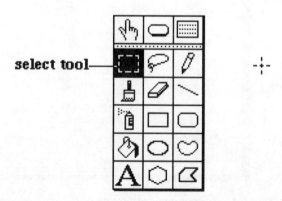

select tool

Figure 6.12   Choosing the Select tool turns the pointer into a crossbar.

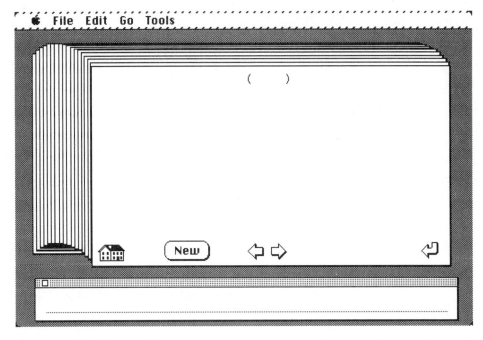

Figure 6.13 Diagonal lines appear in the menu bar when you select a background.

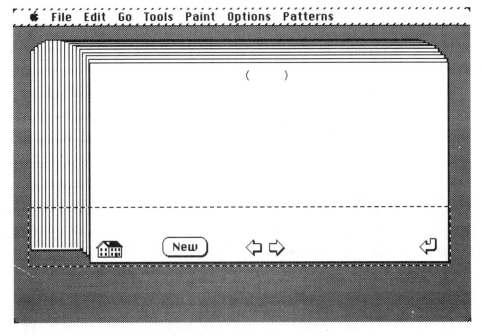

Figure 6.14 Select the bottom portion of the index card to modify.

6. While holding down the SHIFT and OPTION keys on your keyboard, move the pointer inside of the moving dotted line, press the mouse button and drag the selected area downward to lengthen the index card (see Figure 6.15). If you make a mistake, or want to do it over, choose **Undo** *from the Edit menu.*

Tip: The ⌘, SHIFT, and OPTION keys can be used separately or in combination to produce different results. Using the ⌘ key while dragging a selected area stretches the graphic. Using the SHIFT key while dragging keeps objects moving in a straight line, and using the OPTION key while dragging makes a copy of the selection.

---

7. When you're done, release both keys and click outside of the moving dotted line to unselect the area.

Since you modified a picture on the background, every card you add

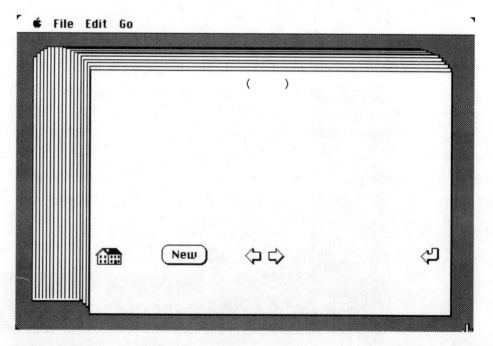

Figure 6.15 The index card now looks like this.

to this stack will have this background picture. Changing a background affects every card in the stack associated with that background.

Lesson 33: USING THE PENCIL TOOL

The Pencil tool is your pen or pencil for drawing freehand. You can create graphics for a specific card by just drawing on that card. Or you can create a graphic that appears on all cards in the stack by drawing it once on the background.

1. Before you can access the background, you must choose the **Browse** tool. Otherwise, the Background command does not appear on the Edit menu. Click on the **Browse** tool in the Tools menu now.
2. Choose **Background** from the Edit menu to see only the background. (Diagonal lines appear on the menu bar to indicate you are in the background.)
3. Click on the **Pencil** tool in the Tools menu. The pointer turns into a little pencil. You can draw freehand with this pencil (see Figure 6.16). Go ahead and draw something on the background such as smoke coming out of the chimney of the Home button.

Tip: Hold down the SHIFT key while using the Pencil tool to draw a straight line. You can also draw a straight line by holding down the SHIFT key while using the Line tool.

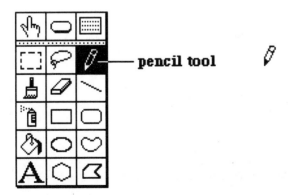

pencil tool

Figure 6.16 Use the Pencil tool to draw freehand.

Lesson 34: USING THE LASSO TOOL

Moving Objects with the Lasso

Another way to select a picture you want to modify is with the Lasso tool (see figure 6-17). This tool helps you select irregular-shaped objects instead of just square areas. You use it just like its name implies.

Erasing with the Lasso

1. Select the **Lasso** tool in the Tools menu.
2. Let's get rid of the parentheses at the top of this card. The parentheses were drawn on the background, so make sure you're viewing the background. (Diagonal lines appear in the menubar when you're in the background.) If you don't see diagonal lines in the menubar, press ⌘-B now to edit the background.
3. Draw a loop around the parentheses with the Lasso tool (see Figure 6.18). The picture that you lasso begins to blink as soon as you complete the loop around the picture.
4. Choose **Cut Picture** from the Edit menu.

> *Shortcut:* To erase a picture, first select it with either the Select tool or Lasso tool, and then just press the BACKSPACE key.

— **lasso tool**

Figure 6.17 Use the Lasso tool to select objects that aren't square.

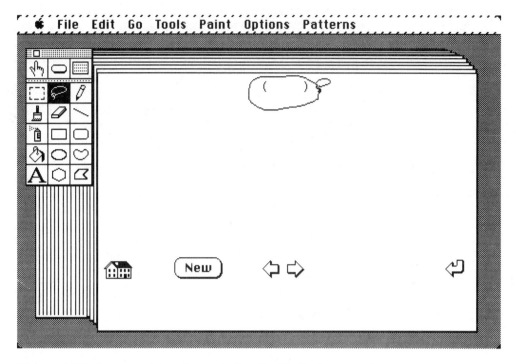

Figure 6.18 Lasso a picture by encircling it with the Lasso tool.

Copying and Pasting Art from the Art Ideas Stack

Use the Lasso tool to copy art from the Art Ideas stack.

1. Go to the Home card and click on **Art Ideas**.

2. Find the card with a graphic you want to copy. For example, click on "Animals, Wildlife, Fish."

3. Lasso the object to be copied such as the rabbit popping out of a magician's hat (see Figure 6.19).

4. Choose **Copy Picture** *from the Edit menu.*

5. Use the Recent card or press the Tilde key to return to the card onto which you'll paste the copied picture—the first card in the HyperCard Tips stack.

6. Choose **Background** *from the Edit menu to paste the picture on the background.*

7. Choose **Paste Picture** *from the Edit menu.*

8. Click inside the picture and drag it to position it on the card. Click outside of the picture when it's placed where you want it.

Figure 6.19 Lasso the rabbit and magician's hat.

Tip: While the picture is selected, choose **Transparent** from the Paint menu if you want other objects to show through this picture, or choose **Opaque** if you want this picture to cover up other pictures and objects.

Lesson 35: USING THE PAINT, OPTIONS, AND PATTERNS MENUS

Whenever you choose a paint tool on the Tools menu, three more menus appear on the menu bar: Paint, Options, and Patterns (see Figure 6.20). Use these menu choices to create special effects and manipulate graphics.

Most of the choices on the Paint menu are explained as you use them in the lessons throughout the rest of this book. You can also find out more about using these commands by looking in the Help stack that is included with HyperCard.

The first three choices on the Options menu require some explanation.

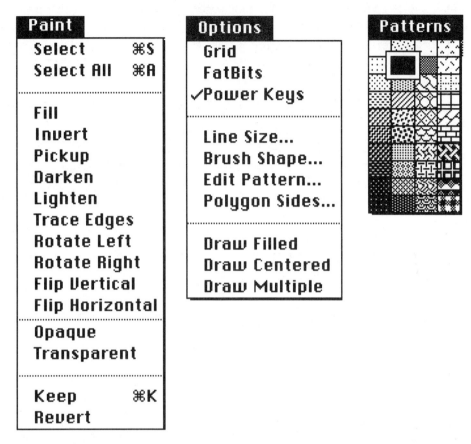

Figure 6.20 The Paint, Options, and Patterns menus.

Grid

Choose **Grid** if you want to draw, paint, or move objects within an invisible grid. You won't see the grid, but choosing it helps you keep graphics aligned as you draw them or move them. You turned the Grid on before modifying the background graphic of your HyperCard Tips stack to keep the selection within those invisible lines as you dragged the mouse. Doing so prevented the selection from having jagged edges.

FatBits

When you choose **FatBits** from the Options menu, the graphics in the middle of the card are magnified. If there are no graphics there, choose **FatBits** from the Options menu again to go back to normal viewing mode. Then choose the **Pencil** tool, hold down the ⌘ key, and click on the picture you want to magnify.

> *Tip:* While the Pencil tool is chosen, you can also jump out of FatBits by holding down the ⌘ key and clicking once.

*1. Choose the **Pencil** tool, hold down the ⌘ key, and click on the picture of the rabbit coming out of the magician's hat.*

Use FatBits to edit small details of your picture, pixel by pixel (see Figure 6.21). FatBits shows you the pixels that make up the picture. For example, if you aren't careful when you copy a picture, stray lines can get copied along with it. Because these lines are so small, they are hard to erase unless you are in FatBits.

> *Tip:* To scroll pictures while in FatBits, hold down the OPTION key and drag the grabber hand that appears. When you release the OPTION key, the grabber hand disappears and the tool you were previously using reappears.

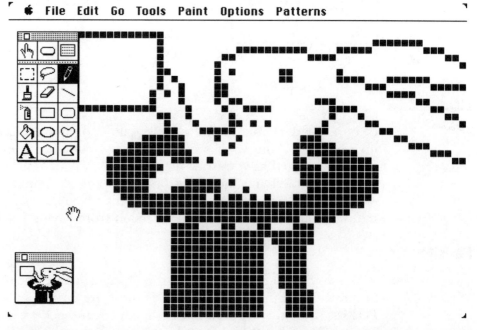

Figure 6.21 Choose FatBits to edit fine details of a picture with accuracy.

2. Use the Pencil tool in FatBits to add or remove one pixel. Clicking on a pixel removes it. Clicking on a white space adds a pixel. You can use any of the paint tools while in FatBits. Practice using different tools in FatBits now. The small window that appears in the bottom left corner of the screen shows the edited portion in normal viewing mode so you can see what you're doing.

Tip: Double-click on the **Pencil** tool to get into and out of Fat-Bits.

---

*3. To get out of FatBits, choose **FatBits** from the Options menu again or hold down the ⌘ key and click once.*

Power Keys

Choosing **Power Keys** enables you to type certain keys on your keyboard to choose a tool or option instead of choosing from menus.

For example, typing "A" with Power Keys checked selects the entire card or background for you to copy or delete. Appendix C at the back of this book lists these keys for quick reference.

Okay, you're finished modifying the background, which is the template for all the cards you'll add to this stack. Now you need a Title card. The first card in the stack is referred to as the Title card because the name, or title, of the stack is usually shown on that card in big bold letters.

Lesson 36: CREATING A TITLE CARD

Now that you are familiar with the Tools menu, you're ready to customize the first card in the stack.

1. Press ⌘-1 to go to the first card in this stack. Notice that whenever you go to another card, HyperCard automatically brings you back to the card level if you were previously displaying a background.

The first card in a stack should tell you what this stack is all about. Commercial stackware developers call the first screen the *Title card* or *Title screen*. It usually has the name of the stack and a copyright notice. Sometimes it also includes a "help" button, which gives you information

Trick: Unfortunately, you cannot add a new card at the very beginning of a stack. If you ever need to do this, follow these steps: 1) add a new card after the first card, and 2) cut the first card and paste it after the second card. The second card becomes the first card!

about what's in the stack or instructions on how to use it. Information on the Title card appears on only the first card in the stack, so make sure you're displaying the card, not its background.

Next you'll type the name of your stack in large letters. But instead of typing text into a field, you'll "paint" it on with the Text tool. There are two kinds of text in HyperCard: Paint text and Field text. *Paint text* is text that is typed on a card or background with the Text tool in the Tools menu. When typed on a background, this text can be shared with several cards. *Field text* is text typed into a field. Field text is easily edited but cannot be shared from card to card. Field text can be used to sort cards and to search for a particular card. You'll learn more about Field text later. For now, you'll be using Paint text.

*2. Choose the **Text** tool from the Tools menu to type text directly onto a card (see Figure 6.22). The current tool chosen turns into an insertion point when you choose the Text tool.*

You can select the font, size, and style of Paint text by choosing **Text Style** from the Edit menu. Do that now:

text tool ———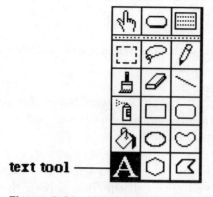

Figure 6.22 Use the Text tool to paint text directly on a card instead of in a field on the card.

*3. Choose **Text Style** from the Edit menu.*

Shortcut: Press ⌘-T or double-click on the **Text** tool to display the Text Style dialog box.

The Text Style dialog box has choices for fonts and styles, alignments, point sizes and line height (see Figure 6.23).

*4. Click in the box for **Bold** under "Style." The text you type with the Paint tool will appear in boldface type.*

*5. Directly below the list of styles are three choices for aligning text: left, right, and centered. Choose the one you want by clicking in the button next to it. Click on **Left** to keep text left-justified when typing.*

*6. Use the scroll bar to find **Times** in the list of fonts. If it appears in this list, click on it to choose it. If not, choose another font. In the next column is a list of numbers. These numbers are all the point sizes available in the font*

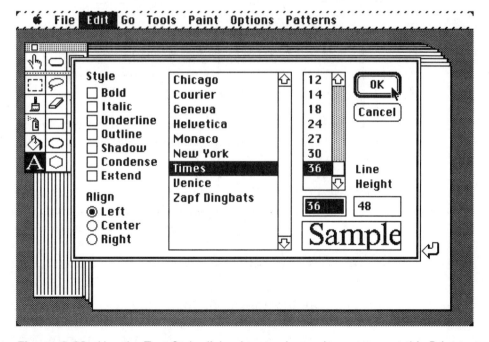

Figure 6.23 Use the Text Style dialog box to choose how you want this Paint text to look.

you chose. Click on 36, if it is in the list, to choose a font size of 36 points. Otherwise, choose the largest font you have. The word "sample" appears in a window in the bottom right corner of the dialog box to show you what the text will look like if you decide to use the Times font at 36 points.

You can also choose a point size not in this list by typing a number in the little box directly below the scroll box. HyperCard will attempt to create a font this size for you.

7. HyperCard measures line height in points (each point is equal to $1/72$ inch) and automatically selects the standard line height for the chosen font. However, you can change this number to one that works best for you. Just double-click inside this box to highlight the old number, and then type a new number.

Tip: Only the fonts in the System file you are using are listed in this dialog box. If you wish to use fonts that are not in this list, use the Font/DA mover to move them into the System file. Refer to your Macintosh User's Guide for instructions about the Font/DA mover.

---

*8. Click **OK** when you're done.*

9. Move the insertion point to the place where you want to begin typing the name of this stack. Click once to mark the starting point, and then type "HyperCard Tips" (see Figure 6.24).

Next you'll add a **byline** to this card. You'll want the byline to have a smaller typeface so it isn't glaring at everyone (unless, of course, you want to be tacky about it).

*10. Move the insertion point over to the right side of the card and click to reposition it. Choose **Text Style** again from the Edit menu and change the size to 12 points instead of 36. Then click in the **Bold** box to uncheck it. Click **OK**.*

Tip: If you change the text style again before clicking to first reposition the insertion point, the text that you just typed—**HyperCard Tips**—will change to the new fonts and style you choose. So make sure to put the insertion point at its new position before changing the text style.

Figure 6.24 Title card for HyperCard Tips stack.

*11. Type **by** followed by your name.*

Tip: For unique stacks that you conceived and created, you would also add "Copyright 1988" and "All rights reserved" after your name.

---

*12. Click on the **Browse** tool in the Tools menu when you're done (see Figure 6.25). You must choose the Browse tool before you can click on buttons or enter text into fields.*

Note: Usually the Title card has its own background, in which case you'd create a new background just for the Title card. However, for now

Browse ———— tool

Figure 6.25 Choose the Browse tool.

it is not necessary to do so. You'll learn how to create more backgrounds in a later chapter. And you'll create more flattering title cards. For now, get used to the basic concepts of building stacks. Once you have a solid foundation, everything else will fit into place.

SUMMARY

HyperCard gives you plenty of tools and menus for customizing graphics or creating your own card designs.

You can make all kinds of modifications with the paint tools. And with the help of special keys like ⌘, SHIFT, and OPTION, you can change the size and shape of a selected object, keep it in alignment with other objects, and make duplicate copies of it in short, simple steps.

When working with graphics, keep these points in mind:

- Most, but not all, graphics are created on the background. To see which graphics are common to all cards in the stack, press ⌘-B to look at the background.
- Diagonal lines appear in the menu bar when you are looking at a background—that's how you know which is the background and which is the card. To edit background pictures, display the background first.
- To work with a picture, first select it with either the Select tool or Lasso tool. Then you can do whatever you want to the selected picture—change its shape by shortening or lengthening it, fill it with a pattern, flip it upside down, move it, or erase it.
- If you create a Title card for your stack, create graphics for it on the card, not its background, so they don't appear on all cards in the stack.
- Text typed onto a card with the Paint tool is referred to as Paint text. Text typed into fields is referred to as Field text. You can choose a typeface and style as well as its point size for either kind of text. (When you use the **Find** command, HyperCard searches for words typed into fields but not words typed with Paint text.)

In the next chapter you'll use more paint tools and two new tools: the Button and Field tools. And you'll finish transforming the old index file into a new one better suited for your needs.

7 Customizing Fields

The boxes in which you type text are called *fields*. In this chapter you'll customize the fields in the HyperCard Tips stack template that you started in Chapter 5. You'll also learn how to create new fields.

The lessons in this chapter show you how to

- Change the look (style) of a field
- Adjust the size of a field
- Move a field
- Create a new field
- Copy a field
- Change the order of fields

Then you'll enter the actual information describing the HyperCard tips you've learned so far.

Open the stack named HyperCard Tips. To open it, choose **Open Stack** from the File menu. Pull down the folder in the dialog box and choose the folder named HyperCard. Find and double-click on the stack named HyperCard Tips.

Lesson 37: CHANGE THE USER LEVEL TO AUTHORING

At the Painting level, you can create all kinds of designs and pictures on your cards, but you're not really authoring a stack—you're designing one. To author a stack, you must be able to create and modify fields and buttons as well as graphics. Fortunately, this is easy to do. So go ahead and change the user level to **Authoring**!

Use the Message Box to Change the User Level

Follow these steps to change the user level to Authoring:

1. If the Message box is not shown on the screen, press ⌘-M to show it.
2. Type **set userlevel to 4** into the Message box. Be sure to type **userlevel** as one word.
3. Press RETURN.

The User Preferences card is now set for Authoring. At the Authoring level you can use the Button and Field tools on the Tools menu to create, copy, and modify buttons and fields (see Figure 7.1).

What's more, you have another new menu available: the **Objects** menu.

The Objects Menu

Use the first group of commands on the Objects menu to see information about each element in the stack currently displayed: the stack itself, backgrounds, cards, fields, and buttons. The next two commands, **Bring Closer** and **Send Farther**, are used to change the order of buttons and fields on a card. Use the last three commands to create new objects: Buttons, Fields, or Backgrounds (see Figure 7.2). These commands are explained in more detail as you use them throughout this book.

Lesson 38: LOOKING AT INFORMATION ABOUT OBJECTS

Stacks, backgrounds, cards, fields, and buttons are known as *objects* in HyperCard. You can view a list of information about each object by using

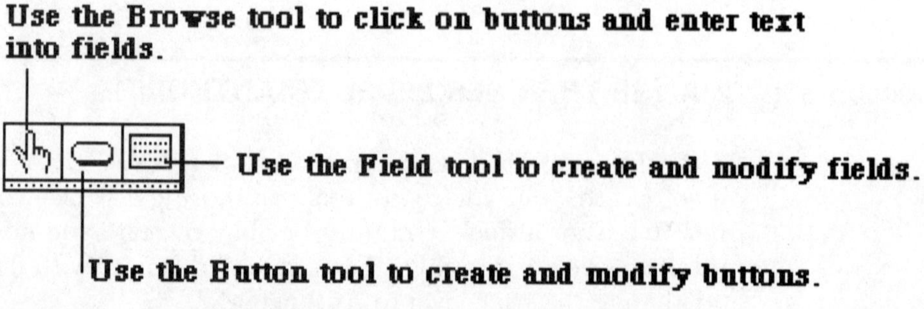

Use the Browse tool to click on buttons and enter text into fields.

Use the Field tool to create and modify fields.

Use the Button tool to create and modify buttons.

Figure 7.1 The Browse, Button, and Field tools.

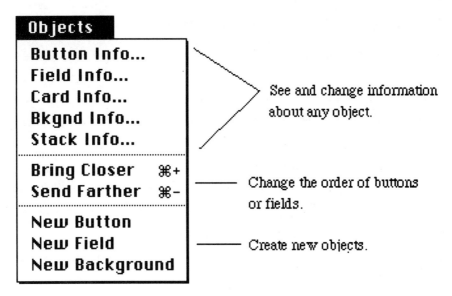

Figure 7.2 The Objects menu.

the Objects menu. In this lesson, you'll look at information about fields. You'll also learn how to change that information. In the next chapter, you'll look at information about buttons, and later in this book, after you've designed your own stack, you'll look at the information boxes for stacks, cards, and backgrounds.

Field Info Dialog Box

The **Field Info...** and **Button Info...** choices are gray, which means you can't choose either one. Why not? Because HyperCard knows which stack, background, and card you are currently looking at on the screen, but not which button or field you want information about until you choose one. So to get information about a particular field, you first choose the **Field** tool and then click on the field you want to know about. Only then can you choose **Field Info...** from the Objects menu.

1. Click on the **Field** tool in the Tools menu. (The Field tool is the rectangle with dots in it.)
2. Click on the largest field on the card.
3. Choose **Field Info...** from the Objects menu.

In the Field Info dialog box, you can enter a name for this field, see its order number on the card (foreground or background), see the

ID number of the card or background on which this field resides, and determine how this field will look on the card (see Figure 7.3). You'll look at all of these choices in more detail in the next lesson.

Lesson 39: CHANGING THE LOOK OF A FIELD

The HyperCard Tips stack has just two fields for entering information: an **Index Number** field and a **Description** field. In this lesson, you'll modify the Index Number field first and then you'll modify the Description field. Since these two fields were created on a background, they will appear on every new card you add to this stack. Any changes you make to background fields affect every card in the stack.

Before modifying fields, you'll add a new card to your stack.

1. Instead of choosing **New Card** *from the Edit menu, click once on the button named* **New**.

This button was preprogrammed not only to add a new card to this stack, but also to automatically enter a sequential number in the Index Number field. The program inside the button tells HyperCard to assign

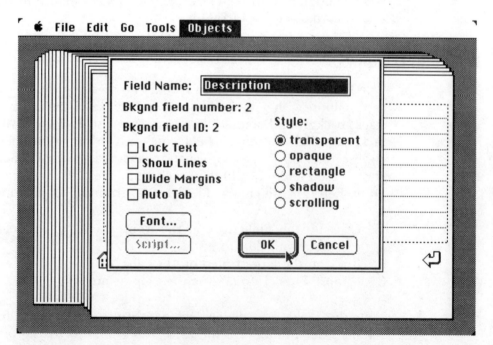

Figure 7.3 Field information is available after you select a specific field.

index numbers automatically to cards as they are created. You'll learn how to program buttons later. For now, you'll learn how to modify fields.

To change the look or style of a field, you must first choose the Field tool and then choose the field to be modified. Do that now.

2. Tear off the Tools menu and put it in the upper left corner of the card.

*3. Click on the **Field** tool in the Tools menu. All fields appear outlined on the card—whether the fields are on the background or a particular card (see Figure 7.4).*

You can modify fields from either the background or card level, no matter where the field actually resides. In other words, you don't have to display the background first to *modify* a field that was created on a card's background. You only have to display the background first to *create* a field on a card's background. Background fields appear on every card in the stack. Card fields appear on one card only.

*4. Click on the **Index Number** field to select it as the one you want to modify.*

*5. Choose **Field Info...** from the Objects menu to see and change information about this field (see Figure 7.5).*

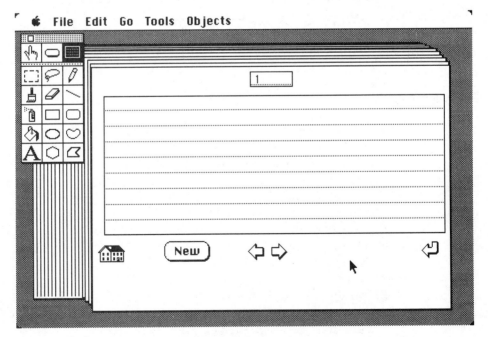

Figure 7.4 All fields appear outlined when you choose the Field tool.

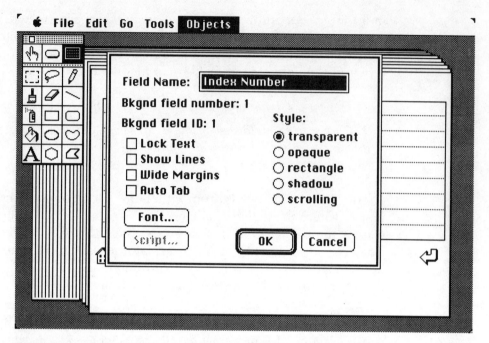

Figure 7.5 Field information for the first field.

Shortcut: After choosing the Field tool in the Tools menu, double-click on a field to see its Field Information dialog box.

Field Styles

The Field Info dialog box gives you several choices for determining how a field should look and how the text within it should look. You'll choose a style for both the field and the text within it after reviewing the choices you have.

These are the choices for field styles (see Figure 7.6):

- Transparent
- Opaque
- Rectangle
- Shadow
- Scrolling

Each style is described below.

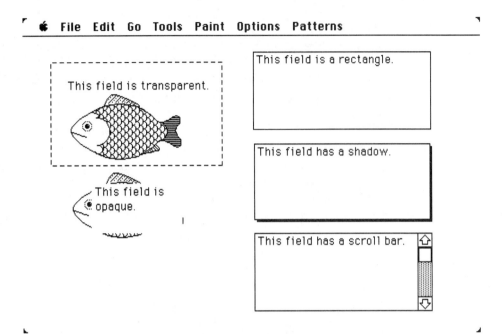

Figure 7.6 You can create Transparent fields, Opaque fields, Rectangular fields, fields with a drop shadow behind them, or fields that have a scroll bar.

Transparent

Normally a HyperCard field covers anything under it and has a border around it so you can distinguish the field on the screen. A *transparent* field lets you see anything under it, and does not have border. In essence, a transparent field is invisible. The field is still there, but you can't tell where it starts or stops. Although you can't see its boundaries, when you press the TAB key to move from field to field, the insertion point will stop in invisible fields as well. And any pictures, buttons, or other fields on the background will show through an invisible field.

You might ask, "Why even have a transparent field if you can't see it?" Well, if you create a box for a field using paint tools, the box will already have its own border and you wouldn't need another one to show the boundaries of that field. In that case, choosing **transparent** for the field style makes the most sense aesthetically. Another use for a transparent field is to show a background object—such as a unique pattern, or a clever picture—through the field. (But use with care! Objects with dark or wild patterns can make text in transparent fields hard to read.)

Opaque

Opaque means you can't see through it. An opaque field hides any object that is under the field. For example, if you move an opaque field over a picture, button, or another field, the opaque field will cover that picture, button, or field. It's like putting a blanket over the other objects.

Opaque fields are white squares with no borders other than the edges of the square. When you type text inside an opaque field, you are typing on a white surface. On a white background, you can't see the borders around an opaque field.

Use opaque fields when the background has a dark pattern that makes text in transparent fields difficult to read, or when you want to hide a button or another field on a particular card.

Rectangle

Rectangle fields are opaque fields that have a black border line. When you type text inside a rectangle field, you are typing in a white box. The rectangle is the most common style of field chosen for text entry, like the blanks you fill in on a form.

Use rectangle fields when you need to define a field's boundaries clearly.

Shadow

A *shadow* field is a rectangle field with a drop shadow behind it. The drop shadow gives the field a 3-D look. Use this field when you want a field to really stand out on a card, for example, when creating *pop-up* fields. (A pop-up field is a field that only appears when you click on something like a button or a word in another field.)

Scrolling

A *scrolling* field is a rectangle field with a vertical scroll bar on its right side. This kind of field may seem like a bottomless pit at first, but it isn't. A scrolling field can hold up to 32,000 characters of information (32 Kilobytes). You can't actually scroll the field until you've first typed in more text than will show in the field at one time. To scroll the field, drag the white square on the sidebar either up or down.

There is no right or wrong choice when choosing a field style. Each choice is mainly aesthetic. However, there are times when choosing **opaque** as opposed to **transparent** is a more logical choice. For example, if you want to hide one field with another field on a specific card, you would choose **opaque** as the field style. Also, if you think a field will hold lots of text—more than will fit on one card—then you should choose **scrolling** as the field style. Which style to choose for a field becomes more apparent as you move to the Scripting level and find more uses for these styles. And, of course, you can always change the field style whenever you like.

Choose Rectangle for the Field Style

Click in the circle next to **rectangle** to select it as the style for the Index Number field.

Other Field Options

You also have options for locking text so no one can edit it, showing the lines in a field, and giving the field a wide margin instead of typing to the edges of the field boundaries. HyperCard Version 1.2 also includes an **Auto-Tab** option that moves the insertion point from one field to another whenever you press the RETURN key.

Lock Text

Don't choose **Lock Text** until you've finished entering text; otherwise, you won't be able to enter text in this field unless you "turn off" the locking by clicking in the lock box again. Lock the text to prevent others from accidentally erasing or changing the text in this field. You'll also lock the text in a pop-up field so you can click on that field to hide it.

Show Lines

Choose **Show Lines** when you want dotted lines to appear on each line in this field (see Figure 7.7). The line height, or space between the lines, depends on which font and line height you choose in the Fonts dialog box.

The Show Lines option does not work with scrolling fields.

Wide Margins

Choose Wide Margins if you want to add one character of white space to the left and right margins of this field. Adding more white space to

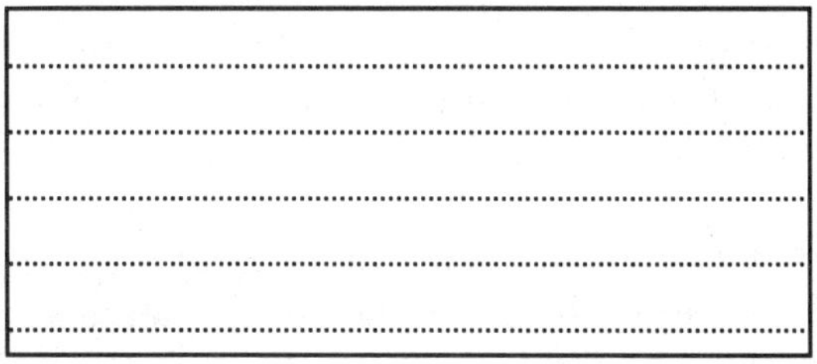

Figure 7.7 Fields with the Show Lines option.

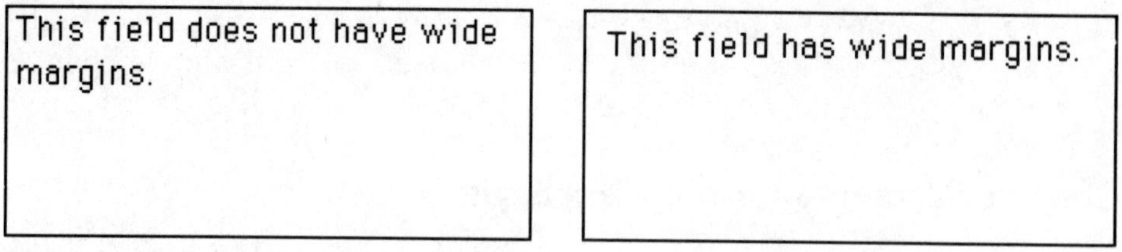

```
┌─────────────────────────────┐   ┌─────────────────────────────┐
│ This field does not have wide │   │                               │
│ margins.                      │   │ This field has wide margins.  │
│                               │   │                               │
│                               │   │                               │
│                               │   │                               │
└─────────────────────────────┘   └─────────────────────────────┘
```

Figure 7.8 Fields with wide margins.

the edges of a field sometimes makes the text within it more visually appealing (see Figure 7.8).

Auto-Tab (Version 1.2 Only)

This option enables you to move from one field to another by pressing the RETURN key instead of the TAB key. Use this option when you have several fields that require lots of text entry—for example, a data base of employee records.

Font

Clicking on the **Font** button gives you a dialog box in which to choose the font size, style, and look of the text within this field. You'll do that in the next lesson. First, you'll change the style of the Description field.

Choose Scrolling for the Field Style

1. Choose the **Field** tool in the Tools menu (if it isn't already chosen).
2. Double-click on the **Description** field. Double-clicking selects the field as the one that you want to modify and also brings up the Field Info... dialog box.
3. Click in the circle next to **scrolling** to select it.
4. Click **OK**. The Description field is now a scrolling field (see Figure 7.9).

Lesson 40:   CHOOSING FONTS AND STYLES FOR FIELD TEXT

Besides controlling how the outside of a field looks, you also have control over the appearance of the text inside the field. You can change the font, font size, and font style any time you like by using the Field Info dialog box.

Unfortunately, you cannot vary the font, size, or style of the text within a field. All the text will look the same. For example, you can't underline one word of text within the field, but you can underline *all* the words in that field.

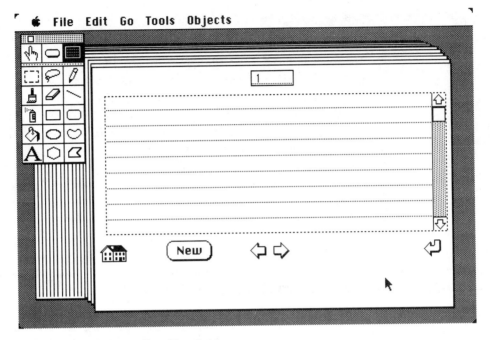

Figure 7.9 Create a Scrolling field.

Trick: To make one word *appear* underlined in the field, you can superimpose one field on top of another. Or you can draw a line on the card using the Line tool in the Tools menu. (Avoid these kinds of tricks in scrolling fields though.) See Figure 7.10.

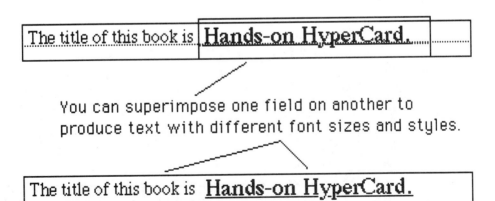

Figure 7.10 Be creative when thinking of ways around HyperCard's limitations.

Choose Text Fonts and Styles for a Field

1. Click on the **Field** tool in the Tools menu.
2. Double-click on the **Index Number** field (the first field on the card).
3. Click on the **Fonts** button. This dialog box should look familiar (see Figure 7.11). It's the same one you used when choosing the text style for the Text tool. The only difference is that here you are choosing a font and style for text inside of a particular field, whereas before you chose a font and style for text typed onto a card with the Text tool.
4. Choose **Times**, 14 point. (If you don't have the Times font, choose **Geneva** instead.)
5. Click **OK**.

Lesson 41: CHANGING THE SIZE OF A FIELD

You can change the size of a field by dragging one of its four corners inward or outward. In this lesson, you'll make the Description field longer so it fills more of the white space on the index card. After all,

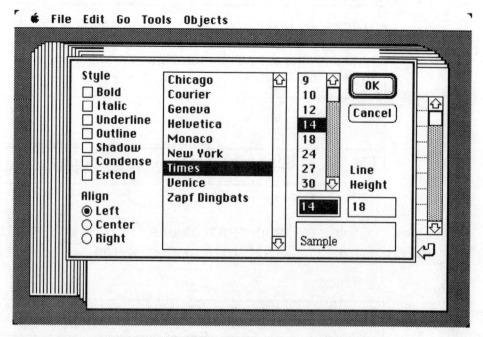

Figure 7.11 Fonts dialog box with Times and 14 point chosen.

that's why you lengthened the white area in the first place—to provide a larger space for the field information.

Make the Description Field Larger

1. Click on the **Field** tool in the Tools menu.
2. Move the pointer to the lower right corner of the scrolling field.
3. Drag the corner down and to the right as shown in Figure 7.12. Keep the field within the boundaries of the index card graphic for aesthetic reasons.
4. Release the mouse button when the field is the size you want it.

> *Tip:* To move a field to another position on the card, choose the Field tool, put the pointer *inside* the field, not on one of the corners, and then drag the field to another location.

Notice that the scrolling field did not cover up the buttons. That's because the buttons were created after the field was created. The last

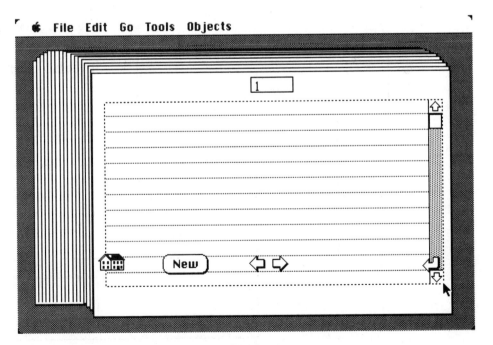

Figure 7.12 Enlarge the Description Field.

object you create appears closest in the stack of invisible layers. Invisible layers? Read on.

The HyperCard Layering System

You know that cards have two parts or layers: a background and a foreground. Another secret about cards is that they really have more than two layers. The truth is that each time you create an object such as a button, field, or picture, that object appears on its own layer. One of the hardest concepts to understand in HyperCard is this invisible layering system. You never see these layers because they are transparent. The only thing they can be compared to are layers of plastic or glass laid on top of each other, each layer having one button or field drawn on it (see Figure 7.13).

So a card is really made up of several layers, not just two, but because you can't physically see these layers, they don't seem real. The only time you even need to keep this in mind is when you change the order of buttons and fields on a card. Later in this chapter, you'll use the **Bring Closer** and **Send Farther** commands on the Objects menu to change the layering order of fields.

Note: The Help stack often refers to these layers as "levels."

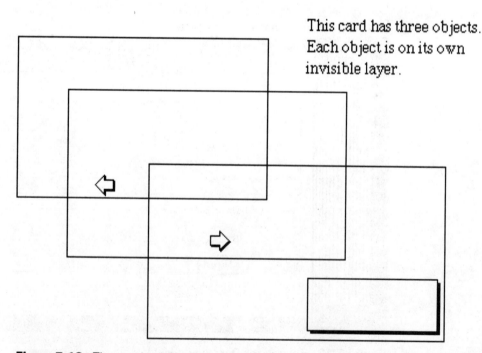

This card has three objects. Each object is on its own invisible layer.

Figure 7.13 The number of layers on a card equals the number of individual objects created on that card, including background objects.

Lesson 42: CREATING A NEW FIELD

In this lesson, you'll create a new field that contains the category of the information you type into the Description field. Since you're going to add either a tip, trick, or shortcut to each card in this stack, the categories you'll enter into the new field you create will be "Tip," "Trick," and "Shortcut." For example, if you type a HyperCard shortcut such as "Press ⌘-B to see a card's background," then you would type the word **Shortcut** into this new field. "Shortcut" is the category of the information on this card.

1. Press ⌘-B to display the background. You'll create a new field on the background so that it will appear on every card you add to this stack.

*2. Choose **New Field** from the Objects menu. A transparent field appears, with a moving dotted line around it, in the center of the card. The moving line tells you that this field is selected (see Figure 7.14). This field stays selected until you click outside of it.*

You'll resize this field and then change its field information.

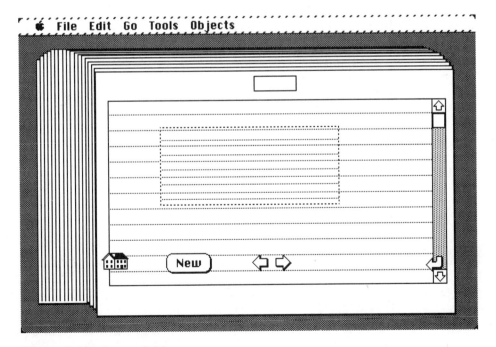

Figure 7.14 A new field.

3. Resize this field by clicking on the lower right corner of it and dragging to the upper left corner of the card. Drag it until it is one line high and about two inches long, as in Figure 7.15.

4. Click inside of this field and drag it to the upper right corner of the screen next to the Index Number field.

*5. Choose **Field Info...** from the Objects menu to see and change information about this field. (Or just double-click on the field to see the Field Info... dialog box.)*

*6. Type **Category** for the name of this field. (You'll refer to this name later when you learn how to program stacks.)*

7. Click in the circle next to rectangle to select it for the field style.

*8. Click on the **Font** button.*

*9. Choose **Bold**, **Times**, and **14 points** for the text font and style. (If you don't have the Times font, choose **Geneva** instead.)*

*10. Click **OK**.*

That's all there is to it! You've customized your new stack and are now ready to enter some information into the fields.

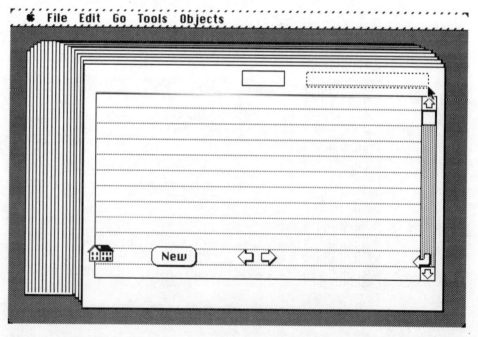

Figure 7.15 Resize the new field and put it in the upper right corner of the card.

Lesson 43: ENTER TIPS AND TRICKS FOR YOUR STACK

You've produced a useful stack and in the process you've learned more about authoring stacks. In this lesson, you'll add a new card for each tip, trick, and shortcut you've learned so far.

Adding More Cards

1. You must choose the **Browse** *tool before you can enter text into fields or click on buttons.*

2. Press the TAB key to move the insertion point into the first field. Since the index number already appears in the first field, press the TAB key again to move into the second field, which is named "Description."

3. Type **Tip** *for the category in which the information belongs.*

4. Here's the first tip you learned in this book:

Tip: Some stacks that you buy contain an installation program that puts an icon for that stack on the Home card. If the Home card is full, just add a new card for storing the other icons.

Type this tip into the Description field. You don't have to press RETURN at the end of each line in this field. HyperCard wraps the text around to the next line as you type past the end of it.

5. Click once on the **New** *button to add another card to this stack.*

The tips, tricks, and shortcuts appear in boxes throughout this book. Go through the chapters and add a tip, trick, and shortcut that you found useful to each card in this stack. You'll find this stack useful in the future as a HyperCard reference tool.

But wait! You don't have to go to all that work! The HyperCard Tips stack is also available on a disk that contains all the stacks in this book plus a few others. You can order the disk using the order card at the back of this book.

Lesson 44: CHANGING THE ORDER OF FIELDS

The order in which you create fields determines the order in which the insertion point moves into fields during text entry. So, for example, if you want the insertion point to move smoothly from left to right and top to bottom, you create the first field at the top left, the next one at center left, and so on. All well and good. But what happens if you finish creating fields and discover that you've left one out, or you want to add a new field in the middle of the rest of them? That, primarily, is what changing the order of the fields is for.

1. Press the TAB key a number of times to see the order in which the insertion point moves into fields.

Pressing the TAB key moves the insertion point into the Index field and then into the Description field and then into the Category field. What if you want to type the name of the category before typing the description of the tip or trick? How can you change the order in which the fields are entered?

The Objects menu gives you two choices for changing the order of a field: **Bring Closer** and **Send Farther**. Each time you choose the **Bring Closer** command when a field is selected, the order number of that field increases by one (see Figure 7.16). For example, if a field currently has an order number of (7) and you choose **Bring Closer** while that field is selected, its order number changes from (7) to (8).

As you create fields, each one appears on its own invisible layer, with the first field on the bottom of these layers. The most recent object is on the topmost layer and therefore has the highest number. When you

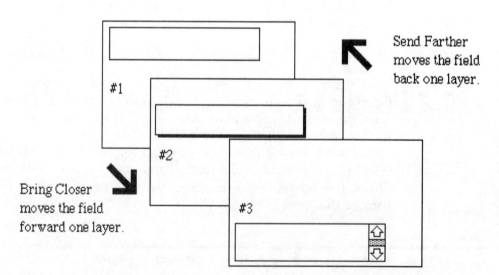

Figure 7.16 The Bring Closer command moves objects to the top of the layering system, increasing its order number.

choose **Bring Closer**, it means "move the object up one layer, thereby increasing its order number in the layer of cards."

*2. To change the order of the Description field from (2) to (3) so you can enter that field last, first choose the **Field** tool on the Tools menu.*

*3. Click once on the **Description** field to select it. Then choose **Bring Closer** from the Objects menu.*

The right arrow button disappeared! Remember the invisible layers discussed earlier? Each button and field is created on a separate layer of the card. These layers are transparent to the eye. But when you use the **Bring Closer** or **Send Farther** command, these layers are shuffled around in another order.

Here, the **Bring Closer** command moved the Description field layer in front of the right arrow button layer on the card.

In other words, the **Bring Closer** command made two changes: it changed the order number of the Description field from (2) to (3), and it changed the position of that field in relation to other objects on the card.

4. To bring the button back in front of the card, click and drag a corner of the card to reduce the length of the field until you can see the missing button (see Figure 7.17).

*5. Choose the **Button** tool in the Tools menu. Click on the button once to select it. Then choose **Bring Closer** from the Objects menu. The right arrow button appears in front of the field again. (Since you selected a button instead of a field, the field order was not affected this time.)*

6. To see if HyperCard really changed the field order from 2 to 3, double-click on the Description field to see the Field Info dialog box.

The field number should be (3) now.

Another way to see the changed order of the fields is by pressing the TAB key a number of times. The insertion bar moves to each field in order.

Besides affecting the TAB order, the **Bring Closer** and **Send Farther** commands also affect the search order when you use the Find command. For example, if there are 10 fields on a card, HyperCard looks for a match in Field (1) first, in Field (2) second, and so on, stopping in each field with a match.

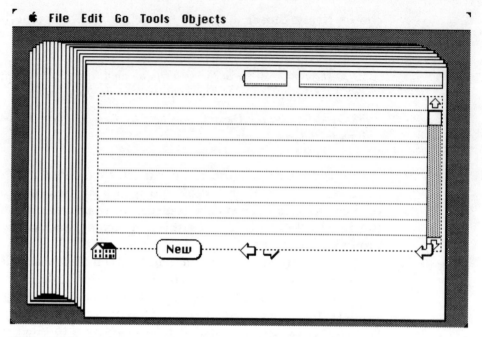

Figure 7.17 Position of the button in relation to the field.

Lesson 45: COPYING FIELDS

The fastest way to create two or more identical fields is by making a copy of a field. To copy a field, follow these steps:

1. Choose the **Field** tool on the Tools menu.
2. Select the field to be copied by clicking once on it. A moving dotted line appears around that field.
3. Choose **Copy field** from the Edit menu.
4. Choose **Background** from the Edit menu if you want to copy the field to the background.
5. Choose **Paste field** from the Edit menu.

Shortcut: With the Field tool chosen, hold down the Option key, click on a field, and drag off a copy of it.

A copy of the selected field appears complete with all the attributes (field style, text style, options, and so on) assigned to the selected field. The only part of the field that doesn't copy is the text within it.

To copy just the text from one field to another, select the text by dragging the mouse through it, then use Copy and Paste from the Edit menu.

The Difference Between Paint Text and Field Text

Before going on, let's review the difference between painting text onto a card like you did on the Title card in the previous chapter, and creating fields in which to type text.

Deciding whether text should be typed into a field or typed on a card with the Text tool is quite simple. If you want the same word or words to appear on every card in the stack, such as the headings of columns or rows, first choose the background and then use the Text tool to paint the text onto the background. If you want different text to appear in the same place on every card, create a field into which you can type text for each card (see Figure 7.18).

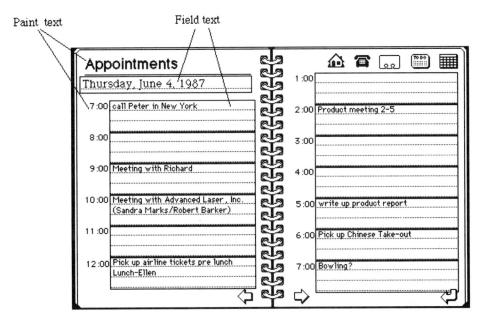

Figure 7.18 Paint text is used for text that doesn't change. Field text is easily edited.

> *Tip:* Field text is more flexible than Paint text. You can't edit Paint text easily once you've typed it on the screen and then moved the insertion point. Paint text is a graphic that you can erase with the Eraser tool, whereas Field text can be easily edited within a field. Paint text is really artwork. Field text is information. If you plan to translate your stacks into foreign languages, you can make this process a lot smoother by putting text into fields instead of typing text with the Text tool.

SUMMARY

Everything is customizable in HyperCard, whether you or someone else created the stack. In this chapter you learned how to modify existing fields and how to create new ones.

When working with fields, keep these points in mind:

- Hold down the SHIFT key while you drag to move a field straight up or down.
- Hold down the OPTION key and drag a field to make a copy of that field.
- Create a field on the background to see it on every card in the stack.
- You can change the text style within a field, but each field can only have one font type, size, and style. Be creative by superimposing one field on top of another to make it look like you used two different text fonts or formats.
- **Bring Closer** means add (1) to the order number of a field. **Send Farther** means subtract (1) from the order number of a field. These commands affect the Tab order, search order, and position of fields in relation to other objects on the card.

In the next chapter you'll learn how to customize and work with buttons.

8 Customizing Buttons

In this chapter, you'll continue modifying the HyperCard Tips stack by changing and removing some of the buttons as well as adding new buttons. You'll also learn how to link buttons to cards, and how to create a button on the Home card. You'll then be able to use that button to go directly to your HyperCard Tips stack.

The lessons in this chapter show you how to

- Move and resize buttons
- Change the look (style) of a button
- Change the text style in the button
- Copy a button from another card or stack
- Create a new button
- Use buttons to create *links* between cards and stacks
- Add a button to the Home card and link it to this new stack

Open the stack named HyperCard Tips by choosing **Open Stack** from the File menu. Pull down the folder in the dialog box and choose the folder named HyperCard. Find and double-click on the stack named HyperCard Tips.

To complete the lessons in this chapter, the user level must be set to **Authoring**. Type **set the userlevel to 4** in the Message box to change the user level to **Authoring** if necessary. (Type **userlevel** as one word, not two.)

Lesson 46: MOVING AND RESIZING BUTTONS

The HyperCard Tips stack has five buttons. The first button looks like a house. It takes you to the Home card when you click on it. The second button, named **New**, adds a new card to this stack and automatically enters a sequential number into the index field of the new card. The third button takes you to the previous card; the fourth button takes you to the next card. And the last button, the **Return arrow**, takes you to the previous stack viewed.

When you lengthened the picture of the index card in Chapter 6, the buttons stayed where they were. That's because buttons are not pictures; they are objects. And since HyperCard treats each button as a separate object, you have to move these buttons one at a time.

In this lesson, you'll move the buttons so they are aligned with the bottom edge of the picture of the index card. Then you'll see how easy it is to change the size of a button.

Moving Buttons

One of the most common mistakes people make when using HyperCard is forgetting to choose the right tool or go to the right card. Before you can work with buttons, you have to choose the Button tool.

*1. Choose the **Button** tool on the Tools menu.*

2. Click on the first button on the card—the Home button. A moving dotted line appears around that button. While holding down the SHIFT key, drag the button to the bottom of the screen so it is aligned with the bottom edge of the index card. (Holding down the SHIFT key while dragging keeps the button aligned as you move it.)

Tip: Once you begin dragging a button vertically, you can't drag it horizontally while holding down the SHIFT key. To switch from vertical to horizontal dragging, release both the SHIFT key and mouse button. Then press them both down again while you drag the button horizontally.

---

3. Click outside of the button to unselect it or just click on another button to select it instead.

4. Repeat these steps to move the other buttons to the bottom of the index card (see Figure 8.1).

By the way, these buttons belong to the background. That's why they appear on every card in this stack.

As with fields, to modify a background button, you don't have to go to the background first because HyperCard already knows where that

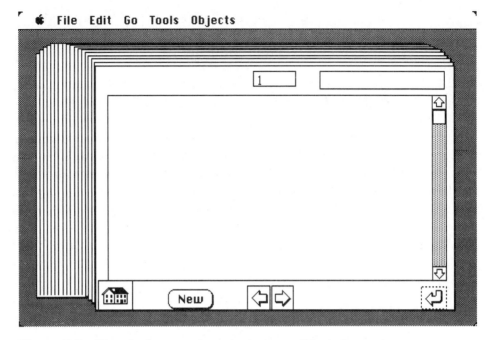

Figure 8.1 Align the buttons along the bottom of the index card.

button is. You can *modify* buttons from either the background or the card level. However, to *create* a button on a card's background, you must first display the background.

Resizing Buttons

Sometimes you'll need to change the size of a button, especially if the name you assigned to it does not fit within the standard size of a button (see Figure 8.2).

You also use the button tool to change the size of a button. Resize the button named **New** by following these steps:

1. First choose the **Button** tool in the Tools menu.
2. Click on the New button to select it.

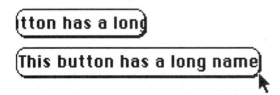

Figure 8.2 To fit long button names within the button, resize the button.

3. Click on the lower right corner of this button and drag down and to the right to enlarge it. Or drag up and to the left to make it smaller. You resize buttons the same way you resize fields.

Lesson 47: CHANGING THE LOOK OF A BUTTON

All the buttons on the HyperCard Tips stack were created on the background. Changes you make to background buttons affect every card in the stack. So when you changed the size of the New button, it appeared that way on every card in the stack.

Not only can you change the size of a button, you can change its style too just as you did with fields. To change the look or style of a button, you must first choose the **Button** tool and then choose the button to be modified. Do that now.

1. Tear off the Tools menu and put it in the upper left corner of the card.
2. Click on the **Button** tool in the Tools menu. All buttons appear outlined on the card—whether these fields are on the background or on the card itself.
3. Click on the **New** button to select it as the one you want to modify.
4. Choose **Button Info...** from the Objects menu to see and change information about this field (see Figure 8.3).

Button Styles

The Button Info dialog box gives you several choices for determining how a button should look. You'll choose a style for the button named New after reviewing the kinds of choices you have.

When changing the way a button looks, you can choose from one of seven distinct styles (see Figure 8.4).

Transparent

A transparent button is invisible. To see its boundaries you must either choose the Button tool, or hold down the OPTION and COMMAND keys to reveal all buttons. Any pictures on the background will show through an invisible button. In fact, often buttons are made invisible for that reason. For example, creating transparent buttons over a picture you've drawn makes it appear as though you can click on that picture to make it function like a button.

The Help Index card in the Help stack has a transparent button over each word on a card. So when you click on a word in the list, the invisible button displays the card with information about that word (see Figure 8.5).

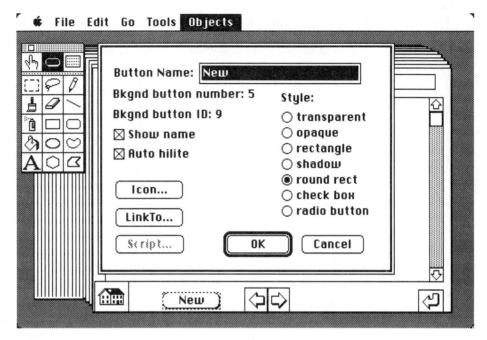

Figure 8.3 Button information for the New button.

Opaque

An opaque button is a just like an opaque field. It hides whatever is under it (see Figure 8.6). You can use opaque buttons to hide pictures, words in fields, or other buttons. An opaque button has no border other

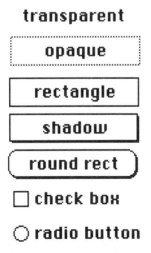

Figure 8.4 You can create transparent buttons, rectangular buttons, buttons with a drop shadow behind them, or buttons that cover up text or graphics.

File   Edit   Go   Tools   Objects

Index

☐ Adding	☐ Apple key
☐ backgrounds	☐ applications
☐ buttons	☐ launching or opening other
☐ cards	☐ arrow or cursor keys
☐ fields	☐ asterisk (*)
☐ stacks	
☐ text, typing	
☐ pictures	
☐ space between text lines	
☐ aiming links	
☐ Apple menu	

Find

Browse ┃ Paint ┃ Copy ┃ Menus ┃ Reference ┃ HyperTalk ┃ Map ┃ Glossary ┃ Index ┃ Exit

Figure 8.5 The Help Index card uses several Transparent buttons.

than its white perimeter. On a white card, you cannot see an opaque button.

Rectangle

A rectangle button is an opaque button shaped like a rectangle with a black line as its border (see Figure 8.7). This style is common for buttons that have names on them and that need to be aligned with other buttons.

Round Rectangle

A round rectangle button is a rectangle button with rounded corners (see Figure 8.8). It is one of the most common button styles used in Macintosh programs.

opaque

Figure 8.6 An opaque button covers up objects beneath it.

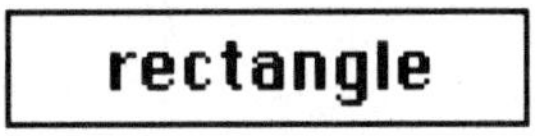

```
┌─────────────────────┐
│  rectangle          │
└─────────────────────┘
```

Figure 8.7 Rectangle button.

Shadow
A shadow button is a rectangle button with a drop shadow behind it (see Figure 8.9).

Check Box
A check box button is a box that you click in to turn something such as a feature on and off. For example, you used a check box when you clicked in the **Text Arrows** option on the Home Preferences card (see Figure 8.10). An X appears within a check box when you click in it the first time. The X disappears when you click in it again. You'll use this button style when you learn how to program with HyperTalk. This button style won't be of any use until you learn how to program a button to do something when you click in it. Then it will be very useful indeed.

Radio Button
A radio button is a small circle that you click in to turn the button on. A black dot appears within the circle when you click in it the first time. The dot disappears when you click in it again. Use this style when you want to provide several choices on a card. For example, the User Preferences card has five radio buttons. You can choose one of the five levels by clicking in the button next to the level you want to use.

Like the check box, this button style isn't of any use until you learn how to program a button to do something. However, when you do learn how to program buttons, you'll find many uses for the radio button style.

Other Button Options

Besides button styles, you have the option for showing the name of a button and for having it appear highlighted when you click on it.

Show Name
If you typed a name into the Button Name field and you want that name to appear on that button, check the box next to Show Name by clicking in it. Clicking in it a second time unchecks the box.

Normally, you'll use the Show Name option with every style except for transparent.

```
╭─────────────────────╮
│  round rect         │
╰─────────────────────╯
```

Figure 8.8 Round Rectangle button.

```
┌─────────────────────┐
│                     │
│    shadow           │
│                     │
└─────────────────────┘
```

Figure 8.9 Shadow button.

Auto Hilite

Choose **Auto Hilite** to have a button appear highlighted (turn black) whenever you click on it. This option does not work well with Check Box or Radio buttons since they need to be programmed to be of use. When you learn how to program them, you'll also learn how to turn the hilite on and off.

Icon

Not all of the pictures on the Home card are buttons. Some of them are pictures that were drawn with paint tools. Then a transparent button was placed on top of each picture so that when you click on it, it functions like a button. When you move a transparent button, the picture beneath it doesn't move with the button.

An icon is a button with a picture encoded into it so you cannot change its shape or size.

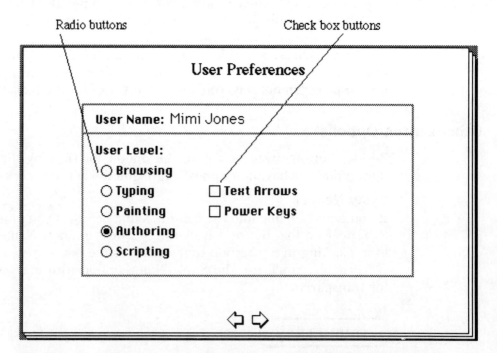

Figure 8.10 Check Box and Radio buttons on the User Preferences card.

All of the buttons in the HyperCard Tips stack are icons, except the New button. You can assign an icon as well as a button style to the same button. But if you don't want a border around your icon, choose **transparent** for the button style.

You can choose from several icons by first clicking on the Icon button in the Button Info dialog box (see Figure 8.11).

Tip: You can modify and create icons with a resource editor such as ResEdit. A HyperCard stack named ResCopier written by Steve Maller of Apple Computer gives novice Macintosh users an easy way to copy icons, sounds, and other resources from one stack to another and one file to another. This stack is free. You can download it from CompuServe or get a copy from a Macintosh Users Group.

You can also obtain a copy from the Apple Programmer's and Developer's Association, which also has other useful stacks and utility programs. Their address is APDA, 290 SW 43rd Street, Renton, WA 98055.

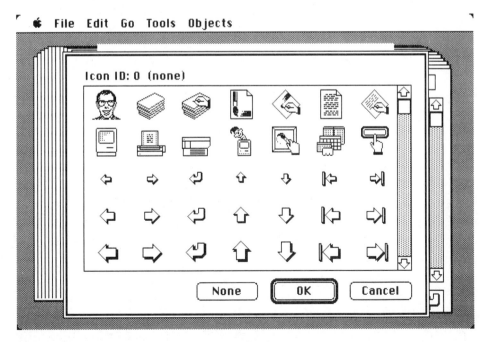

Figure 8.11 Icons available with HyperCard.

One of the limitations of HyperCard buttons is that all the buttons are square or rectangular. For example, you cannot create a round button. And you can't create odd-shaped buttons.

You'll learn how to use the **Link to** and **Script** button options later in this book.

Choose Rectangle for the Button Style

1. Click in the circle next to **rectangle** to select it as the style for the New button.
2. Click **OK**.

Shortcut: After choosing the Button tool in the Tools menu, double-click on a button to go directly to its information dialog box.

Lesson 48: CHANGING THE TEXT STYLE OF BUTTON TEXT

For some reason, there is no choice in the Button Info dialog box for changing the style of text that appears within a button. Don't worry. You can change the text style, but it involves a trick.

Change the Style of the Button Text

As you probably guessed, you can use the Message box to change the text style of a button. The Message box lets you do practically anything in HyperCard. The magic words are **set textStyle of** <**card** or **background**> **button** <name or number> **to** <style>. If the button is on a background, you must type **background** before **button** in the Message box. For <name or number> type either the name you assigned to the button in the Button Info dialog box or the button number, which is also shown in the Button Info dialog box.

For example, since the New button is on the background, typing **set textStyle of background button "New" to italic** changes it from plain to italic. Do that now.

1. Go to the card that has the button you want to change. In this case, go to any card in the Tips stack. (The New button is a background button so it shows on every card in this stack.)

2. Press ⌘-M to display the Message box.
3. Type **set textStyle of background button "New" to italic** and press RETURN (see Figure 8.12).

You can change the button style from its default setting, Plain, to any of the following:

> **bold**
> *italic*
> <u>underline</u>
> outline
> shadow

You can also use a combination of styles, for example, **set textStyle of background button "New" to bold, underline.**

More examples:
set textStyle of background button "New" to outline, italic
set textStyle of background button "New" to bold, italic
set textStyle of background button "New" to plain

Change the Font of the Button Text

To change the font, type **set textFont of <card or background> button <name or number> to <font name>**. You can use any font stored in either the HyperCard stack on which the button is located or in the System file.

For example, typing **set textFont of background button "New" to Times** changes the New button from Geneva to Times. Do that now. (If this button was not on the background, you'd type **set textFont of card button "New" to Times**.)

1. Go to any card in the HyperCard Tips stack.
2. Press ⌘-M to display the Message box.
3. Type **set textFont of background button "New" to Times** and press RETURN. (If you don't have the Times font, type **Venice** instead of **Times**.)

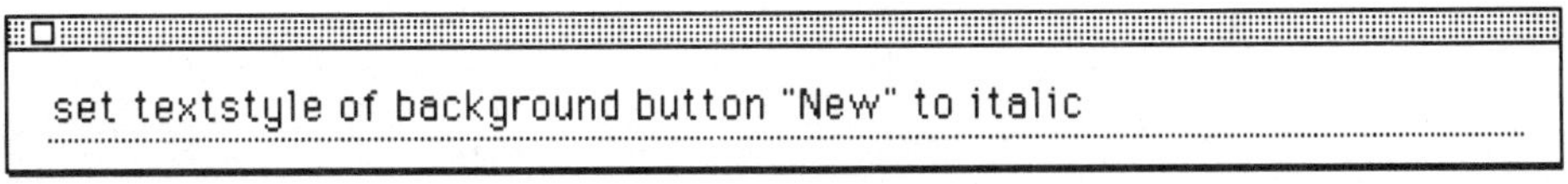

```
set textstyle of background button "New" to italic
```

Figure 8.12 Use the Message box to change a button's text style.

Change the Size of the Button Text

To change the size of the text, type **set textSize of** <**card** or **background**> **button** <name or number> **to** <point size>.

For example, typing **set textSize of background button "New" to 10** changes the New button from its current point size to 10 points. Do that now.

1. Go to any card in the HyperCard Tips stack.
2. Press ⌘-M to display the Message box.
3. Type **set textSize of button background "New" to 10** and press RETURN.

If you make the button text so large that it no longer fits within the button, just resize the button.

Lesson 49: COPYING A BUTTON

A button is more than just the little symbol that you click on; it also includes all the programming that the click sets in motion. For instance, clicking on the **Save** button in any Macintosh application makes the computer save a file, which involves turning on the disk drive to read the file, reading it, checking to make sure there's enough room to save it on the designated save disk, turning on the disk drive to save the file, saving it, checking for errors, and then returning to the screen. All of those actions—and more—are programs that are part of the Save button.

In HyperCard, copying a button gives you all of its underlying programming that you can then use for other purposes. That's the purpose of the Button Ideas stack. It has a whole host of buttons complete with programming that you can copy into your own stacks to use as is. The Button Ideas stack is part of the standard HyperCard program. An example is a button that you can click on to flip through all the cards in a stack, so you can view them all quickly.

Copying a button means you don't have to go to all the trouble of creating it, by programming, yourself. Later on, when you get proficient with HyperTalk programming, you may want to use the buttons in the Button Ideas stack as starting points for creating your own button ideas. And to take the concept one more step: if you buy a HyperCard program that has buttons that you like, maybe you'll want to use them too.

Here are the steps for copying a button from the Button Ideas stack:

1. Press ⌘-H to go to the Home card.

*2. Click on the **Button ideas** stack. This stack has many buttons for you to copy and paste on cards in the stacks you create. Of course, if a button that you need doesn't exist, you'll have to create it yourself. That's simple enough to do.*

*3. Click on the line with **Business button ideas**.*

*4. Choose the **Button** tool on the Tools menu. All the buttons have dotted outlines around them so you can see which objects are buttons.*

Tip: A common mistake is using the Select tool in the Tools menu to copy a button. You can actually select and copy a button (except for icons) with the Select tool. But it won't function because you really only copied *a picture of the button*, not the button itself with all its underlying programming.

Choosing the Button tool tells HyperCard that you are going to copy, cut, paste, change, or just look at a button.

*5. Click on the **View** button to choose it. A moving dotted line appears around it.*

*6. Choose **Copy Button** from the Edit menu. HyperCard copies the button but doesn't give you any confirmation that it has done so.*

You can copy a button to one card or you can copy it to all cards in the stack. It is important to know the difference between the background and card level of a card, and to remember to choose one or the other when editing stacks. Once again, buttons, fields, and art that you put on a background appear on *all cards* in the stack. What you put on a card at the card level appears on that card only.

Now return to the HyperCard Tips stack.

*7. Choose **Recent** from the Go menu and click on the HyperCard Tips stack.*

Tip: Remember to choose Background *before pasting* a button onto a background. Otherwise, you'll paste it on only the card that's currently displayed.

---

*8. Choose **Background** from the Edit menu. You can tell when you're in the background because the menubar in the background has diagonal stripes.*

*9. Choose **Paste Button** from the Edit menu.*

10. Drag the button to the lower right of the card, next to the Return arrow button.

*11. Choose the **Browse** tool in the Tools menu so you can test the button. Click on the **View** button.*

Congratulations! You've finished modifying the HyperCard Tips stack. To make this stack really useful, add all the tips, tricks, and shortcuts in this book to the cards in this stack. And as you discover new tips and tricks, add them to your HyperCard Tips stack. Then this information will be available on your computer while you are creating stacks in HyperCard.

Lesson 50: ADDING A BUTTON TO THE HOME CARD

Now that you have this great stack, you might want to access it from your Home card. You can do so by creating a new button, pasting it on your Home card, and then *linking* it to the HyperCard Tips stack. That's what you'll do next.

Create a New Button on the Home Card

1. Press ⌘-H to go to the Home card.

The buttons on the Home card are linked to the stacks included with HyperCard. When you buy or create a stack that you plan to use often, add a button to the Home card for that stack. In this lesson, you'll add a button to the Home card. Then you'll tell HyperCard to open the HyperCard Tips stack when you click on this button.

*2. Choose **New Button** from the Objects menu. Move the button to a white area on the Home card.*

*3. Choose **Button Info...** from the Objects menu (see Figure 8.13). Type **Tips** for the name of this button.*

*4. Check the boxes for Show Name and Auto Hilite. The name you type for this button will show beneath the button style or icon you choose. When you click on it, this button will turn black until you release the mouse button. Click on **Transparent** for the button style.*

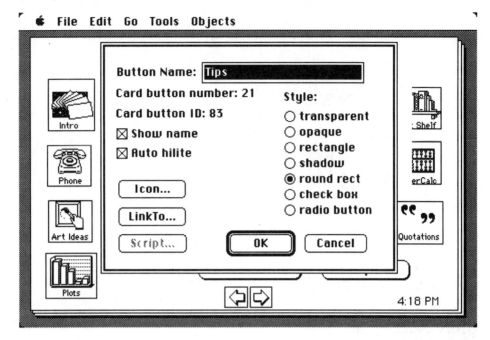

Figure 8.13 Button Info dialog box.

After selecting *Transparent* for the button style, you can select an icon to represent a new button.

*5. Click on **Icon...** to see what kind of icons you can choose from to represent this stack. Use the scroll bar to see more icons.*

*6. Click on any of the icons listed to choose it. Then click **OK** to save your changes.*

7. Drag the button to a white area on the Home card (see Figure 8.14). You can resize the button if you like by dragging one corner of it up, down, right, or left. Try it.

Link This Button to the HyperCard Tips Stack

Okay, so you've created a new button but it doesn't do anything yet. In this exercise, you'll see how easy it is to link that button to a card. *Linking* is the only way to program a button without using HyperTalk.

When you use the **Link to** button in a Button Info dialog box, you're telling HyperCard that you want to connect that button to a specific card. You can link a button to any card in any stack.

Figure 8.14 Move your new button to a white area on the Home card so it blends in with the other stack icons.

Follow these steps to link the Tips button on the Home card to the first card in the HyperCard Tips stack:

*1. Make sure the Button tool is selected on the Tools menu. Then double-click on the **Tips** button to see the Button Info dialog box.*

2. In the button Info dialog box, click on the Link to... button. A dialog box with choices appears. It will stay on the screen until you click in it.

*3. Now find and open the stack to be linked. Choose **Open Stack** from the File menu. Pull down the appropriate folder. Find and open the HyperCard Tips stack. Double-click to open it.*

You may need to move this Destination dialog box out of the way because it appears on top of card information. To move this box, click on the gray bar at the top of the dialog box and drag it to another location.

*4. Click on **This Stack** in the dialog box (see figure 8.15). This choice links the button to the first card in this stack. The other choice, This Card, is for linking a button to a specific card.*

After you've clicked on **This Stack** in the dialog box, HyperCard takes

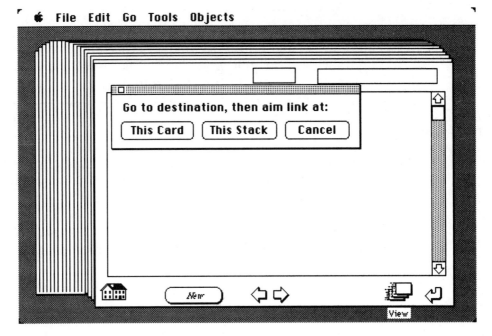

Figure 8.15 The Link dialog box follows you to the Destination card.

you back to the card with the button you just linked. Now you can test this button to make sure it's linked to the right card. When you click on this button, it should go to the first card in the HyperCard Tips stack.

> *Tip:* If you link a button to the wrong card, it's no big deal. To unlink a button, just repeat the linking procedure to link it to the correct card. If you decide that you don't want the button linked to any card for the time being, *link it to itself* to unlink it.

*5. Choose the **Browse** tool from the Tools menu. Click on the **Tips** button to go to the HyperCard Tips stack.*

Linking a button to a card is a one-way ticket. The button takes you to the linked card but doesn't bring you back. The HyperCard Tips stack just happens to have a Home button to bring you back to the Home card. However, stacks you create won't automatically have a Home button or any other button, for that matter. But you can create a button anywhere you like and link it to any stack by following the procedures you used in this lesson.

> *Tip:* A button can be as large as the card itself. You can create an invisible button that covers the entire card and link it to another card so that when you click anywhere on the card, it automatically goes to the card you linked it to.

Delete Buttons

If you decide that you don't like the way a button looks, you can always modify it in the Button Info dialog box. But if you'd really rather erase that button and start all over, you can do that too.

The quickest way to delete a button is to choose the **Button** tool, click on the button to be deleted, and then press the BACKSPACE key. Of course, you can also use the Cut Button and Clear Button menu choices that appear on the Edit menu when you select the Button tool.

SUMMARY

In this chapter you learned how to modify, copy, and create buttons and to link them to cards in other stacks. And you're finished modifying your HyperCard Tips stack.

When working with buttons, keep these points in mind:

- Hold down the SHIFT key while you drag to move a button straight up or down.
- You can copy ready-made buttons from the Button Ideas stack. You don't have to go to the background to copy a background button. However, to paste a button on a background, you first must display that background.
- You can change the text style within a button by typing special commands in the Message box.
- You can create buttons on your Home card and link them to any stacks you like. You can use buttons to link cards in the same stack or in other stacks.
- Buttons will become more useful to you when you learn how to program them.

In the next chapter, you'll learn how to design a stack.

9 Designing a Stack

Before designing a stack you should think about a few things like what kinds of information you want to put in the stack. This chapter covers some basic design guidelines to follow in creating a stack.

The lessons in this chapter show you how to

- Outline a design for a stack
- Organize your design into cards

In previous lessons, you created stacks by copying and modifying an existing stack. You don't have to use an existing stack. You can create stacks by beginning with a blank screen. But keep in mind that you don't have to "reinvent the wheel." Creating HyperCard stacks is usually a process of borrowing buttons and art from other cards.

Lesson 51: BEFORE DIGGING IN

Before creating a new stack, it's best to outline on paper what you plan to do. When writing this outline, you should have an idea of

- who will use this stack
- why someone would use it
- what kind of information it will contain
- how you intend to organize the information

Audience

Think about who would use this stack. Are they experienced Macintosh users? Are they students? Are they HyperCard experts?

Why Use This Stack?

Why are you creating this stack in the first place? Will it be used to teach someone how to do something like fix a flat tire? Will it be used like a data base for storing and retrieving information? Will it be used to sell a product like a sales demo or presentation tool? Will it be a help system accompanying a Macintosh software program?

Content

Decide what information you will include. For example, if you're creating a sales catalog, you'll include information such as the name of the product, what it looks like, its order number and price. You should create a detailed outline before creating the stack.

Lesson 52: ORGANIZING CARDS

How will users get from one card to another in your stack?

You can organize cards in any way you want. For example, cards can be organized in a line (*linear order*) with right and left arrow buttons that you click on to go forward and backward through the stack. Designing stacks in linear order is the simplest way to organize cards used for simple presentations, like a slide show (see Figure 9.1).

Do you want to create menus for users to choose from? Or do you want to create a card with pictures that users can click on to branch to different cards? If so, you can organize cards with a *menu structure* as in Figure 9.2.

Use this method of organization for stacks that are tutorials or that contain reference material. Quizzes are commonly organized using a menu structure.

You can get as crazy as you like, and organize cards so that you can get to any card from any other card, as in Figure 9.3.

Next you should draw a map of how the cards will be organized. Draw lines from one card to another to indicate how the cards will be linked.

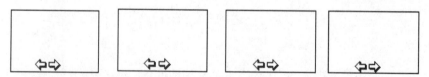

Figure 9.1 Linear organization

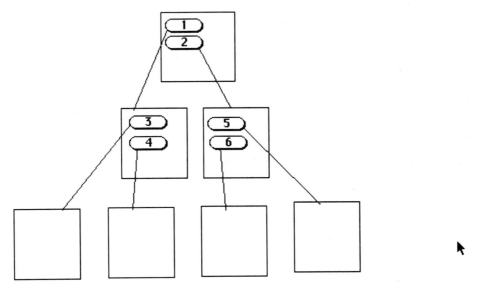

Figure 9.2 Main menu with buttons branching off to other cards.

It's important that the people who use your stack don't feel lost within it. So in addition to buttons taking you from one card to another, you should create a button that takes you back to a card.

After organizing the cards and determining how you'll navigate through them, decide how many backgrounds you'll need to use. Think

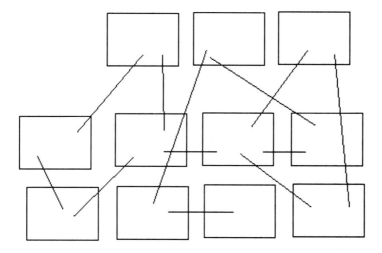

Figure 9.3 Link cards any way you like.

about which objects (buttons, fields, and graphics) can be shared from card to card. Backgrounds give your stacks consistency, making them easier to navigate through. Also, sharing buttons, fields, and graphics takes up less disk space than recreating them on each card.

You can also think of backgrounds as an extension to the pull-down menus: a group of options clearly available to the user. For example, you can create several buttons on a background so that these buttons are available from any card with that background.

Also, keep common buttons (such as navigation buttons) in the same place on every card.

SUMMARY

This chapter was intended to provide you with some basic guidelines for creating a stack. It is by no means a complete guide to designing stacks.

Okay, now what? Once you've thought out, outlined, and mapped out your stack, all you have to decide is how best to do it with HyperCard.

The fastest way to create a stack is to copy and modify an existing one. However, you can always create one from scratch if you can't find one you want to copy. The next chapter shows how to create a stack from scratch.

10 Put Your Resume on a Stack!

In this chapter you'll learn how *easy* it is to put your resume on a stack. Since resumes are divided into categories of information, they are already outlined for you. And you know who your audience is—a potential employer. Of course, not everyone is going to know how to use a Macintosh, or own one, for that matter. Putting your resume on a stack will help *you* organize and update the information.

And besides, it's an easy way to learn how to create a stack in HyperCard. In previous chapters you created new stacks by copying and modifying existing ones. This chapter shows you, step by step, how to create a stack from a blank screen.

The lessons in this chapter show you how to

- Design a stack template for a resume
- Create a frame with a double border
- Add background buttons
- Create a field without using a menu

To complete the lessons in this chapter, the user level must be set to **Authoring**. Type **set the user level to 4** in the Message box to change the user level to **Authoring**.

Lesson 53: WHERE DO I START?

When designing a stack to put your resume on, think of an easy way for someone to find specific information about you. Categorize your skills just like you do on a resume: Objective, Experience, Education, Membership, Awards, and Publications (see Figure 10.1).

Then create buttons, one for each category, that are linked to cards with that information.

John Doe   **415/555-9899**
100 Elm St.
San Francisco, CA 94000

Objective: To obtain a writing position that will eventually lead me to become the right-arm of the president of a large corporation.

Experience   <u>**Technical Writing**</u>

Colorful Corporation, Mountain View, CA **1987-1988**
Technical writing and consulting.

- Designed, developed, wrote, and programmed sales demos.

- Answered questions about designing, developing, writing, and programming sales demos.

A-1 Computer   **1986-1987**
Technical writing and consulting.

- Wrote training courses for new, innovative, and revolutionary software and hardware products.

- Attended dozens of meetings and parties.

MonEye Software   **1982-1985**
Technical Writing

- Managed, created, directed, wrote, edited, and produced a manual for the MonEye word processor.

- Created hundreds of help screens for the intuitive, easy-to-use MonEye word processor.

Education   **M.A. in Technical Writing,** *March 1982*
                     Any University

                     B.F.D. in Creative Writing, *August 1979*
                     Any University

Membership   Society for Clear Writing
                     Society Against Bad Writing
                     Society for Social Justice
                     Society for Societies

Figure 10.1   A sample resume.

Lesson 54: DRAWING A DIAGRAM

We can't emphasize enough how important it is to draw a diagram or map of the general layout of the stack. It gives an order to the stack and helps you see if the cards will flow smoothly. The diagram will also be useful later if you decide to make a lot of modifications to this stack.

See Figure 10.2 for a sample diagram for a resume.

Lesson 55: PUTTING IT ON A STACK

As you know, there are several ways to create a stack. When designing a stack, keep in mind that the person looking at it needs an easy way to get from one card to the next. So keep it simple and make buttons obvious.

Here's one way to do it:

1. Start HyperCard if you haven't already. It doesn't matter which stack is open when creating a new stack from scratch.

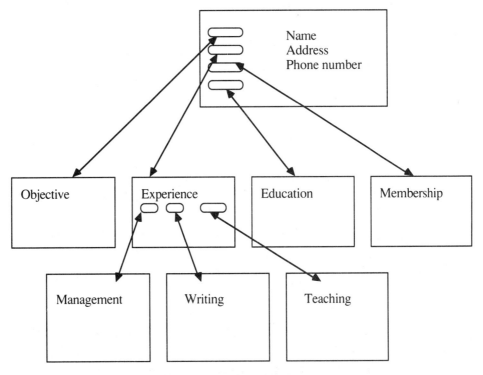

Figure 10.2 A sample diagram of cards laid out.

2. Choose **New Stack** from the File menu. To give yourself as much creativity as possible, create this stack from a blank screen.
3. Uncheck the box next to **Copy current background** since you don't want to copy the background of the stack currently shown.
4. Pull down the HyperCard Stacks folder and choose the folder named HyperCard. That's where you'll save this new stack.
5. Type **Resume** for the name of this stack and press RETURN to start building a new stack. You should see a blank white screen.

Lesson 56: FRAMING A CARD

You're staring at a white screen (see Figure 10.3). Both the background and the first card in this stack are white. Since this resume will have only one background, you'll put graphics, fields, and buttons common to all cards on the background.

*1. Choose **Background** or press ⌘-B to display the background.*

Before adding buttons or fields to this background, decide what kinds

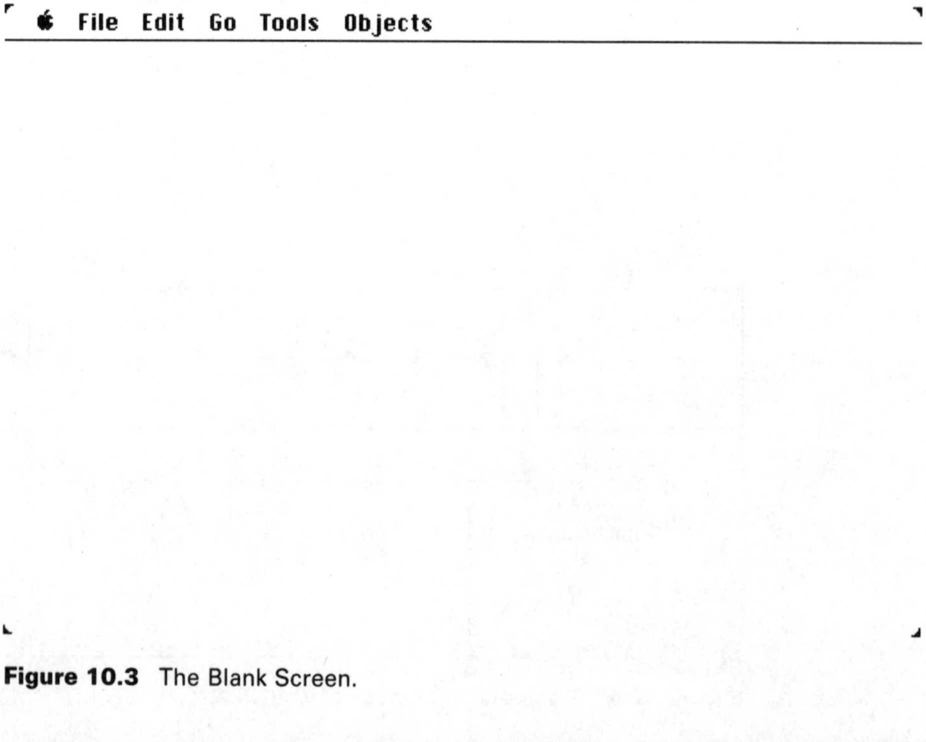

 File Edit Go Tools Objects

Figure 10.3 The Blank Screen.

of graphics you'd like, if any. You can use the paint tools to draw graphics yourself, or copy them from the Art Ideas stack to this background.

Add a border if you like. A border is to a card what a frame is to a picture. To draw a border inside the card, do this:

*2. Choose the **Rectangle** tool on the Tools menu (see Figure 10.4). Use this tool to draw a rectangle or square with a black border.*

*3. You can choose the thickness of the line by choosing **Line Size** from the Options menu (see Figure 10.5). Then click on the one you want. Do that now.*

Tip: Double-click on the Line tool in the Tools menu instead of choosing Line Size to see the chart of line sizes.

---

4. Move the crossbar to the upper left corner of the screen and click to mark the starting position. Then drag diagonally to the lower right (see Figure 10.6). Release the mouse button when you're done.

*5. To make a double border around the square, choose **Select All** from the Paint menu. Then choose **Trace Edges** from the Paint menu (see Figure 10.7). This frame will appear on every card you add to this stack.*

You can create many different frames by choosing **Trace Edges** several times when a picture is selected.

If you'd like to add a picture to this stack, you can copy one or more from the Art Ideas stack. Remember to use either the Select tool or Lasso tool on the Tools menu to select an object to be copied. Then simply

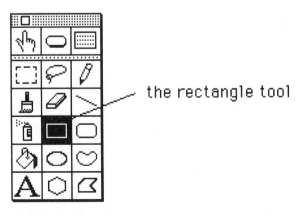

the rectangle tool

Figure 10.4 The Rectangle tool.

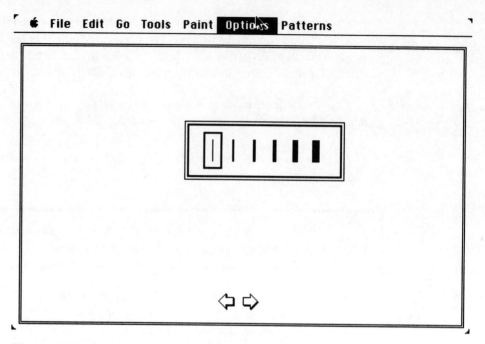

Figure 10.5 Choose from several line sizes.

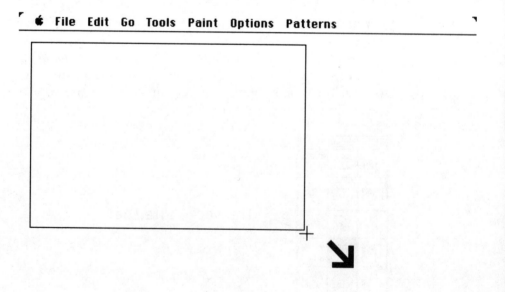

Figure 10.6 Drag diagonally to draw a square.

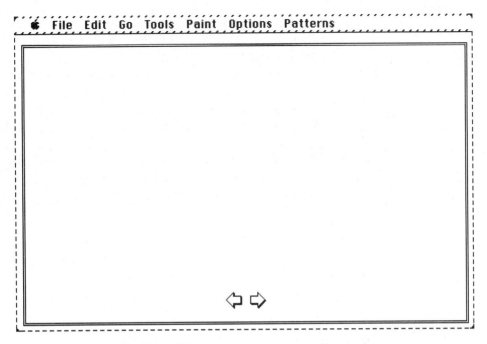

Figure 10.7 Choose Trace Edges once to draw a double border.

choose **Copy Picture** from the Edit menu. Return to your resume stack. Then choose **Paste Picture**. Don't paste this picture on the background unless you want it to appear on every card in this stack.

6. Go to the Art Ideas stack. Find and copy a picture of the Macintosh. Paste this picture on the first card of your resume stack.

Lesson 57: ADDING BACKGROUND BUTTONS

You should add navigation buttons—buttons you click on to get from one card to another—to a background. Always put these buttons on the background so they'll be in the same place on every card.

You'll add the standard HyperCard navigation buttons—the right and left arrow buttons—to this background. Instead of creating a new button, you might as well copy these buttons from the Button Ideas stack. Follow the steps below to do this:

1. Go to the Home card.
2. Click on the **Button Ideas** icon.
3. Click on the first line in the Button Ideas stack, "First, Previous, Next, Last, Return," to go to the card with all the arrow buttons.

4. Choose the **Button** tool on the Tools menu.
5. Click on one of the arrow buttons pointing left to select it.
6. Press ⌘-C to copy that button.
7. Go back to your resume stack. To get back quickly, choose **Recent** from the Go menu and click on the picture of your resume, or press the tilde key a few times to retrace your steps.
8. Press ⌘-B to display the background. You'll paste this button on the background so it will appear on every card you add to this stack.
9. Press ⌘-V to paste this button. The button appears in the same place on this card that it was on the card from which you copied it.
10. Repeat Steps 1 through 9 to copy the Right Arrow button.

Lesson 58:   WHAT TO PUT ON THE FIRST CARD

Usually you'll type the name of a stack on the first card to indicate what this stack is all about. That is not a hard and fast rule, though. For example, you don't have to type "Resume" on the first card, and in this case it might look silly. Other words, pictures, and buttons that you add to the first card can make the purpose of the stack obvious. On the first card in your resume stack, you'll type your name, address, and phone number. Then you'll add buttons for the major categories of your resume.

1. Go back to the card level if the background is still shown on your screen. The information you type on this card will appear on this card only.
2. Choose the **Text** tool. Next you'll choose a font, point size, and style for your name, address, and phone number.
3. Press ⌘-T to see the Text Style dialog box. Choose a font such as Geneva and choose at least 14 points so your name will be easy to read. Choose **Bold** for the style. Click **OK** to save the changes.
4. Click the insertion point once to mark the place on the card where you want to start typing. Type your name on the card. Press RETURN to go to the next line. Type your address. Press RETURN. Type your phone number, including the area code (see Figure 10.8).

When you're finished designing your first card, add another card to this stack. The second card will contain information that you want the users to see when they click on the first button on the first card.

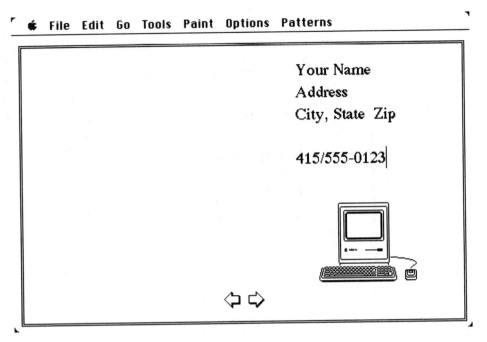

Figure 10.8 Type information about yourself.

Add a Button for Each Category

Besides personal information, you'll add several buttons to this card, one for each category of information: Objective, Experience, Education, Membership, and Publications. These buttons will serve as an index to the other cards in this stack.

*1. Choose **New Button** from the Objects menu.*

*2. Double-click on the button to see the Button Info... dialog box. Type **Objective** for the name of this button. Click on Round Rect for the button style (see Figure 10.9).*

*3. Leave the **Show Name** box checked. Click in the box next to **Auto Hilite** to turn that feature on.*

*4. Click **OK** to save your changes. Move this button anywhere you like on the card.*

Duplicate This Button

Next you'll make four copies of this button so the copies will have all the features you just assigned to the Objective button.

5. Hold down the OPTION key, and click on the new button to select it. While

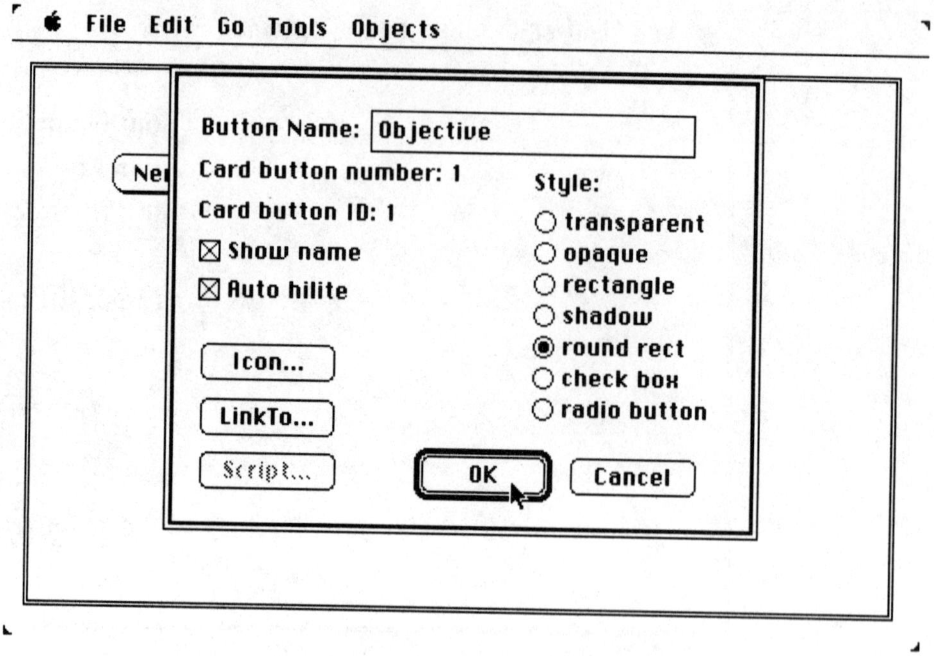

Figure 10.9 Button Info dialog box for button named Objective.

holding down the OPTION key, drag the mouse below the new button to "peel off" a copy. Now you have two copies of the same button.

6. Center the copied button below the Objective button. Repeat this procedure four times to make four more buttons (see Figure 10.10).

Unfortunately, there is no command for aligning buttons with each other. However, there is a utility stack named "Groupies" that you can use to align buttons and fields. This stack was created by Sioux Lacy of Apple Computer's HyperCard Test Team. This stack is free and is available from most Macintosh User's Groups.

Tip: To align buttons, overlap the first button with the second button. Then hold down the SHIFT key and drag vertically or horizontally to align the two buttons.

Name Each Button

7. All you'll need to do is change the name of each button. Double-click on each button to see its Button Info dialog box. Assign a name to each button; for example, type **Experience** *for the second button (see Figure 10.11).*

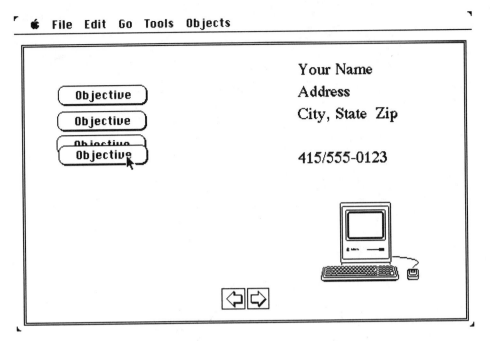

Figure 10.10 Hold down the Option key and drag to copy a button.

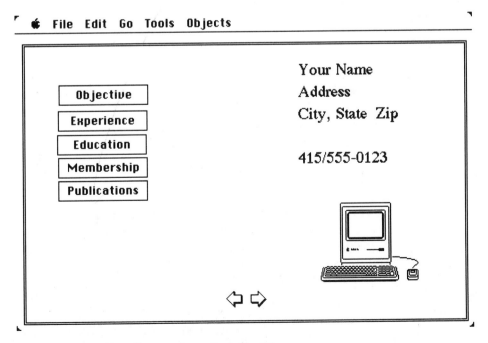

Figure 10.11 Your first card can look like this.

After you've created all the cards for this stack, you'll link these buttons to the appropriate card. Right now you don't have any cards to link them to.

Copy and Paste Pictures from Art Ideas

Just like you copied buttons from Buttons Ideas, you can also copy art from Art Ideas, or from any other stack.

1. Go to the Home card.
2. Click on the **Art Ideas** icon.
3. Click on a **category** to go to a card with the pictures you want to copy.
4. Choose the **Lasso** tool on the Tools menu.
5. Lasso what you want to copy. For example, lasso the picture of the Macintosh computer.
6. Press ⌘-C to copy your selection.
7. Go back to your resume stack.
8. Press ⌘-V to paste this button on the card. Move the pointer inside of the copied picture and drag to a place on the card where you want the picture to be. Click outside of the picture to unselect it.

Next, you'll add more cards to this stack.

Lesson 59:   ADD CARDS AND FIELDS

Your Objective

1. Press ⌘-N to add a new card to this stack. This card will contain your objective—what kind of job you are interested in.
2. Choose the **Text** tool. Press ⌘-T to select a text style you like. Then type **Objective:** somewhere near the top of this card (see Figure 10.12).

As you add to your list of skills, you'll change information about your objective depending on what type of job you're applying for. Whenever you know the text will change from time to time, you should always type that text into a field instead of typing it with the Text tool.

Create a Field

Now that you're an experienced HyperCard user, we'll show you faster ways to create fields and buttons. The fastest way to add a field to a

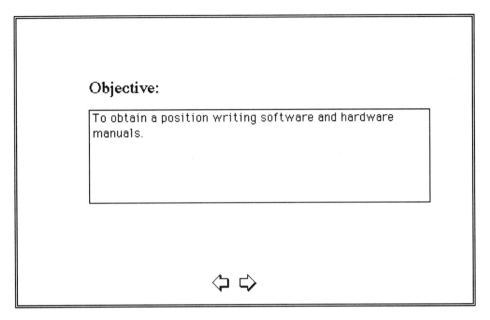

Figure 10.12 The Objective card can look something like this.

card is by choosing the Field tool, and then holding down the ⌘ key and dragging the mouse diagonally. Try it now.

1. Choose the **Field** tool on the Tools menu to tell HyperCard you want to create or modify a field.
2. Position the pointer about three lines below the word **Objective** that you just typed. Hold down the ⌘ key and drag the mouse diagonally to create a new field. Then double-click on this field to assign information such as field style, type of font, and so on.

Experience

1. Add another card to this stack. This card will contain information about your experience.

*2. Choose the **Text** tool. Press ⌘-T to select a text style. Then type **Experience** at the top of this card.*

You can create as many fields as you like to hold the information about your experience. If you have several categories of experience, your stack will flow more smoothly if you separate each category onto different cards. Always try to keep each card simple so you don't overwhelm the reader. A general rule of thumb is to keep one idea per card.

The information you type for the Experience category will undoubtedly take more room than will fit on one card, so you might want to add another menu card with buttons for each category as in Figure 10.13. Then add cards that correspond to each button.

3. Add these buttons just like you did in the previous lesson. (Choose the Button tool first, then hold down the OPTION key and drag off copies.)

4. Add one card for each button you create on this card. Add one or more fields on each card and label each card with the name of the button it will be linked to.

Education

1. Add another card to this stack. This card will contain information about your education.

2. Choose the Text tool. Press ⌘-T to select a text style. Then type **Education** *at the top of this card.*

Since your educational background may change, it's best to create a field in which to enter and update your degrees and coursework (see Figure 10.14). Instead of creating one field, you may want to create several fields, one for each degree you've earned. You could also add a field for listing additional coursework such as workshops or other classes you've attended.

3. Type the names of your degrees on this card. Then create a field by choosing

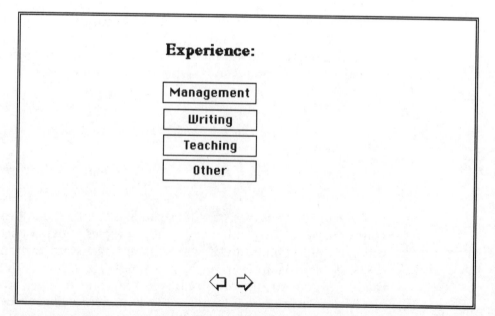

Figure 10.13 Any card can contain buttons to branch off to other cards.

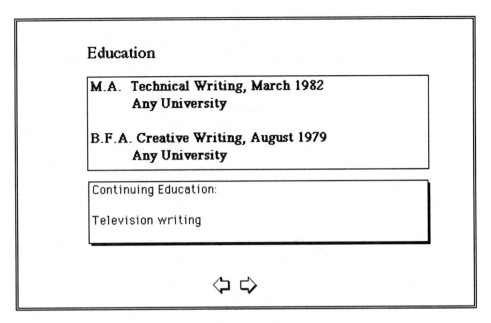

Figure 10.14 List your educational background.

*the **Field** tool, holding down the ⌘ key and dragging the mouse diagonally until the field is as large as you need. Double-click on this field to assign information such as field style, type of font, and so on.*

Membership

1. Add another card to this stack.
2. Choose the Text tool. Press ⌘-T to select a text style. Then type **Membership** at the top of this card.
3. Create a field on this card. Double-click on this field to assign field information if you like. In this field, you'll enter the names of professional organizations to which you belong.

Publications and Awards

1. Repeat Steps 1 through 3 above to create cards that list any articles or books you've published, and any awards or honors you've received.

Lesson 60: FILL IN THE BLANKS

Once you've added all the cards you need for your resume, start typing information into the appropriate fields.

1. Choose the **Browse** tool.
2. Press ⌘-1 to go to the first card in this stack. If there are no fields on this card, click the right arrow button to go to the next card—the Objective card.
3. Press the TAB key to move the insertion point into the first field. Type information into the field on this card. Click the right arrow button again to go to the next card. Fill in all the fields with the appropriate information, skipping cards that have no fields.

When you're through entering information into the fields on all the cards, you're ready to link the buttons to the appropriate cards.

Lesson 61: LINK BUTTONS

When building a stack, it is best to link buttons last. You should add all the cards you need to this stack and fill in all the fields first. Then when you know how it's all going to work together, you link buttons.

You already know how to link buttons, but here's a quick list of the steps you need to follow in case you've forgotten:

1. Go to a card with buttons to be linked. In this case, go to the first card in your stack.

*2. Choose the **Button** tool on the Tools menu.*

*3. Double-click on the **Objective** button to see the Button Info dialog box.*

*4. In the Button Info dialog box, click on the **Link to...** button.*

5. Go to the card that the button will be linked to. In this case, the next card.

Remember, you can move the dialog box by dragging it to another location on the card.

*6. Click on **This Card** in the dialog box.*

Trick: There's no command to unlink a button. If you accidentally link a button to the wrong card, just relink it to the correct card by repeating Steps 1 through 5.

*7. Choose the **Browse** tool in the Tools menu. Click on the **Objective** button to make sure it's linked to the right card.*

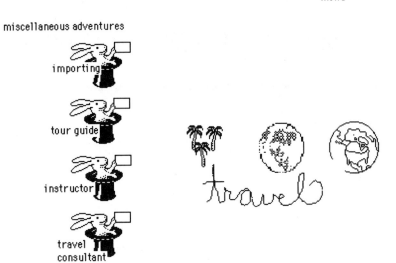

click here to
return to education
menu

Figure 10.15 A card from Elaine Winter's Resume stack.

Now that you're a pro, go ahead and link the other buttons on this card.

The template you've just created is only one way to do it. You can create a resume stack any way you like. For example, Figure 10.15 shows one card in a resume stack created by Elaine Winters, an educational consultant in Berkeley, California.

SUMMARY

You've learned how to create a stack from scratch as well as some fundamental rules for designing stacks. When designing a stack from scratch, keep these points in mind:

- Create the background first. It is really your template.
- Add navigation buttons to the background.
- Buttons should look the same on a particular card so they are intuitive to the user.
- Link buttons last.

Designing a stack involves a lot of different skills. The user interface—what the user sees and how the user is supposed to use the stack—is the most important ingredient in designing a stack. If the users can't understand the buttons, they won't know how to get to the information they need.

11 Importing and Exporting Files

In this chapter, you'll learn how to copy files from other programs onto cards. You'll also learn how to copy text and pictures from cards into files that you can use with other programs.

The lessons in this chapter show you how to

- Import pictures directly onto cards.
- Import text and data from other applications into fields on cards.
- Export text from HyperCard fields into a file you can use with other programs.
- Export data from HyperCard fields into a file you can use with other programs.

To complete the lessons in this chapter, you must set the user level to Authoring. Type **set the userlevel to 4** in the Message box to change the user level to Authoring if necessary.

Also, you'll need a paint file, a document file created by a word processor, and a data file created by a data base or spreadsheet program to complete the lessons.

TEXT FILES

You can import text files created with any word processing program as long as they were saved as text only; that is, the files must contain only characters, no formatting code. Text-only files are also referred to as ASCII (American Standard Code for Information Interchange) files. Most word processing programs let you save your files as ASCII files. For example, MicroSoft word has a Text Only file format option (see

Figure 11.1). Use this option to save a file you want to import onto a card in HyperCard.

DATA FILES

You can import data files created with a spreadsheet or data base program such as MicroSoft Excel, MicroSoft Works, or any file with fields and records as long as that file was saved in text-only or ASCII file format. Most applications give you the option of saving data as text only.

Lesson 62:   IMPORTING A PAINT FILE ONTO A CARD

Suppose you have a picture saved as a MacPaint file and you want to put it on a card in a HyperCard stack. You could copy it into your Scrapbook while using the MacPaint program. And then you could open the HyperCard stack and copy the picture from the Scrapbook onto a card.

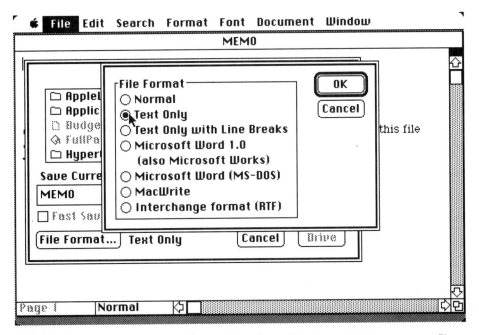

Figure 11.1 Use MicroSoft Word's Text Only file format option to save files as ASCII files.

You aren't limited to using the Scrapbook or Clipboard for copying text and pictures onto cards. HyperCard has menu choices for importing and exporting paint files. **Importing** means copying information from one file into the one you're currently using. **Exporting** means copying information from the file you're using and creating a new file with that information in it. (See Figure 11.2.)

In this lesson, you'll create a stack of pictures imported from files created with MacPaint or other similar painting programs. To practice importing paint files in this chapter, you'll need a picture saved as a MacPaint file.

Creating a New Stack for Imported Pictures

1. Choose **New Stack** from the File menu.
2. Uncheck the box next to **Copy current background**. There's no need to copy a background since importing files covers up all objects on the card anyway.
3. Type **Imports** for the name of this stack and press Return to start building a new stack. You should see a blank white screen.

Why Create a Stack with MacPaint Pictures?

You might be thinking now, "If you can import files directly onto cards, then why create a whole new stack just for imported pictures?" The

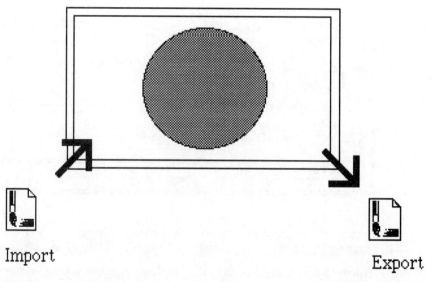

Import   Export

Figure 11.2 Importing and exporting files.

answer to that question is "To prevent you from importing pictures onto cards with information you need." When you import a file, it covers up all pictures and objects (buttons and fields) on the current card. So, to save yourself a lot of time trying to recover lost objects, you must add a new card on which to import the picture. Then you can cut and paste the picture onto other cards. And, when you're through, you can just delete the card with the imported picture.

If you plan to use lots of pictures that are currently in file formats other than HyperCard, create a stack just for those pictures. Then copy the pictures you need from one stack to another. Creating and using this temporary stack will prevent you from accidentally covering up useful cards with imported pictures.

What Kinds of Paint Files Can I Import?

You can import any file created with MacPaint or a similar paint program such as FullPaint or SuperPaint. (If using SuperPaint, be sure to save the picture as a MacPaint file.) You can also use special hardware products to create paint files from printed materials or video images.

You can scan images from the pages of a book or magazine with scanners such as the Apple scanner or the Abaton scanner. These scanners can create MacPaint files from the printed pictures that you feed into the scanner. A product called MacVision enables you to create MacPaint files from images on your television. Figure 11.3 contains icons representing paint files you can import.

What's So Special about MacPaint Files?

MacPaint files are bit-mapped graphics. Bit-mapped graphics are pictures created with paint programs that enable you to edit each dot (or pixel) in a given picture. The Import Paint command does not work with files created with programs like MacDraw because those programs do not create bit-mapped graphics. These kinds of programs are called **object-oriented** because they store each drawing as one object instead of as a group of bits.

Figure 11.3 Icons representing paint files you can import.

Note: Bit is short for **binary digit**. A bit can be either a 1 or a 0. The value of the 0 or 1 can be either positive or negative, true or false, on or off. The word **bit-mapped** means creating a picture by turning bits on or off. Each dot on your computer screen is assigned either on or off, black or white.

Importing MacPaint files also gives you two advantages: (1) you can browse through imported images using HyperCard's navigational tools and (2) HyperCard automatically compresses imported pictures, which saves you disk space and enables HyperCard to load those pictures into memory faster.

How to Import a Paint File

*1. Starting with your new Imports stack on the screen, choose any paint tool on the Tools menu, for example, the selection rectangle. Doing so gives you two new menu choices on the File menu: **Import Paint** and **Export Paint**. These commands appear on the File menu only when a paint tool is selected first. (See Figure 11.4.)*

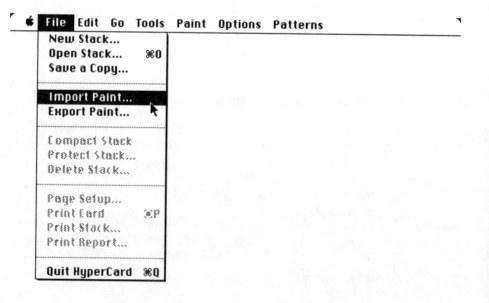

Figure 11.4 New menu choices appear when you choose a paint tool.

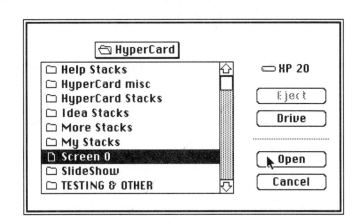

Figure 11.5 Import Paint dialog box.

*2. Choose **Import Paint** from the File menu. The dialog box appears asking you which file you want to import. Only those files that are possible to import will be listed in this dialog box. (See Figure 11.5.)*

3. Find and open a MacPaint file by double-clicking on it in the Import Paint dialog box. Your MacPaint picture is now on your new card. If the new card would have had a picture already on it, importing the MacPaint file would have replaced the old picture with the imported one.

4. Add a new card and repeat steps 1, 2, and 3 to import another MacPaint file. If you don't add a new card, the next card you import will replace the picture on the card currently displayed.

Lesson 63: EXPORTING A PAINT FILE FROM A CARD

Export means you can copy graphics created with HyperCard paint tools into files usable by programs like MacPaint. In this lesson, you'll export one of the pictures in the Clip Art stack included with HyperCard.

To export a picture on a card in the Clip Art stack into a file of its own, do this:

1. Go Home. Click on the Clip Art icon on the Home card. Display a card with a picture you want to export.

*2. Choose any paint tool on the Tools menu so the **Import Paint** and **Export Paint** choices appear on the File menu.*

*3. Choose **Export Paint** from the File menu. The dialog box (Figure 11.6) appears asking you to type a name for the file that will contain the exported picture.*

*4. Type a name for this file (**Exports**, for example) and press Return.*

Exporting the picture doesn't remove it from the HyperCard stack. This picture has been copied to a file named Exports. You can open the file named Exports using MacPaint or another paint program that is compatible with MacPaint formatted files.

In addition to importing and exporting pictures, you can import and export text. HyperCard versions 1.1 and 1.2 include three new buttons for importing and exporting text files: Import, Export Text, and Export Data.

These buttons are in the Button Ideas stack. Copy and paste them into any stack you like. Or use them directly from the Button Ideas stack. The next three lessons show you how to use these new buttons.

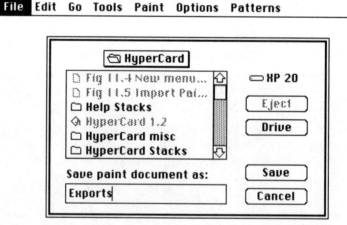

Figure 11.6 Export Paint dialog box.

Lesson 64: USING THE IMPORT BUTTON

The Import button imports documents and data files from other programs into scrolling fields in a HyperCard stack. The Import button adds new cards with scrolling fields as well as copies text into those fields.

You can use the Import button to import an ASCII file as either data or text. HyperCard lets you specify which when you click on the Import button.

Importing Text Files

To complete this lesson, you'll need a file saved as text only (or ASCII). If you don't have a text-only file to import, create one now and name it Memo. In this lesson, you'll import a text file named Memo into a new stack named Import Text.

Once you have a text-only file to import, follow these steps:

1. Press ⌘-H to go to the Home card.

2. Click on Button Ideas.

3. Click on Text to go to the card with text buttons. There you'll find the Import buttons. (See Figure 11.7).

4. Choose the Button tool from the Tools menu. Click once on the Import button to choose it. Then press Command-C to copy it.

*5. Create a new stack named Import Text. (Choose **New Stack** from the File menu, leave the **X** in the box labeled **Copy current background**.)*

6. Press ⌘-V to paste the Import button and move it onto the new stack as shown in Figure 11.8.

Before clicking on the Import button, you need to know the pathname (that is, the names of all the disks and folders in which the file to be imported is stored) of the file named Memo. Use the Find File desk accessory in the ￼ menu to find Memo, as shown in Figure 11.9.

The pathname for Memo as shown in the Find File dialog box is XP 20:Memo. XP 20 is the name of the hard disk. Write down the pathname so you don't forget it.

Now you're ready to import the file named Memo that you created earlier. (If you want to import a different text-only file, type the name of that file instead of Memo.)

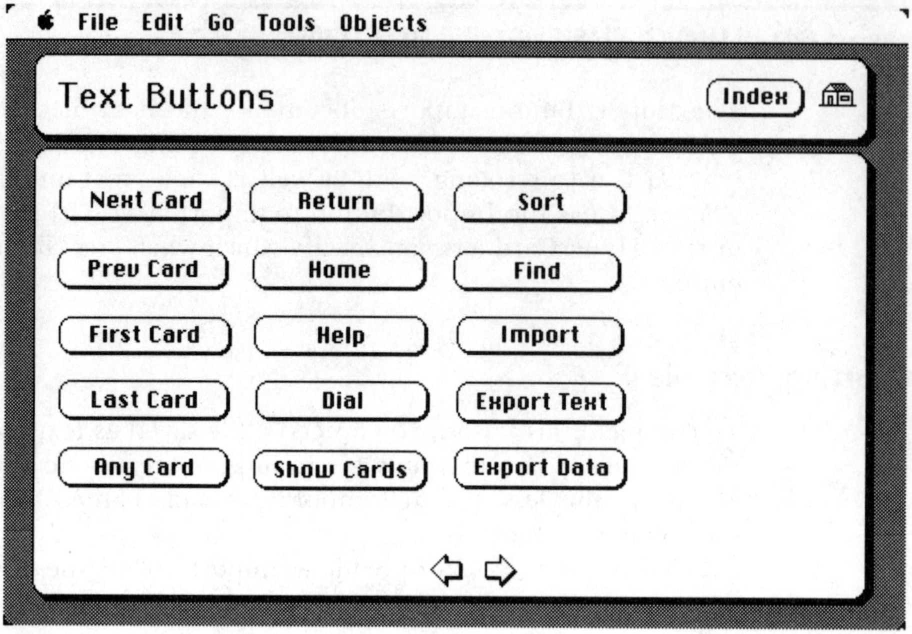

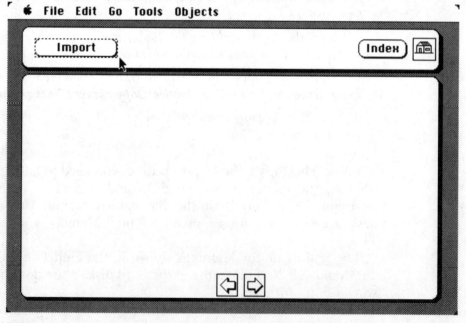

Figure 11.7 The Import and Export buttons are in the Button Ideas Stack.

Figure 11.8 Copy the Import button to a new stack named Import Text.

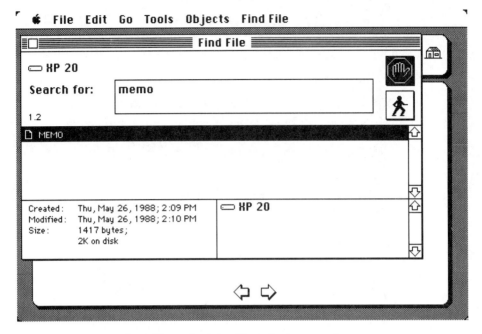

Figure 11.9 Use Find File to find the file to be imported.

7. Click on the Import button. HyperCard asks if you want to import a file as data or text.

8. Click on Text to import a text-only file.

Next, HyperCard asks if you want Header information included at the top of the card with imported text. Header information includes the following:

number of cards created

name of the original file

number of lines in the file

total number of characters imported

9. Click Yes to include header information.

10. Type the name of the file you want to import, including its pathname, as shown in Figure 11.10.

HyperCard creates a new background that includes a scrolling field and then copies the text into that field, as Figure 11.11 shows.

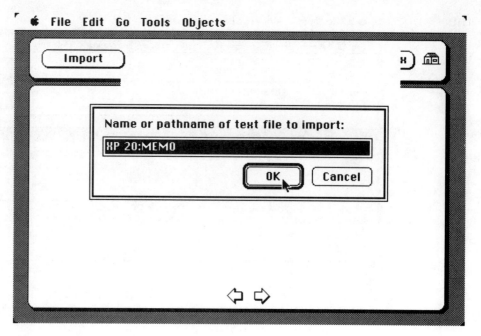

Figure 11.10 Enter the name of the file with its pathname.

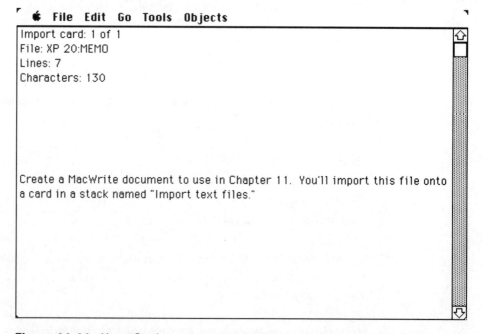

Figure 11.11 HyperCard creates a new background with a scrolling field and then copies the imported text into that field.

Importing Data Files

A data file contains pieces of information created with a data base or spreadsheet program. Each piece of information stored in a field or cell is separated by a comma, semicolon, or other character. This character is referred to as a **delimiter**.

If you don't have a data file to import, you won't be able to complete this lesson. If you have a data file you can use to practice using the Import button, make sure you've saved it as a text-only or ASCII file before going on with step 1. Figure 11.12 shows how to save Excel files as text only. Figures 11.13a and 11.13b show how to save files created with MicroSoft Works as text. (If you attempt to import data files that haven't been saved as text only, you'll either get an error message or import garbled letters and symbols.)

1. Click on the Import button. HyperCard asks if you want to import a file as data or text.

2. Click on Data to import files created with a spreadsheet or database program.

Next, HyperCard asks whether you want to use Tab and Return as delimiters.

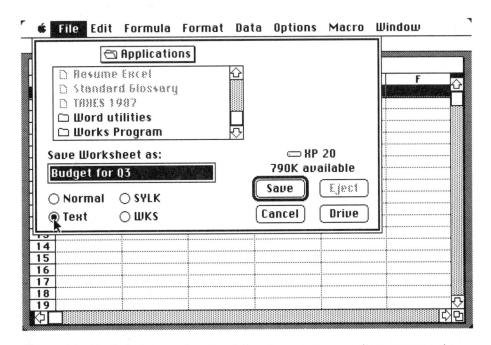

Figure 11.12 Before importing Excel files, be sure to save them as text only.

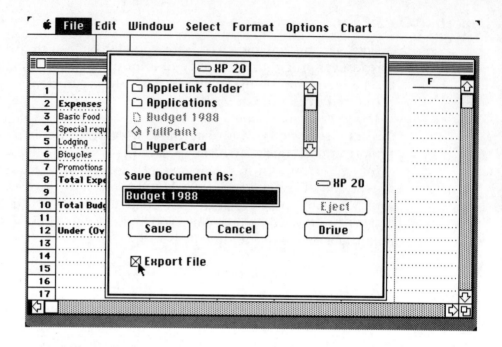

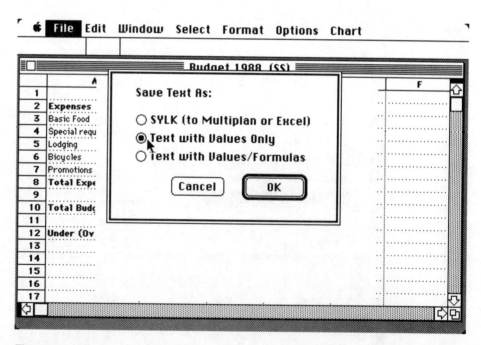

Figure 11.13a and b Saving MicroSoft Works files as text is a two-step process.

3. Click on Yes unless you want to specify a different ASCII character to use for the delimiter. Clicking on Yes automatically chooses the standard delimiter for fields, which is the Tab character (ASCII 9), and the standard delimiter for records, which is the Return character (ASCII 13).

4. The Header information for data files is the same as it was for text files. If you want this information included, click Yes.

5. Enter the name of the file you want to import, including its full pathname.

HyperCard creates a new background with a scrolling field and adds a new card to that background for each record in the file, as shown in Figure 11.14.

Each card contains one record. However, each record may have several fields. When you import a file, the fields are created one on top of the other so you'll have to drag the fields off of each other to see the fields underneath.

6. To drag one field off of another, choose the Field tool. Then select the field by clicking once on it and dragging it to the side or down (see Figure 11.15).

Lesson 65:   USING THE EXPORT TEXT BUTTON

Use the Export Text button to send text from one or more background fields to a new or existing file. Before using this button, copy it to a stack that contains text you want to export.

```
 🍎  File  Edit  Go  Tools  Objects
```

```
┌─────────────────────────────────────────┬──┐
│ Field 3 of 3                             │⇧ │
│ Record 1 of file: xp 20:budget 1988      │──│
│                                          │▓ │
│ Budget                                   │▓ │
│                                          │──│
│                                          │⇩ │
└─────────────────────────────────────────┴──┘
```

Figure 11.14 HyperCard creates a new background with a scrolling field and adds a new card for each record, copying each record onto a different card.

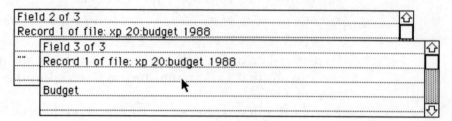

Figure 11.15 Fields are imported on top of each other, so you need to separate them by dragging them off one at a time.

1. For this lesson, copy the Export Text button from the Button Ideas stack to the stack named File Index. You'll export the text in the fields of this stack to a file named Exported Text.

2. Click on the Export Text button.

3. Choose the fields in the current background that you want to copy to another file.

4. Enter the name of the file to contain the exported text. (If the name you enter already exists, HyperCard will replace the contents of that file with the exported text, but, before doing so, it will ask if that's what you really want to do.)

Tip: In case you're wondering, the Export Text button will not append the exported text to an existing file. It will replace that text.

The Export Text button won't create files that can be used by a data base or spreadsheet program. Use the Export Text button to create files you can then edit with a word processing program.

Lesson 66: USING THE EXPORT DATA BUTTON

Use the Export Data button to create files that can be used in applications that put text into fields and records such as data base and spreadsheet programs. The Export Data button copies text along with record and field delimiters from HyperCard fields to a new or existing file.

1. For this lesson, copy the Export Data button from the Button Ideas stack to the stack named Address. You'll export the data in the fields of this stack to a file named Exported Data.
2. Click on the Export Data button.
3. Choose the fields in the current background that you want to copy to another file.
4. Enter the name of the file to contain the exported text. (If the name you enter already exists, HyperCard will replace the contents of that file with the exported text, but, before doing so, it will ask if you're sure that's what you want to do.)
5. Click on Yes when asked whether you want to use Tab and Return as delimiters unless you prefer to enter other ASCII characters to use.

SUMMARY

This chapter explained how to import and export paint, text, and data files.

- The **Import Paint** and **Export Paint** commands appear on the File menu whenever you choose a paint tool or any tool on the Tools menu except for the Browse, Button, or Field tools.
- To import document or data files, first save them as text only. Then use the Import button.
- To copy text from the fields of a HyperCard stack into a text file that can be used by word processing programs, use the Export Text button.
- To copy text from the fields of a HyperCard stack into data files that can be used by spreadsheet and data base programs, use the Export Data button.

The next chapter explains how to create a stack with more than one background.

12 Creating a Stack with More than One Background

In this chapter, you'll learn how to create a stack used to sell the products of a fictitious company. This stack will be a sales catalog on disk. In the process of creating this stack, you'll learn how to add more than one background to it as well as practice using more paint tools and menu commands.

The lessons in this chapter show you how to

- Design a stack
- Use the Patterns menu
- Use the Bucket tool
- Revert to the previous version
- Create white letters on a black card
- Create a new background
- Look at the information about a stack
- Look at the information about a card
- Look at the information about a background

To complete the lessons in this chapter, you must set the user level to Authoring. Type **set the userlevel to 4** in the Message box to change the user level to Authoring if necessary.

Lesson 67: DESIGNING A STACK FOR A PRODUCT CATALOG

In Stack Ideas, there are some good examples of product catalogs. One stack idea is for an auto supply catalog as shown in Figure 12.1. If you created a stack from this stack idea, you would need to create more than one background for each button linked to different information such as Inventory and Suppliers. Or you could create several smaller stacks linked to one another. The other is a catalog of collectibles, as shown in Figure 12.2.

In this lesson, you are going to design a stack for a fictitious company called Bargain Baubles. This company wants to put its catalog of products on a HyperCard stack. It sells items such as automobile hood ornaments, costume jewelry, plastic flowers, and other strange things people give you for Christmas.

The cards in this stack will contain the name, price, and order number of each product as well as a picture of it. This stack will also contain an index that lists each product.

Outlining the Bargain Baubles Stack

Before creating this stack, outline on paper what you plan to do. Your outline might look like this:

Audience: People who use Macintosh computers

Use: To show available products and provide ordering information

Information: Pictures, names, prices, and order numbers for each product

Organization: Menu structure

Then draw a map like the one in Figure 12.3.

Determining How Many Backgrounds Are Needed

Once you've drawn a map, you can see which cards will most likely share the same buttons, fields, and graphics. Those cards will share the same background.

The first card, which is the title card, identifies the contents of the stack. The next card in your hierarchy will be an index that lists all the categories of products to be sold. Each index item will be linked to a different card listing specific names of products. These cards will be referred to as **subindex cards**. Each product in this subindex will be linked to a card with information about that product.

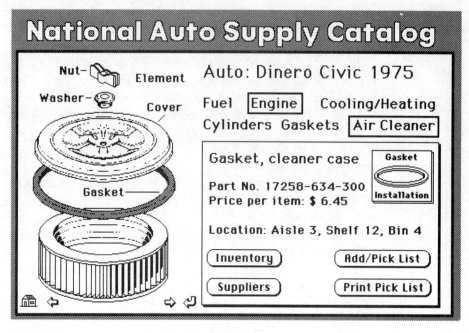

Figure 12.1 Auto supply products catalog.

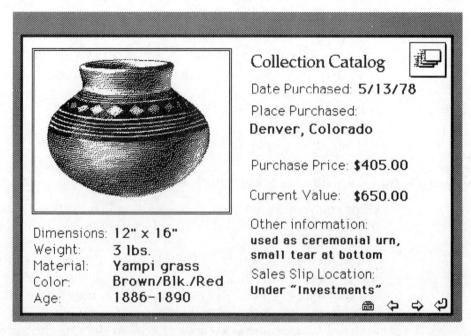

Figure 12.2 Collectibles product catalog.

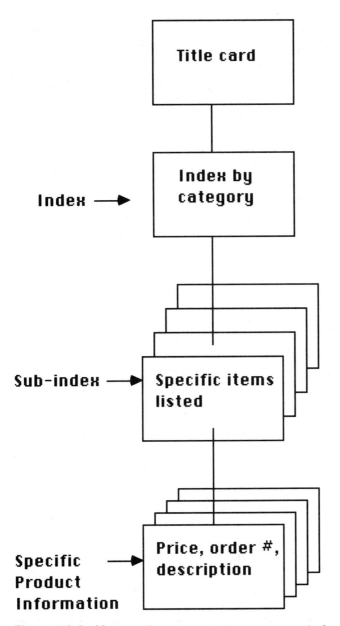

Figure 12.3 Map out the menu structure on paper before creating a stack.

The title card and index card will share the same background. (You'll create a dark pattern on the title card that will cover up any background pictures or objects, so it won't be necessary to give the title card its own background.) You'll need a new background for the subindex cards and another one for the cards with product information.

So you'll create three backgrounds for this stack: one for the title card

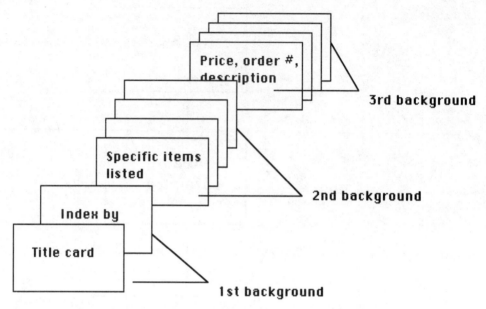

Figure 12.4   Create three backgrounds, one for each card layout.

and first index card, one for the subindex cards, and one for the product information. Figure 12.4 illustrates this procedure.

Why Share Backgrounds?

Sharing backgrounds saves disk space, especially if you share graphics. It is important to know that the more graphics you put on a card and the darker they are, the larger the stack will be. For example, a black card takes up more disk space than a white card.

The size of the stack is important when you think about how you're going to distribute it. If a stack won't fit on one 800K floppy disk, it will be more difficult for others to copy it. (They'll have to copy it from one hard disk to another hard disk, since it won't fit on a floppy disk.) If you plan to create a huge stack, break it down into several smaller stacks with common backgrounds and then link them.

Tip: Making some decisions now can save you time later. Of course, you can always change your mind and modify objects at any time. But if you create several fields and buttons on a card and then decide you want those objects on the card's background, you'll have to cut and paste each object one at a time to move them to the background.

Creating a Product Catalog

Follow these steps to begin building the product catalog stack:

1. Choose *New Stack* from the File menu.
2. Uncheck the box next to *Copy current background* since you don't want to copy a background.
3. Type *Bargain Baubles* for the name of this stack and press RETURN to start building a new stack. You should see a blank white screen.

Lesson 68: USING PATTERNS

The first card you are going to create is a title card. On this card, you'll paint the name of this stack and then link it to the next card. The second card will contain a list of choices that link to the other cards in this stack.

You can be as creative as you like with the title card. Colette Kehoe created the title card in Figure 12.5 while keystroke testing the lessons in this book.

To add some spice to your title card, you'll use some paint tools and the Patterns menu.

Figure 12.5 Title card for Bargain Baubles.

1. Tear off the Tools menu and put it somewhere on the screen.

2. Choose a paint tool on the Tools menu to see the three paint menus: Paint, Options, and Patterns.

3. The Patterns menu is also a tear-off menu. Tear it off and put it somewhere on the screen. It's easier to work with paint tools and patterns if they are visible at all times.

4. To select a pattern, click on one of the patterns in the Patterns menu. For now, select the solid black pattern.

You can fill the screen with a pattern by using the Bucket tool on the Tools menu.

5. Choose the Bucket tool on the Tools menu. (See Figure 12.6.) Now imagine the bucket filled with black paint (your chosen pattern).

6. Click once to pour the contents of the bucket onto the card.

Typing paint text onto a pattern can be tricky. Try that now to see for yourself.

7. Choose the Text tool. Click the insertion point somewhere on the card and type **Bargain Baubles**. *Notice the white areas that cover up parts of the pattern in Figure 12.7.*

Trick: Instead of using the text tool, you can create a transparent field with Outline as the chosen font. Then when you type text into this field, it appears as white letters on a black pattern. (See Figure 12.8.)

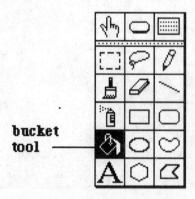

bucket
tool

Figure 12.6 Bucket tool.

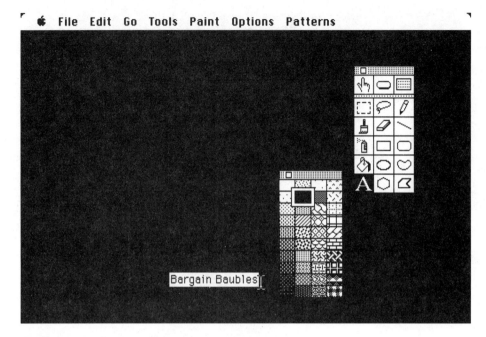

Figure 12.7 Typing paint text on a black pattern.

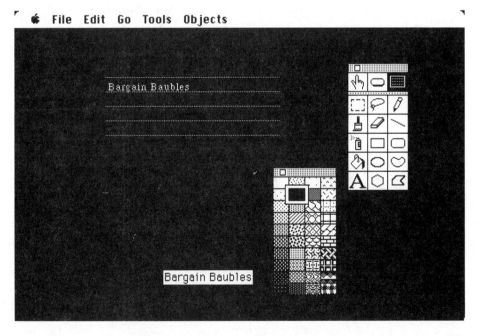

Figure 12.8 Use the Outline font in a text field to see letters on a black pattern.

Next, you'll learn an easy way to use paint text to create white letters on a black background.

Reverting to the Previous Version

For now, put this card back the way it was.

1. Choose a paint tool to access the Paint menu from the menu bar.
2. Choose *Revert* from the Paint menu. This choice undoes all the changes you just made with the paint tools.

If you go to another card and then return to this one later, choosing **Revert** won't undo the changes you made to this card. To wipe out the paint on the card if **Revert** didn't work, do this:

1. Choose *white* in the Patterns menu
2. Choose the Bucket tool and click once on the card.

Lesson 69:   TYPING WHITE LETTERS ON A BLACK PATTERN

What you're going to do next is type white letters on a black pattern with the text tool. There's a trick to doing this that may be obvious to you and may not. Here's how to do it, starting with a white background:

1. Click on the text tool in the Tools menu. If the black pattern is not selected in the Patterns menu, select it now.

*2. Choose **Text Style** from the Edit menu. Then choose **New York, 18 points, bold** for the text style. Click OK.*

*3. Move the insertion point to the place on the card where you want to type and click once. Then type **Bargain Baubles**.*

The title card sometimes includes instructions to click on a button or somewhere on the screen so others know what to do when they see this screen. Next, you'll add a sentence that tells others what to do.

*4. Click somewhere below **Bargain Baubles** to position the insertion point for one line of instruction. Press ⌘-T to change the text style for this line of instruction. Choose **New York, 12 points**. Click OK. Type **Click anywhere on this card to begin**.*

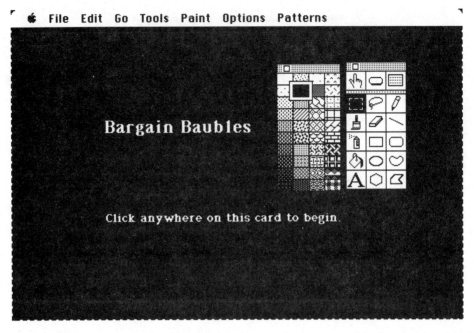

Figure 12.9 Invert black letters on a white card to create white letters on a black card.

*5. Choose **Select all** from the Paint menu.*

*6. Choose **Invert** from the Paint menu. What was black is now white; what was white is now black. (See Figure 12.9.)*

Lesson 70: CREATING AN INDEX CARD

When you're finished designing your title card, add another card to this stack.

1. Press ⌘-N to add a new card.

Since you didn't make changes to the background of the previous card, you're facing a white card again. This card will contain an index of products by category. First, you'll add some fields to create columns in which to type names of categories for the products.

*2. Using the text tool, type **Bargain Baubles Super Catalog** at the top of this card.*

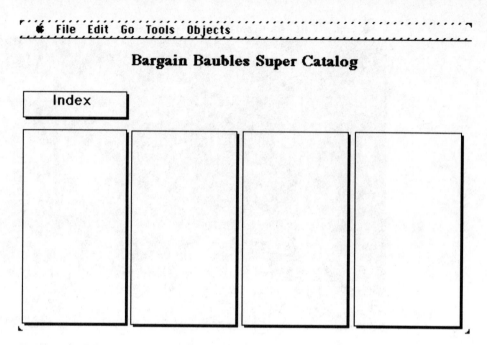

Figure 12.10   Create fields for the Index card.

3. Choose the Browse tool to see the Objects menu in the menu bar.

*4. Choose **New Field** from the Edit menu. Position and resize each field as shown in Figure 12.10.*

5. Type the product categories into the fields as shown in Figure 12.11.

Next, you'll add transparent buttons over each name in the fields. Later, you'll link those buttons to their associated second or subindex cards.

Adding Transparent Buttons Over Each Item

1. Choose **New Button** from the Objects menu.
2. Double-click on the New button to see the Button Info dialog box. Since you don't want this button to cover up the text, choose **transparent** for the button style and click in the **Show name** box so the **x** disappears.
3. Click OK.
4. Position this button over the first word in the list—Antlers.
5. Copy this button by holding down the Option key and dragging off a copy. Position the copied button over the next word in the list. (Hold

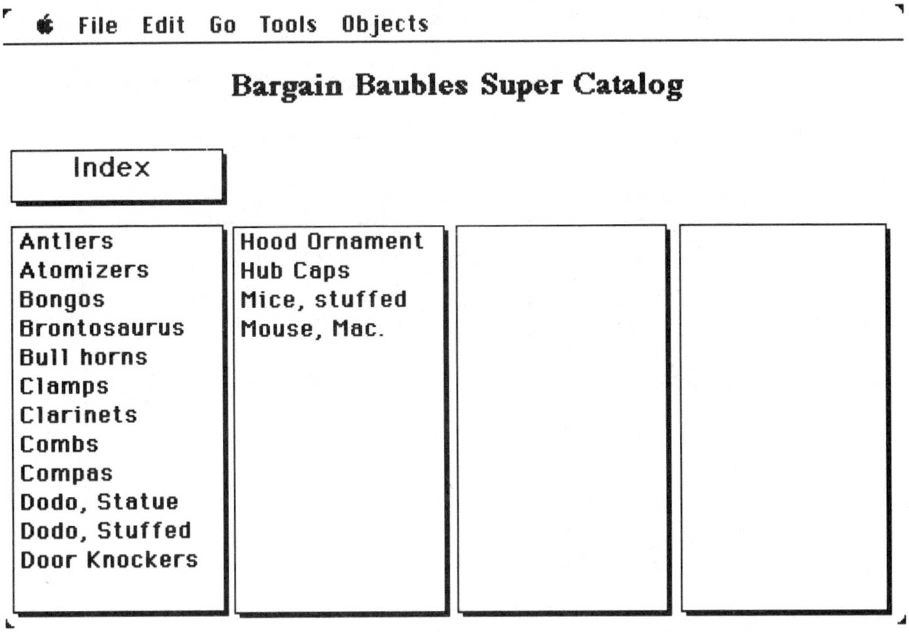

 File Edit Go Tools Objects

Bargain Baubles Super Catalog

Index

Antlers	Hood Ornament		
Atomizers	Hub Caps		
Bongos	Mice, stuffed		
Brontosaurus	Mouse, Mac.		
Bull horns			
Clamps			
Clarinets			
Combs			
Compas			
Dodo, Statue			
Dodo, Stuffed			
Door Knockers			

Figure 12.11 Type categories of information.

down the Shift key while dragging to keep the copied button aligned with the original.)

6. Repeat step 5 until you have created a transparent button on top of each word in the index.

Figure 12.12 illustrates transparent buttons.
Next, you'll create a new background for the subindex cards.

Lesson 71: CREATING A NEW BACKGROUND

The subindex cards in this stack will all share the same background information: pictures, buttons, and fields. However, the layout or template for these cards will be different from the Index card. The new background will have a different number of fields and some navigation buttons.

*1. While the Index card is displayed, choose **New Background** from the Objects menu. This command adds both a new background and new card.*

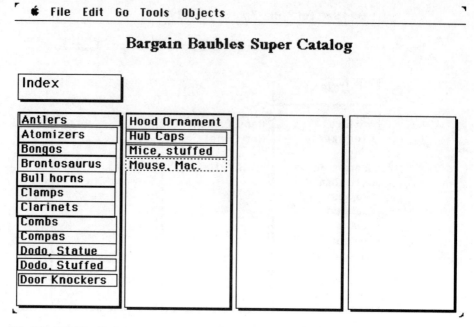

Figure 12.12   Create transparent buttons over each item listed.

Tip: Before adding a new background to a stack with several cards, first go to the last card of the current background. Then choose **New Background** from the Objects menu. Otherwise, you'll split the stack, causing it to have three backgrounds instead of two.

Adding Background Fields

You can create background fields and card fields. A **background field** appears on every card associated with a particular background. It has the same size, shape, and position on every card; what changes from card to card is the text in a field. A **card field** appears only on the card on which you create it.

Next add some fields to the background, as shown in Figure 12.13.

*2. Choose **Background** from the Edit menu to display the background if it isn't displayed already.*

*3. Choose **New field** from the Objects menu.*

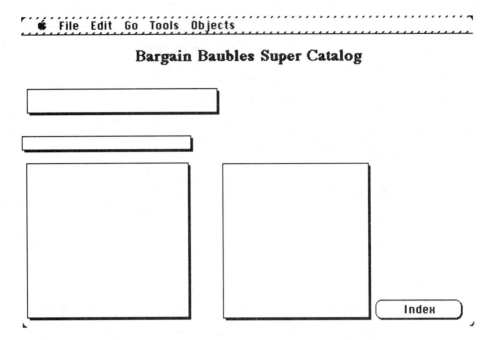

Figure 12.13 Fields on background of subindex.

To move a field to another position on the card, put the pointer inside the field and drag it to the new location.

4. Double-click on the field and assign field information to it.

5. Click OK.

6. To make duplicate copies of a field, hold down the Option key, click on the field, and drag off a copy. Resize and position the fields any way you like.

Next, fill in the fields of this card with information about one of the categories of products. For example, one of the index items listed in the previous card is Hood Ornaments. So one of the cards in the subindex will list all the kinds of hood ornaments for sale.

8. Type the names of hood ornaments available into the fields as shown in Figure 12.14.

Adding Background Buttons

Next, you'll add some simple navigation buttons to the background.

1. Go to the Home card

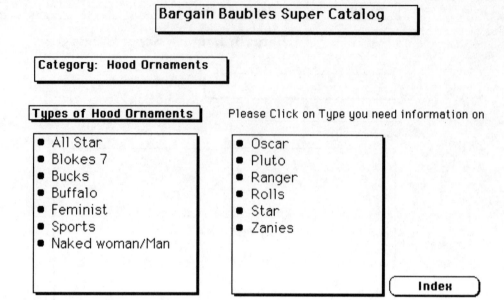

Figure 12.14 Enter types of hood ornaments available.

2. Copy the right arrow button
3. Return to the subindex card in the Bargain Baubles stack
4. Choose **Background** from the Edit menu
5. Paste the right arrow button

Repeat steps 1 through 5 to copy the left arrow button from the Home card.

Next, you need to link the Index card to the subindex card. To do so, you'll link the transparent button over the item named Hood Ornaments in the Index card to this card.

1. Go to the Index card.
2. Choose the Button tool. Double-click on the Hood Ornaments button.
3. Click on **Link to**.
4. Go to the subindex card that lists the types of hood ornaments.
5. Click on **This Card**.
6. Choose the Browse tool and click on the Hood Ornaments button to make sure it's linked correctly.

Next, create a button to take you back to the main Index card.

1. Be sure you are editing the background. (Lines appear in the menu bar when the background is displayed.) Choose **New Button** from the Objects menu.
2. Double-click on the New button to see the Button Info dialog box. Click **round rect** for the button style and type **Index** for its name.
3. Click OK.
4. Move the Index button to the lower right corner of this card. Then double-click on that button to see the Button Info box again.
5. Click on **Link to**. Then press ⌘-1 to go back to the first card in the stack. Press ⌘-3 to go to the next card, the Index card.
6. Click on **This Card** in the destination box.

HyperCard automatically returns you to the card to which you added the new button.

7. Choose the Browse tool from the Tools menu.
8. Click on the Index button to return to the Index card.

Before creating the third background, add transparent buttons over the name of each kind of hood ornament. You'll link each button to the card with information about that hood ornament later. (Before you can link these buttons, you'll need to create the cards to link them to!)

Adding Transparent Buttons Over Each Item

1. Choose **New Button** from the Objects menu.
2. Double-click on the New button to see the Button Info dialog box. Since you don't want this button to cover up the text, choose **transparent** for the button style and click in the **Show name** box so the **x** disappears.
3. Click OK.
4. Position this button over the first word in the list—All Star.
5. Copy this button by holding down the Option key and dragging off a copy. Position the copied button over the next word in the list. (Hold down the Shift key while dragging to keep the copied button aligned with the original.)
6. Repeat step 5 until you have created a transparent button on top of each word in the subindex.

All that's missing now is the information about each product listed on the subindex cards.

Lesson 72: CREATING A BACKGROUND FOR PRODUCT INFORMATION

The rest of the cards in this stack will all share the same background information: pictures, buttons, and fields.

1. If you have created more than one subindex card, go to the last card with that background before adding a new background.
2. Choose **New Background** from the Objects menu. This command adds both a new background and new card.

Adding Background Fields

Next, you'll add five fields to the background. You'll name these fields category, price, order number, type, and description, in that order.

*1. Choose **New field** from the Objects menu.*

To move a field to another position on the card, put the pointer inside the field and drag it to the new location.

2. Move this field to the top left corner of the card.

3. Double-click on the field to see the Field Info dialog box.

*4. Type **Category** for the name of this field.*

*5. Under Style in the dialog box, click on **shadow**.*

6. Click on the Font button in the Field Info box to choose the text style.

*7. Choose **Bold, Geneva**, and **14 points** for the text.*

8. Click OK.

*9. Hold down the Option key, click on the new field, and drag off a copy. Repeat this procedure until you have five fields as shown in Figure 12.15. Double-click on the second field and type **Price** for its name. Double-click on the third field and type **Order #** for its name. Name the fourth field **Type** and the last field **Description**.*

Add Background Buttons

Add left and right arrow buttons to the background. You can copy these buttons from the previous background.

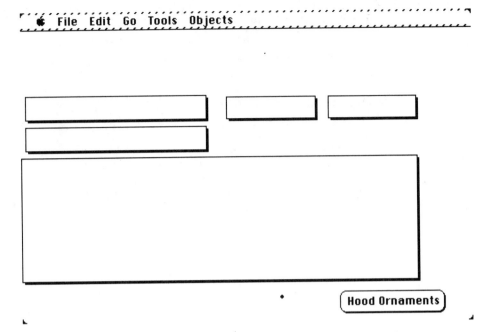

Figure 12.15 Add fields to background of product information cards.

Create a button to take you back to the subindex card.

*1. Be sure you are editing the background. (Lines appear in the menu bar when the background is displayed.) Choose **New Button** from the objects menu.*

*2. Double-click on the New button to see the Button Info dialog box. Click **round rect** for the button style and type **Hood Ornaments** for its name.*

3. Click OK.

4. Move the Hood Ornaments button to the lower right corner of this card. Then double-click on that button to see the Button Info box again.

*5. Click on **Link to**. Go to the subindex card that lists all the categories of hood ornaments.*

*6. Click on **This Card** in the destination box.*

HyperCard automatically returns you to the card to which you added the new button.

7. Choose the Browse tool from the Tools menu.

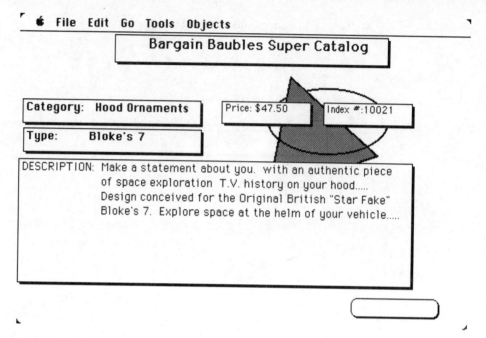

Figure 12.16   Product information for Bloke's 7.

Entering Information

Type information into the fields for the hood ornament named Bloke's 7, as shown in Figure 12.16.

Your background template for the product information is complete. Next you can copy pictures of the products onto each card, then enter information into the fields on the cards. And, finally, link the cards and buttons.

Lesson 73:   CREATING INVISIBLE BUTTONS

One way to link the Title card to the Index card is to create a large invisible button that covers the entire Title card and links it to the Index card. This enables you to click anywhere on the Title card to go directly to the Index card.

To create a large, invisible button over the Title card, do this:

1. Display the Title card on the screen.

2. Choose New Button from the Objects menu.

3. Position the new button in the upper-left corner of the title card.

4. Point to the lower right corner of the new button and drag it to the lower right corner of the card until it covers the entire card (See Figure 12.17).

Tip: Here's a faster way to create a transparent button. Choose the Button tool. Hold down the ⌘ key and position the pointer in the upper left corner of the card. While still holding down the ⌘ key, drag diagonally to the opposite corner of the card.

---

*5. Double-click on the card to select the button. The Button Info dialog box appears. Choose Transparent for the style and uncheck the Show Name Option. Click on the **Link to** button. Then press ⌘-3 to go to the next card—the Index card. Click on **This Card** in the destination dialog box.*

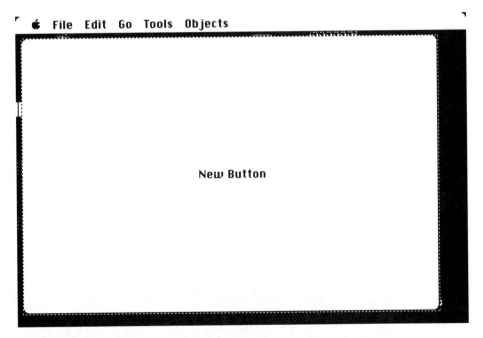

Figure 12.17 A button can be as large as a card.

Lesson 74: LOOKING AT STACK INFORMATION

To see information about the stack you just created, do this:

*1. Choose **Stack Info . . .** from the Objects menu about the stack currently open.*

The Stack Info dialog box (Figure 12.18) lists the following information:

The name of the stack

The pathname of this stack (where it's located)

The number of cards in this stack

The number of backgrounds in this stack

The size of this stack

The amount of space free in this stack

The Stack Info dialog box gives you an idea of how this stack is structured: how many backgrounds it has and how many cards it has on top of those backgrounds. This information will be more useful when

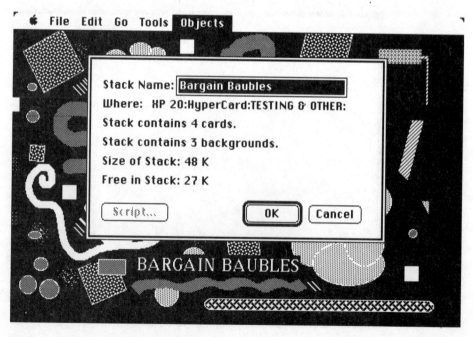

Figure 12.18 The Stack Info dialog box.

you create more complicated stacks and start writing scripts for stack elements like backgrounds and cards.

But even now you can find a good use for this information. For example, knowing the size of a stack tells you whether you need a 400K or an 800K floppy disk to make a copy of this stack. If the stack is over 800K in size, you'll need to copy it to a hard disk.

The Script button is available at the Scripting level but not at the Authoring level. You'll learn how to write programs for stacks in Section Three, Advanced Applications. For now, ignore this button.

2. Click OK or Cancel to get out of the dialog box.

Lesson 75:   LOOKING AT CARD INFORMATION

To see information about the card currently on the screen, do this:

1. Choose **Card Info...** from the Objects menu to see information about that card.

The Card Info dialog box (Figure 12.19) lists the following information:

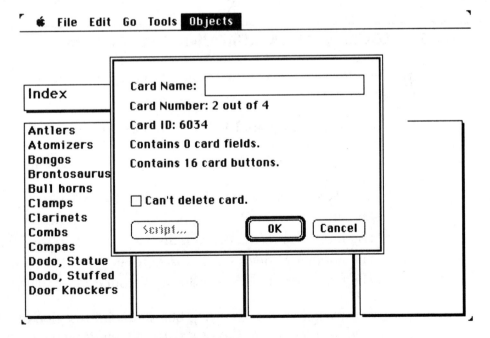

Figure 12.19 The Card Info dialog box.

The name of this card (useful when scripting)

The order number of this card in the stack

The unique ID number assigned to this card

The number of fields on this card only (not on the background behind it)

The number of buttons on this card only (not on the background behind it)

The Card Info dialog box shows information about the card currently on the screen: its name, order number, ID number, and the number of fields and buttons it has.

The card number tells you its current order in the stack. HyperCard numbers each card sequentially as you create it. But, when you delete a card from the stack, all cards are automatically renumbered. Therefore, you can't rely on a card's number enough to refer to it in a button or card script, for example. That's where the unique ID comes into play. You can rely on the ID number because it never changes. Once a card is assigned an ID number, no other card in that stack will have that number, even if the card is deleted.

Lesson 76:   LOOKING AT BACKGROUND INFORMATION

For information about the background associated with the card currently on the screen:

1. Choose **Background Info . . .** from the Objects menu.

The Background Info dialog box lists the following information:

A name for this background (useful when scripting)

The unique ID number assigned to this background

The number of cards that use this background in this stack

The number of fields on this background

The number of buttons on this background

The Background Info dialog box shows information about the background associated with the card currently on the screen. You can assign a name to this background by typing in the space next to **Name**. You can refer to objects by name when you write a script or program for an object.

This dialog box also gives you a choice to protect the background from being modified or deleted by someone looking at this stack. Clicking in the box next to **Can't modify background** prevents anyone from making changes to this background. Clicking in the box next to **Can't delete background** prevents anyone from deleting this background.

SUMMARY

In this chapter, you learned how to create a sales catalog on a stack. Stacks that are more complex than those used for collecting research notes or other simple tasks usually need more than one background. Before adding a new background, remember to go to the last card of the current background and then choose **New Background** from the Objects menu. Otherwise, you'll split the stack, causing it to have three backgrounds instead of two.

You also used more paint tools and learned some tricks for typing white text on a black pattern. Experimenting with paint tools doesn't mean you're stuck with the graphics you've created. The **Revert** command brings back the last version of a card should you make a mistake or change your mind about changes you make with the paint tools.

Finally, you looked at information about your stack, the current card, and the current background.

13 Everyone Wants a Second Home

In this chapter, you'll create a second Home card. When you've outgrown your Home card or run out of space, you can easily add a second Home card right behind the first one. And, if you like, you can move it in front of the original Home card so your new Home card appears first when you start HyperCard.

The lessons in this chapter show you how to

- Create a second Home card
- Cut and paste cards to reorder them
- Duplicate buttons
- Write scripts for buttons
- Open applications with buttons

To complete the lessons in this chapter, you must set the user level to Authoring. Type **set the userlevel to 4** in the Message box to change the user level to Authoring if necessary.

Lesson 77: ADDING A SECOND HOME CARD

When your original Home card is full, you can always add another Home card right behind the first one. You don't have to run out of room first. You might want to create a second Home card as a launching pad for just the stacks you create or use most often.

Follow these steps to create another Home card:

1. Go to the Home card.
2. Press ⌘-N to add a new card. (Same as choosing **New Card** from the Edit menu.)

HyperCard inserts a new card with the same background information (fields, buttons, and pictures) as the Home card.

Cutting and Pasting to Reorder the Cards in the Home Stack

You can put this new Home card in front of the one that comes with HyperCard if you like. To cut and paste a card, use the **Cut Card** and **Paste Card** choices on the Edit menu.

When cutting and pasting cards, keep in mind that *you cannot paste a card in front of the first card in a stack.* You can paste a card only after whichever card is shown on the screen. So, for the second card in the stack to become the first card, you'll have to cut the Home card and then paste it back again.

To move your new Home card to the head of the stack, follow these steps:

1. Display the original Home card on the screen.
2. Choose **Cut Card** from the Edit menu. The Home card disappears and your new Home card is now shown on the screen.
3. Choose **Paste Card** from the Edit menu. The original Home card is pasted *after* the card shown on the screen.

When you open HyperCard, your new Home card will appear on the screen. To get to the original Home card, just click the right arrow button once.

Go to your new Home card for now. Next you'll create buttons, align them in a row on this card, and then link each button to a different stack.

Lesson 78: DUPLICATING BUTTONS

You can create several different buttons one at a time and assign each its own button information. But, to create five identical buttons, it's faster to duplicate them than to create them one at a time. In this lesson, you'll create five identical buttons, changing only the name of

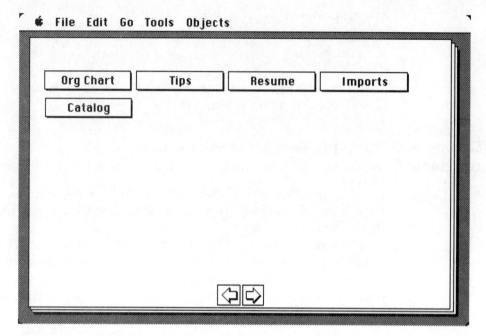

Figure 13.1 Create five buttons, one for each stack you've created.

each button. (See Figure 13.1.) Then you'll link each button to one of the stacks you've created so far: Org chart, Tips, Resume, Imports, and Catalog.

1. Go to the second Home card.
2. Choose **New Button** from the Options menu. (HyperCard automatically selects the button tool when you choose **New Button**.)
3. Double-click on the button to choose the button style.
4. You don't have to assign a name to this button, but it's usually a good idea to do so. Otherwise, you or another person using your stack might not know what the button is for. Type a name for your button in the Name field.
5. Choose from the styles available. For example, choose **shadow** by clicking in the circle preceding it. You can alter this shape later.
6. Point to the new button with the mouse. Hold down the Option key and drag off a copy. Do this five times to create five buttons.

Tip: Hold down the Shift key while dragging horizontally or vertically to keep the new button aligned with the original button.

Duplicating buttons can save time when you are creating several buttons that all look alike. For example, when creating an invisible button, you usually uncheck the **Show Name** feature in the Button Info dialog box, so copying this button produces an identical button without a name within it.

As you know, you can connect two cards or two stacks with buttons. Next you'll link each button to a different stack.

Lesson 79: LINKING TO STACKS

When you're through modifying the buttons, link them to the appropriate stacks.

*1. Click the **Link to** button in the Button Info dialog box.*

Go to the card that you want to appear when you click this button.

> *Tip:* You can move the Destination box anywhere on the screen just by dragging it.

*2. Choose **Open Stack** from the File menu. Or use the Recent card to go to a stack you've looked at recently. Find the stack you want to link the button to.*

*3. To link the button to a specific card, find and display that card, and then click on **This Card** in the destination box.*

To link the button to the first card in this stack, just click on **This Stack** in the destination box.

> *Tip:* If you mistakenly link a button to the wrong card, it's no big deal. To unlink a button, just repeat the linking procedure to link it to the correct card. If you decide that you don't want the button linked to any card for the time being, *link it to itself* to unlink it.

4. Choose the Browse tool from the Tools menu. Click on one of the new buttons to test it.

Lesson 80:   DOUBLING BACK

Okay, I'm linked. Now how do I get back to my second Home card? You have several options, among them:

- Choose **Open Stack** and select the stack to return to.
- Press the Tilde (or Esc) key.
- Press ⌘-R to see the Recent card. Then click on the card to return to.
- Press ⌘-H to go Home. Then press ⌘-3 to go to the next card, which is your second Home card.
- Create a button that links you to the second Home card.

On the background of the first card in each stack you've linked, follow these steps to create a button that links you back to the second Home card.

1. Choose **New Button** from the Objects menu.
2. Double-click on the button to see the Button Info dialog box. Choose **transparent** for the style, uncheck **Show Name**, and click on **Icon**. Choose a Return Arrow icon. Then click the **Link to** button.
3. Go to the second Home card.
4. With the second Home card displayed, click on **This Card** in the destination box. HyperCard automatically goes back to the previous stack displayed.
5. Choose the Browse tool from the Tools menu. Click on the Return Arrow to return to the second Home card.

Buttons can do much more link you from one card to another. Buttons can also perform functions such as sorting cards, viewing cards, or printing cards. Next, you'll learn how to program buttons to do more than link cards.

Lesson 81:   ADDING SCRIPTS TO BUTTONS

A **script** is a program you write with a programming language called HyperTalk. Scripting is the term HyperCard uses for programming. HyperTalk is HyperCard's very high-level, easy-to-learn programming language. Every time you used the Message box, you were actually using HyperTalk. You have been typing one-line scripts into the Message box all along.

You don't have to know everything about scripting (alias programming) to create scripts for stacks. There is no such thing as one big long list of code in HyperCard. You program buttons one at a time. You program fields one at a time. And it's the same for cards. So it's a piecemeal effort that's really effortless.

What's more, not all button, fields, cards, or other objects have to be programmed. You can program just one button in the whole stack if you like. Or you can add a program to each and every object. The secret is that you can program everything, anything, or nothing in HyperCard.

And, yes, it's time to change the user level to Scripting. So pat yourself on the back—you've made it to *StackWare Author*!

Changing the User Level to Scripting

You can now move to the next skill level: Scripting. Use the message box to change the user level from Authoring to Scripting.

1. Press ⌘-M to display the Message box.
2. Type **set userlevel to 5**. Press RETURN.

At this level, you can write a script for each HyperCard element: Stack, Background, Card, Field, and Button. To add a script to an object, you simply click the Script button in the Information dialog box for that object.

In this lesson, you'll create several buttons for your new Home card. And then you'll program them by adding a few words to each button's script. These words will tell HyperCard what to do when you click on the button. For example, let's look at the script that's attached to the Home button.

1. Go to the Address stack. The Address stack is just one of many HyperCard stacks that include a Home button.
2. Choose the Button tool.
3. Double-click on the Home button to see its Button Info dialog box.
4. Click on **Script**, as shown in Figure 13.2.

You'll see the script shown in Figure 13.3.

This script tells HyperCard to show the visual effect named **iris close** and then go to the Home stack whenever you click on the Home button. Visual effects provide visual transitions between cards and stacks. You'll learn all about visual effects in Section 3 of this book. For now, just concentrate on how scripts are put together.

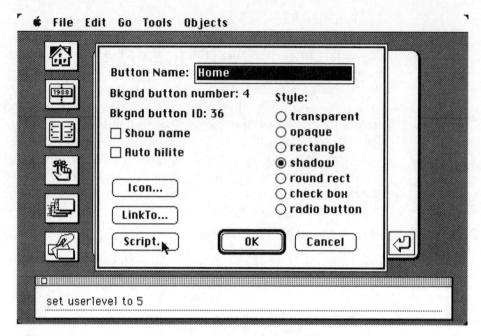

Figure 13.2 Click on the Script button to see its script.

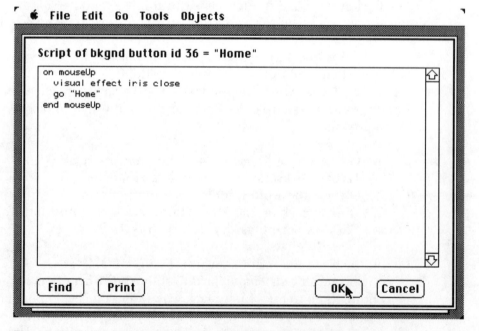

Figure 13.3 The script attached to the Home button in the Address stack.

When you press the mouse button down while the pointer is on the Home button, HyperCard receives a message from the computer that says "the mouse is down right now." When you release that button, HyperCard receives a message that says "the mouse is up now." Once the mouse is up, HyperCard executes the commands that follow in order: "visual effect iris close" and "go home". When HyperCard looks for instructions following "go home," it sees "end mouseUp." "End mouseUp" tells HyperCard "that's all I wanted you to do."

Besides programming buttons to open other stacks, you can program buttons to choose items from pull-down menus. You'll do that next.

Creating Buttons That Display Desk Accessories

1. Choose New Button from the Objects menu.

2. A button appears with a moving dotted line around it to indicate that it is still selected. Double-click on the new button to see its Button Info dialog box. You are going to program this button so that, when you click on it, it displays the Macintosh Control Panel.

3. Type Control Panel for the name of this button and click in the box next to Show Name.

4. Choose either the rectangle or round rect button style. (You can choose any style you like.)

5. Click on the Script button in the Button Info dialog box. The Script box appears with the words on mouseUp and end mouseUp already within it and the insertion point blinking in the correct place for you to begin typing.

On mouseUp tells HyperCard to execute the next command once the mouse button has been released while on top of the button that contains this script.

6. Type doMenu Control Panel and click on the OK button at the bottom of the Script box.

The **doMenu** command simply tells HyperCard to look in all the menus on the menubar and find the word that follows **doMenu** in the script. If it finds that word on a menu, it chooses it just as if you had pulled down the menu and chosen it manually.

7. Choose the Browse tool in the Tools menu so you can test the button. Click on the Control Panel button.

Lesson 82:   OPENING APPLICATIONS WITH BUTTONS

How would you like to open an application like Microsoft Word from within HyperCard and then return to your Home card when you quit the application?

Being able to access all your other software programs from a card in HyperCard seems like a real programming chore. But the truth is, it's one of the easiest ways to program a button.

You don't even have to tell HyperCard the pathname where each program is located on your hard disk. HyperCard will ask you only once, the first time you click on a button, and then remember the path.

Before programming buttons to open applications, write down the names of all the applications you want to open. Write these names exactly as they are spelled beneath their icons in the Finder. HyperCard will look for the name that matches that.

Then create a new button for each application you want to open from within HyperCard.

*1. Choose **New Button** from the Objects menu.*

2. Double-click on the new button to see its Button Info dialog box.

You are going to program this button so that, when you click on it, it opens Microsoft Word.

*3. Type **Word** for the name of this button and choose **transparent** for its style.*

4. Click on the button named Icon. Click on the icon that represents a word processing application (Figure 13.4). (You can choose a different icon if you like.) Click OK.

*5. Resize the button if necessary. Then double-click on it again to get back to the Button Info dialog box. Click on the Script button. The Script box appears with the words **on mouseUp** and **end mouseUp** already within it and the insertion point blinking in the correct place for you to begin typing.*

*6. Type **open Microsoft Word** and click on the OK button at the bottom of the Script box, as shown in Figure 13.5. (Be sure to type the quotation marks around the name of the application.)*

The Open command tells HyperCard to look on your hard disk for the named application.

7. Choose the Browse tool in the Tools menu so you can test the button. Click on the Word button.

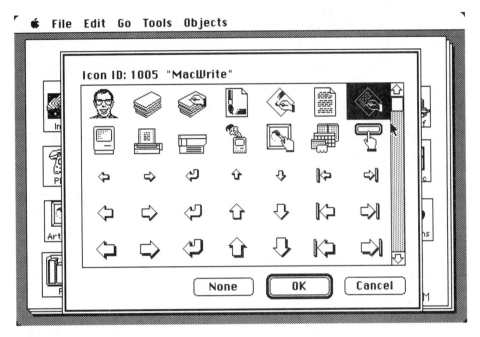

Figure 13.4 Word processing icon.

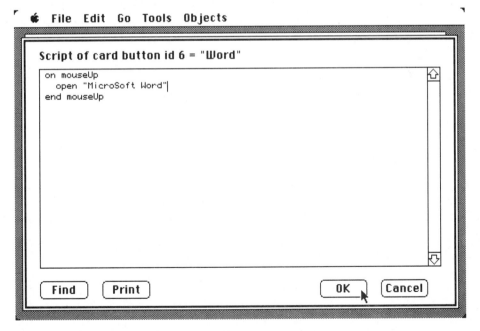

Figure 13.5 Script for opening the MicroSoft Word application.

8. If the application is buried within some folders, HyperCard will first ask you to locate this file.

Locate Microsoft Word in the window and double-click on it to open it. HyperCard stores this pathname on a card in the Home stack for future reference. (So it won't ask again.)

9. Microsoft Word opens as if you had double-clicked on its icon in the Finder.

*10. Quit the application by choosing **Quit** from its File menu.*

You've returned to your Home card! Follow the steps listed above to create a button for each application you want to access from within HyperCard.

SUMMARY

In this chapter, you learned how to create your own Home card and make it the first card you see when you open HyperCard. You also practiced creating and linking buttons to stacks. But, more important, you learned how easy it is to program a button in HyperCard. You've been using the HyperTalk programming language all along, but now you know how to put those commands into button scripts. In Section Three of this book, you'll learn how to use more advanced programming techniques for developing HyperCard applications.

SECTION III ADVANCED APPLICATIONS

Scripting is HyperCard's fancy word for programming with HyperTalk. **HyperTalk**—HyperCard's programming language—consists of about 45 commands that can make your Macintosh sit up and whistle, or sing, or show cartoons and other animation. This chapter introduces you to scripting and shows how to write some simple scripts for buttons, fields, cards, backgrounds, and stacks. *Caution:* This is not a chapter that teaches you how to be a programmer. This chapter shows you how to program *without being a programmer*.

What's more, knowing about half of HyperTalk will do about 90 percent of the things you'll ever want or need to do with programming. When you're through with this last section of the book, that 90 percent will be yours.

You'll see how to write scripts (a.k.a. *programs*) for objects in stacks to make them more useful. Each of these objects can both send and receive messages from HyperCard and from each other. You'll learn how to write scripts to send messages that tell HyperCard what to do.

Specifically, you'll learn how to create

- Visual effects
- Flashing cards and buttons
- Check box and Radio buttons
- Pop-up fields
- Fields with running totals
- Fields that display the time or date
- Sort buttons
- Sounds
- Animation

233

- Dialog boxes
- Quiz stacks
- Passwords
- Your own HyperTalk commands

The HyperTalk examples in this section cover the 35 most-used commands:

add	divide	get	pass	set
answer	doMenu	go	play	show
ask	drag	hide	pop	sort
beep	edit script	if	print	subtract
choose	exit	multiply	push	type
close printing	find	open	put	visual
click	flash	open printing	repeat	wait

Some of these commands no doubt look familiar because you've already used them in previous chapters (**find**, **doMenu**, **go**, **open**, **open printing**, **print**, **close printing**) either by clicking on a preprogrammed button or by typing them into the Message box. In this section, you'll learn how to add one or more of these commands to the scripts of HyperCard objects—buttons, fields, cards, backgrounds, and stacks—to make your stacks more useful.

Appendix B lists all HyperTalk commands with a definition and example of each one. It also lists *functions*, *properties*, and *variables*. If you don't know what functions, properties, and variables are, don't worry about it. They're simply more fancy HyperTalk words that will be explained as you learn to script (yes, program) in the lessons in this section.

A note about HyperCard programming tricks: Perhaps the greatest accolade one HyperCard programmer can pay to another is to say, "Gee, how did you do that?" To which the other programmer will reply, beaming: "Oh, that was a trick." Just knowing how the HyperCard commands work isn't enough. You also have to know how to use them or, more importantly, what their "tricks of the trade" are. This whole last section of the book explains a number of common HyperCard programming tricks. They take a lot of the mystery out of why HyperCard programs act as they do.

14 HyperTalk Basics

To be a little more formal about the definition of a script: a **script** is a series of commands assigned to a button, field, card, background, or stack that tells HyperCard what to do. For example, adding the following script to a button tells HyperCard to go to the stack named Address whenever you click on the button:

```
on mouseUp
   go to stack address
end mouseUp
```

When you press the mouse button down, HyperCard receives a message from the computer that says "the mouse is down right now." When you release that button, HyperCard receives a message that says "the mouse is up now." Once the mouse is up, HyperCard reads the next command (go to stack Address) and executes it. When it looks for further instructions, it finds "end mouseUp." **End mouseUp** tells HyperCard "Stop. There are no more commands here."

In this chapter, you'll look at some typical button scripts and create a few scripts of your own. You'll see how to

- Write scripts that help you navigate.
- Add visual effects to scripts.
- Mark cards for fast retrieval later.
- Search fields for a whole word.
- Search a specific field for a word.
- Search more than one stack for a word.
- Execute commands only on certain conditions.

You'll use these commands:

go

visual

pop

push

find

put

if

get

To complete the lessons in this chapter, you must set the user level to Scripting. Type **set the userlevel to 5** in the Message box to change the user level to Scripting.

Lesson 83: LOOKING AT SCRIPTS

You already know how to write scripts that tell HyperCard to display desk accessories and open applications when you click on buttons. Now you'll see the scripts associated with typical navigational buttons that appear on a background in most stacks, for example, the Right and Left Arrow buttons. In this lesson, you'll become familiar with the scripting window as you look at the scripts attached to buttons, fields, cards, backgrounds, and stacks.

Scripts for Buttons

Each button has a script associated with it. Here's how to see the scripts for the navigation buttons on the Home card:

1. Go to the Home card now.
2. Choose the Button tool from the Tools menu.
3. Double-click on the Right Arrow button to see the Button Info dialog box.
4. Click on the Script button to see the script, as shown in Figure 14.1.

When you click on a Right Arrow button, you usually go to the next physical card in the stack. That's because the script for this button says:

```
on mouseUp
   go to next card
end mouseUp
```

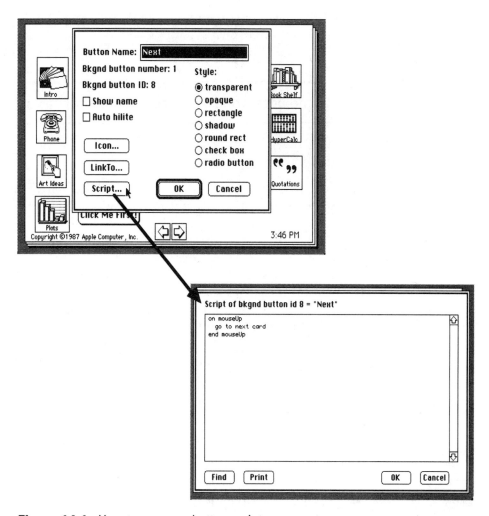

Figure 14.1 How to access a button script.

The Components of a Script

Scripts are made up of one or more **message handlers**. A message handler begins with the word **on** and ends with the word **end**. The word **on** is referred to as a **handler**. It tells HyperCard when to execute the commands. The **on** handler is followed by a message such as **mouseUp**, **openField**, **openCard**, or **openStack** to name a few. The next few lines contain commands that tell HyperCard what to do. And the last line in a message handler begins with the word **end** followed by the same message used in the first line. **End** tells HyperCard when to stop. For example, the **on openStack** message in a button tells HyperCard to execute any commands between **on openStack** and **end openStack** whenever you open a stack with that script.

The components of a script are illustrated in Figure 14.2.

Tip: Some books refer to a message handler as an **event**.

Where Does the Script Belong?

Where you put the script—in a button, field, card, background, or stack—depends on how many objects you want to control and the result you're trying to achieve.

HyperCard executes commands in a button script only when that button is clicked. The same goes for a field—if you want a command to be executed only when the field is entered or clicked on, put the script in that field. You can, however, write a script that affects more than one button. If you want a script to affect all buttons on a card, add the script to that card. Likewise, if you want a script to affect *all* objects on all cards with the same background, add the script to the background. And last but not least, to execute commands when you open a stack, or anywhere in a stack, put them in the stack script.

These rules are pretty important, so Figure 14.3 states them with a little more emphasis.

1. Button and Field Scripts

The message that you'll use most often in a button script is **mouseUp**. Buttons aren't the only objects with mouse messages. You can also add

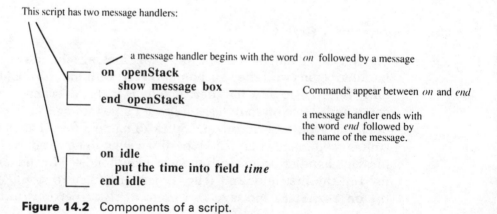

This script has two message handlers:

a message handler begins with the word *on* followed by a message

```
on openStack
    show message box ——————— Commands appear between on and end
end openStack
```

a message handler ends with the word *end* followed by the name of the message.

```
on idle
    put the time into field time
end idle
```

Figure 14.2 Components of a script.

A button or field script affects only the button or field to which it is attached.

A card script affects the card to which it is attached and any fields or buttons on that card.

A background script affects all cards with that background and any buttons or fields on those cards.

A stack script affects all objects in the stack.

Figure 14.3 Which object does the script belong to?

mouseUp messages to the scripts of fields and cards. So, when you click on a particular field or card, HyperCard executes the commands in that script. The only restriction on using **mouseUp** in field scripts is that you must lock the field before HyperCard can recognize the mouse click. To lock the field, you just check the box next to **Lock field** in the Field Info dialog box.

2. Card Scripts

The message that you'll probably use most often in a card script is **openCard**. It means that, each time the card is opened or displayed on the screen, HyperCard follows the commands between **on openCard** and **end openCard**. Adding a **mouseUp** message to a card script tells Hyper-Card to execute those commands when you click the mouse anywhere on the card, including any object on that card. The following example tells HyperCard to show card field one, if it's currently hidden, when this card is displayed.

```
on openCard
   show card field one
end openCard
```

Let's look at the card script attached to the Phone card.

1. Go to the Phone card now.
2. Choose **Card Info** from the Objects menu.
3. Click on the Script button to see the script for this card, as shown in Figure 14.4.

Shortcut: In version 1.2, you can press ⌘-Option-C to go directly to the card script.

---

3. Background Scripts

Messages added to background scripts usually manipulate buttons and fields added to a background. Common field messages are

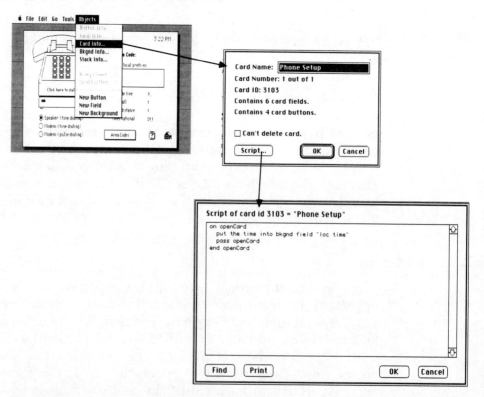

Figure 14.4 Card script attached to Phone card.

openField and **closeField**. Common button messages are **newButton** and **mouseUp**.

1. Go to the Address stack. You'll look at its background script next.
2. Choose **Background Info** from the Objects menu.
3. Click on the Script button to see the script for this background, as shown in Figure 14.5.

Shortcut: In version 1.2, you can press ⌘-Option-B to go directly to the background script attached to the card currently on the screen.

On CloseField tells HyperCard to execute the commands between **on closeField** and **end closeField** only if the text in a background field has been changed.

On NewCard tells HyperCard to move the insertion point into the first field whenever a new card is added to this background.

4. Stack Scripts

Scripts you assign to stacks are executed as soon as you open the stack. Often, commands that tell HyperCard to clean up a stack are added to the stack script. For example, you can add commands that tell Hyper-Card to change the user level, hide or show one or more fields, hide or show the Message box, hide or show the menu bar, push or pop a card, and so on.

Look at the stack script attached to the Address stack.

1. Go to the Address stack if it isn't already open.
2. Choose **Stack Info** from the Objects menu.
3. Click on the Script button to see the script for this stack, as shown in Figure 14.6.

Shortcut: In version 1.2, you can press ⌘-Option-S to go directly to the stack script attached to the stack currently open.

As you get used to writing scripts, the object you should attach them to will become more obvious.

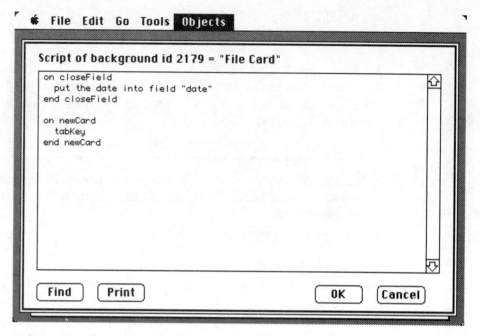

Figure 14.5 Background script attached to Address stack.

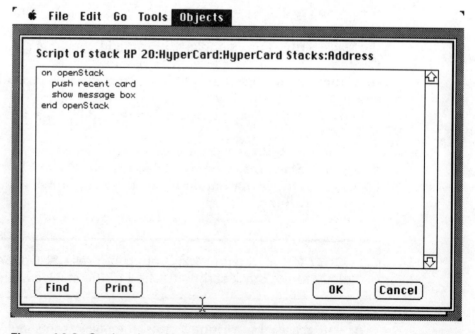

Figure 14.6 Stack script attached to Address stack.

> *Tip:* HyperCard doesn't know the difference between uppercase and lowercase letters, so you can type your scripts using either or both.

The Script Window

You can edit scripts in the script window with the edit commands for **Cut**, **Copy**, and **Paste**. That means you can copy messages from one script window to another. For example, you can copy a button script to a field script. And you don't have to copy the whole script. You can copy any part you like.

You cannot choose these commands from the Edit menu while you're in the script window. You must use their keyboard equivalents: ⌘-X to cut, ⌘-C to copy, and ⌘-V to paste.

> *Tip:* Press ⌘-A to highlight the entire script. (Doing so saves you time when selecting a long script to cut or copy.)

Notice the buttons in the script window: Find and Print. The Find button helps you quickly locate a word in a long script. *Scripts can contain up to 30,000 characters!* To find a specific word in a script, click on the Find button and then type the word you want to find.

> *Tip:* To find the next occurrence of a word in the script, press ⌘-G.

To print just the script in the current script window, not any cards in the stack, press the Print button.

> *Tip:* If you don't want to print the whole script, just part of it, highlight the words you want to print and then click on the Print button, as shown in Figure 14.7.

Now that you are familiar with all the parts of the script window, it's time to start writing scripts of your own.

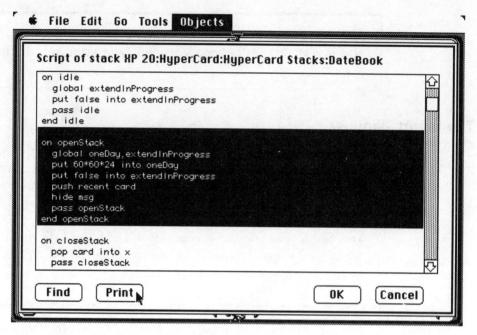

Figure 14.7 Highlight a group of commands to print.

Lesson 84: USING THE GO COMMAND IN SCRIPTS

Buttons, fields, cards, and backgrounds can be referred to by name, number, ID, or position on a card or in a stack. When referring to objects with the **Go** command, you can be as general as **go to next card** or as specific as **go to card 9 of background 2 in stack "Sample."**
Examples:

    go back
    go Home
    go to last card of Home
    go to card 17 of background 3
    go to card 10 of stack "Tips"
    go to card ID 2435 of stack "Home"

Use the **Go** command in a script to display a different card or stack when you click on a button, in a field, or anywhere on a card.

1. Go to the Plots stack.
2. Choose **New Button** from the Objects menu to add a new button to the Plots card.
3. Double-click on the new button to see the Button Info dialog box. Type **Plots** for the name of this button. Assign it any other characteristics you like.
4. Click on the Script button to display its script. The insertion point should be blinking between **on mouseUp** and **end mouseUp**.
5. Type **go stack clip art** and click OK.
6. Move the Plots button to an out-of-the-way place on the Plots card.
7. Choose the Browse tool and click on the Plots button to make sure it works.

Now that you can go quickly to the Clip Art stack from the Plots stack, you might want to copy the different charts you create to the Clip Art stack for later use.

Scripts can be as simple as that. Of course, you can add more than one command to a script. For scripts with **Go** commands, often a visual effect command is added before the **Go** command. If you're like most people, you'll find HyperTalk's visual effects more fun to play with than any of the other commands. Go to the next lesson for more about visual effects!

Lesson 85:   ADDING VISUAL EFFECTS

> *Tip:* If you are using a Macintosh II computer with a color monitor, choose **Control Panel** from the menu now, click on Monitors, black & white/grays, and choose 2 (2-bit mode). Otherwise, you won't be able to see the visual effects work. (Of course, when the color version of HyperCard becomes available, you won't need to do this. There have been rumors about a color version of HyperCard, but don't look for it in version 2.0.)

In movies and television, when the camera cuts from one scene to the next, there is always some sort of visual transition. For example, right before a commercial, the last scene you see almost always fades to black. HyperTalk has a special command that lets you add similar visual transitions between cards and stacks. It is called the **visual** command.

This command is often used in combination with the word **effect** followed by one of the visual effects listed in Table 14-1.

For example, the **barn door open** visual effect opens the card from the center, progressively uncovering the card like curtains parting on a stage. (See Figure 14.8.)

Creating Visual Effects

Commands for visual effects are commonly added before **Go** commands in scripts.

Visual Effect	When Used (examples)
iris open	To go to a card with detailed information about the current topic. Opens from center of card.
iris close	To return to the card shown before an **iris open**.
zoom open (or zoom out)	To go to a card with detailed information about the current topic. Opens from the position of the mouse click.
zoom close (or zoom in)	To return to the card shown before a **zoom open**.
dissolve	To fade from the title card to the first card. To make a gradual transition from card to card. To represent the passage of time.
checkerboard	To go from one card or stack to another.
venetian blinds	To go from one card or stack to another.
wipe left	To continue to next card on same topic.
wipe right	To return to card shown before a **wipe left**.
wipe up	To continue to next card on same topic.
wipe down	To return to card shown before a **wipe up**.
barn door open	To introduce a topic.
barn door close	To end a topic.
scroll left	To move to a card with a different topic.
scroll right	To return to the card shown before a **scroll left**.
scroll up	To move to a card with a different topic.
scroll down	To return to the card shown before a **scroll up**.

Table 14.1 Visual effects.

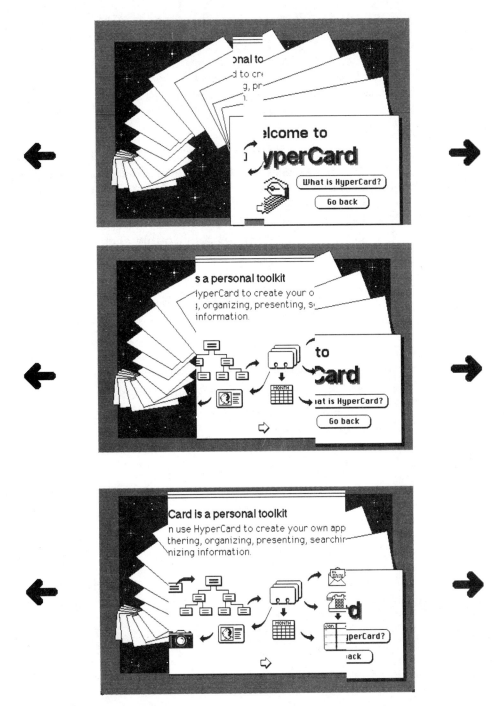

Figure 14.8 The barn door visual effect gradually opens the card from the center.

1. Go to the stack you created named HyperCard Tips. You'll add visual effects to the navigation buttons on this stack.

2. Choose the Button tool on the Tools menu. To display the button script of the right arrow button, double-click on that button to see the Button Info dialog box. Within that box is a button named Script. Click on the Script button to see the script window.

> *Tip:* To bypass the Button Info dialog box and go directly to the script window if you're using version 1.2, hold down the ⌘ and Options keys and click once on a button to see its script. If you're using version 1.0.1 or 1.1, choose the Button tool, then hold down the Shift key and double-click on the button.

3. Click after the on mouseUp message to position the insertion point. Then press RETURN to insert a blank line between on mouseUp and go to next card.

> *Tip:* Place the visual effect just before the Go command, not after. Otherwise, the visual effect will be ignored.

4. Type visual effect dissolve. Click OK.

5. To see your visual effect now, first choose the Browse tool from the Tools menu or press ⌘-Tab to switch to the Browse tool. Now click on the Right Arrow button and watch the visual transition from one card to the next.

6. For experimentation, repeat steps 2 through 5 above, substituting dissolve with one of the other effects listed in Table 14-1.

Varying Speed

You can also vary the speed of the effect by adding one of these modifiers after the effect and intensity chosen:

```
fast
very fast
slow
```

```
slowly
very slow
```

For example, you can add **visual dissolve slow** or **visual zoom open fast** to the script of a card or button.

Next, modify the script of the right arrow button to give it some speed.

1. Display the script of the right arrow button.

*2. Click after the word **dissolve** in the visual effect message to position the insertion point. Then type the words **very slowly** as shown below:*

```
visual effect dissolve very slowly
```

3. Click OK.

4. Switch to the Browse tool and click once on the right arrow button to see the visual transition.

Varying Intensity

In addition to typing a visual effect and the speed of that effect, you can add one of these phrases for an added effect:

```
to black
to white
to gray
to inverse
to card
```

For example, you might add **visual dissolve to black** or **visual zoom close to card** to the script of a button. (You don't have to type **effect** after **visual**. The word **effect** is just added for readability.) To control both the speed and intensity of the effect, you can create commands such as **visual iris close slow to gray**.

Tip: When you add both an intensity and a speed, the order in which you list them following the effect is important. *You must add the intensity last.* For example, HyperCard won't understand **visual dissolve to black very slowly**, but it will understand **visual dissolve** very slowly to black. Welcome to programming.

Lesson 86:   MARKING CARDS FOR LATER RETRIEVAL

You've already looked at the scripts of right and left arrow buttons. Now look at the script of a return arrow button. The Home card does not have a return arrow button, but the Address stack does. Go to the Address stack now and look at the script associated with its return arrow button.

1. Press ⌘-M to see the Message box. Type **go address** and press Return.
2. At the Address stack, choose the Button tool, hold down the Shift key and double-click on the return arrow button to see its script. (If using version 1.2, hold down the ⌘ and Option and click once to see a button script.)

```
on mouseUp
   pop card
end mouseUp
```

This script doesn't use the **Go** command. It uses a command called **Pop**. Huh? Pop what? The **Pop** command **pops a card** out of the computer's memory and back onto the screen. **Pop** doesn't work alone. It works with the **Push** command. The **Push** command was added to the stack script. When you opened the Address stack, HyperCard first read the stack script. Look at that script now:

1. Click Cancel to close the script window for the button script.

*2. Choose **Stack Info** from the Objects menu.*

3. Click on the Script button to see the script for this stack.

```
on openStack
   push card
end openStack
```

Push means "push the card into memory for now." That's how Hyper-Card marks a card for later retrieval. It just shoves it into memory. So, when you opened the Address stack, HyperCard pushed the first card in the Address stack into memory. Then, when you clicked on the return arrow button, HyperCard read the button script, which says "pop card," and popped the first card in the Address stack from memory back onto the screen.

4. Click Cancel to close the script window for the stack script.

You can push more than one card in memory. The last card pushed into memory is the first one popped out. **Pop** means "go back to the last card pushed." (See Figure 14.9)

The trick to using the **Push** and **Pop** commands is that the **Push** command is usually added to a card or stack script so that, when you first open a card or stack, it is pushed into memory. The **Pop** command, on the other hand, is usually added to a button script, such as the Return Arrow button.

Pop and **Push** make it easy for you to retrace your steps much as the tilde (~) or esc key does.

Look at the **Pop** and **Push** commands in the Clip Art stack:

1. Go to the Home card. (Press ⌘-H.) Click on the Clip Art icon to go to the stack of Clip Art.

The stack script contains the **Push** command, so you'll look at that script first.

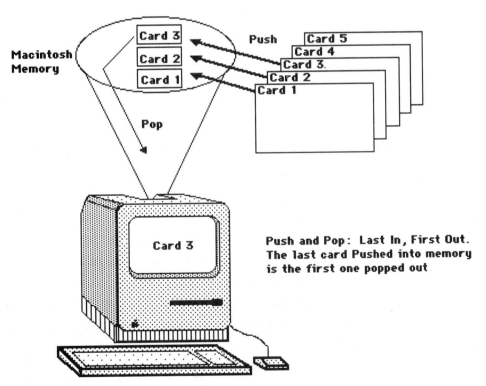

Figure 14.9 The last card pushed is the first card popped onto the screen

*2. Choose **Stack Info** from the Objects menu and then click on Script to see the stack script.*

Shortcut: If using version 1.2, press ⌘-Option-S to see the stack script. If using a previous version, hold down the Shift key and choose **Stack Info** from the Objects menu.)

```
on openStack
  push recent card
end openStack
```

This stack script tells HyperCard to mark the card it just came from (in this case, the Home card) as the one to display when HyperCard next sees a **Pop** command.

3. Click OK or Cancel to go back to the card.

The Return arrow button has a **Pop** command. Look at its script now:

4. Choose the Button tool on the Tools menu.

5. Hold down the Shift key and double-click on the Return arrow button. Its script looks like this:

```
on mouseUp
  visual effect iris close
  pop card
end mouseUp
```

6. Click OK.

7. Press ⌘-Tab once to choose the Browse tool. Click on the Return Arrow button to see which card it displays.

The Home card appears. That's because the word **recent** preceded the **Push** command.

You don't have to use **recent** with the **Push** command. If you add **push card** or **push this card** to your stack script, instead of **push recent card**, HyperCard displays the first card in the Clip Art stack when it sees a **pop card** command instead of going back to the Home card. Try it now. Remove the word **recent** from the Clip Art stack script.

1. Go to the Clip Art stack.

*2. Choose **Stack Info** from the Objects menu. Click on Script.*

*3. Double-click on the word **recent** in the script and press the Backspace key to remove that word. Click OK.*

The script for this stack should now look like this:

```
on openStack
  push card
end openStack
```

4. Press ⌘-Tab to choose the Browse tool. Then go back to the Home card.

5. Click on the Clip Art icon. Click on the Right Arrow button a few times to display a few cards. Then click on the Return Arrow button to go back to the card pushed.

You return to the first card in the Clip Art stack because it was pushed into memory when you opened the Clip Art stack.

*6. But click on the Return Arrow button again and you go back to the Home card! Why? Because the Home card was pushed into memory when you opened the Home stack. Then, when you opened the Clip Art stack, the first card of clip art was pushed on top of the Home card. So the first **Pop** command popped the clip art card back onto the screen and the second **Pop** command popped the only card left in memory—the Home card—onto the screen.*

As you can see, if you plan to use a lot of **Push** and **Pop** commands in your scripts, keeping track of the next card in memory can get a little dicey. So here's a programming trick to help you keep track: Number your **Push** and **Pop** commands, and then sketch a picture on a piece of paper that shows you which card is next in memory. It's much easier to visualize which card will appear next.

Adding a Return Arrow Button to Your Resume Stack

You linked buttons named Objective, Experience, Education, and others to specific cards in the resume stack you created in an earlier chapter. But the only way to get back to the card that listed all the buttons was either to use the tilde (or esc) key on your keyboard or to press the left arrow button several times.

Now that you understand how the **Pop** and **Push** commands work, you can add them to your card and button scripts. By adding **push card** to the card script of the card you named Main Menu, you can mark it as the one to return to when you click on the Return Arrow button. But you don't have a Return Arrow button yet! No problem; you'll create one now:

*1. Go to the Resume stack you created. Type **go resume** in the Message box.*

2. Go to the card named Main Menu, the one that lists the buttons Objective, Experience, etc.

*3. While the Main Menu card is shown, hold down the Shift key and choose **Card Info** from the Objects menu.*

> **Shortcut:** In version 1.2, you can press Command-Option-C to go directly to the card script.

Add this script to the card:

```
on openCard
  push card
end openCard
```

4. Click OK.

This script tells HyperCard to mark the Main Menu card for later retrieval whenever it appears on the screen. To retrieve this card, you'll need a script with the **Pop Card** command. This command is usually added to the script of a button such as the Return Arrow button. Next you'll create a Return Arrow button on the background and add a **Pop Card** command to its script.

*1. Choose **Background** from the Edit menu.*

*2. Choose **New Button** from the Objects menu. Double-click on the button to show the Button Info dialog box. Click on **transparent** for the button style. Click in the Show Name box to uncheck it. Then click on Icon to go to the Icon window.*

3. Choose a Return Arrow icon for its shape. Click OK.

4. Go directly to the script window by holding down the Shift key and double-clicking on the Return Arrow button.

*5. The **mouseUp** messages are already there with the insertion point positioned for you to type a command. Type **pop card** into the button's script. The script will look like this:*

```
on mouseUp
  pop card
end mouseUp
```

(You can also add a visual effect before the **Pop** command if you like.)

6. Click OK.

7. Press ⌘-B to get out of the background. Then drag the Right Arrow button to the bottom right of the card.

8. Press ⌘-Tab to choose the Browse tool so you can click on buttons again. Click on the Right Arrow button a few times to go to another card. Then click on the Return Arrow button to return to the Main Menu card.

(Pressing the Return Arrow button when the Main Menu card is displayed returns you to the previous card or stack popped with the Pop Card comments.)

Comment Lines

The double-hyphen in the script below is referred to as a **comment line**.

```
on mouseUp
  pop card    --go back to last card pushed
end mouseUp
```

Any line with two hyphens in front of it is a comment line and is ignored by HyperCard. You'll want to add comment lines to document why you added specific commands to a script or what a group of commands is supposed to do. That way, if you forget what the script was meant to do, the comment lines will remind you. Documenting your programs also helps others figure out your scripts so they can easily modify them.

Lesson 87: SEARCHING WITH LIMITS

You already know how to use the **Find** command to search for information. Now you'll learn some different ways to use the **Find** command in a script. When you choose **Find** from the Go menu, it searches all fields on all backgrounds in a stack for the characters you typed between the quotation marks. This command is so efficient that it not only finds the word but also finds any word that begins with those characters. For example, if you type **Find "John"** and the word **"Johnson"** is in a field in the stack, HyperCard will stop at Johnson too.

But with scripting, you can change how the **Find** command works. By adding some key words either before or after the word or characters you want to find, you can:

- Limit the search to a specific field.
- Limit the search to whole words, not parts of words.
- Expand the search to find those characters within any word.
- Expand the search to look for those characters in other stacks.

Go to the HyperCard Tips stack you created earlier to practice using the **Find** command to limit or expand a search.

Searching a Specific Field

By including the name or number of the field when using the **Find** command, you speed up the search time. (HyperCard doesn't bother searching any other field.)

For example, typing **Find "tip" in bkgnd field "category"** into the Message box tells HyperCard to search only the field named Category for the word *tip*.

Searching for a Whole Word

Using **word** with **Find** speeds up the search because HyperCard will look only for the whole word you specify. That prevents HyperCard from stopping in fields with words that only begin with those letters.

1. Go to the HyperCard Tips stack.
2. Add the words **do, double, down, use, cause, users,** and **mouse** in the description fields of this stack so you can complete the **Find** exercises in this lesson.
3. Press ⌘-M to display the Message box.
4. Type **Find word "do"** and press RETURN. HyperCard will not stop at any word that includes **do**, for example, **double** or **down**. If you type a word or phrase that includes a space, HyperCard ignores any letters following the space when you use the **Find word** command.

Shortcut: Press Shift-⌘-F to find a whole word.

> *Tip:* In version 1.2, you can use **Find whole "text"** instead of using **Find word "text"**. Use **Find whole** to find a word or phrase that matches exactly what you type between quotes, including spaces. For example, **Find whole "Apple Computer"** stops at any card with *Apple Computer* but doesn't stop when it finds only *Apple* or *Computer*.

Searching for Characters as Part of Any Word

Using **chars** with **Find** tells HyperCard to stop in any field that includes those characters within a word. If the characters you want to find include a space, HyperCard ignores any letters following the space.

1. Go to the stack named HyperCard Tips if it isn't already displayed.
2. Press ⌘-M to display the Message box.
3. Type **Find chars "use"** and press Return. HyperCard stops at any word that includes use as part of it, for example, mouse, cause, and users.

> *Tip:* In version 1.2, you can use **Find string <text>** instead of using **Find chars <text>**. Using **Find string** results in a faster search than **Find chars**. (Any group of characters in sequential order is a referred to as a **string**.) Use **Find string** to find a string that matches exactly what you type between quotes, including spaces.

Now that you know ways to limit a search, it's time to learn how to expand a search across more than one stack.

Lesson 88: USING QUOTES, VARIABLES, AND CONTAINERS

Before you can write a script that searches more than one stack, you must know how to use *variables* and *containers*.

Quotes

Always put quotation marks around text in scripts so that HyperCard recognizes what is text and what is not. When HyperCard sees quotes around text in a script, it doesn't mistake that text for a command, variable, or object.

Using Variables

A **variable** is a word or character that holds a value temporarily. The classic illustration of what a variable is occurs when two scientists get together and one says, "Now just for the sake of argument, let **x** equal 100..." In this case, **x** is the variable because its value is strictly arbitrary or, well, variable. The value of a variable changes as the conditions in a script change. For example, the word *total* is a variable in this command: **put field 1 + field 2 into total**. The contents of the variable "total" change as the contents in field 1 and field 2 change.

A variable name can be any name as long as it's not a HyperTalk command or other special word reserved for use by HyperTalk. All the words listed in Appendix B are HyperTalk words that you cannot use as variable names. Check Appendix B if you're not sure whether the name you want to use for a variable is a reserved word.

A variable name cannot include spaces or begin with a number or symbol. For example, **8temp** is not a variable. Neither is **#32** nor **VAR 32**.

Any letter of the alphabet can be a variable in HyperTalk, so right there you have 26 variables to choose from. Here are some examples of other words you can use as variables: **temp**, **rightword**, **anotherone**, **myname**, **myaddress**, **yrtodate**.

Putting Information into Containers

Containers are objects that contain information. The Message box and fields you create are containers.

Tip: Although they are not visible objects, variables are also referred to as **containers** in HyperCard because they contain information.

The **Put** command is used to put information into a container. For example, typing **put "hello" into message box** tells HyperCard to put the word *hello* into the message box. You'll practice putting words into the Message box next.

1. Open the HyperCard Tips stack if it isn't already open. Press ⌘-M to display the Message box.

2. Type **put "the message box is a container" into message box** *and press RETURN. See Figure 14.10.*

Tip: The Message box can be abbreviated as **msg**, **msg box**, **message**, **message box**, **message window**, and **msg window**. You can also add the word **the** in front of any name for the message box, for example, **the msg box**.

---

3. Select the words in the Message box by dragging the insertion point through them, and then type **put "every field is a container" into field "description"** *and press Return.*

When a container does not contain any words or characters, it contains a value called **empty**. You're probably very familiar with at least one of the uses of the concept of "empty" because that's basically how the **Clear** command works on a lot of Macintosh programs. Choosing **Clear** puts the "empty" value into something on the screen. In HyperCard, for

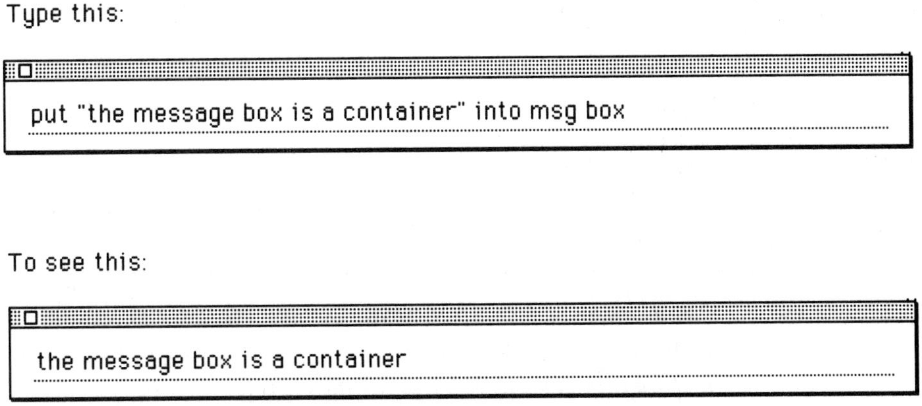

Type this:

```
put "the message box is a container" into msg box
```

To see this:

```
the message box is a container
```

Figure 14.10 You can use the **Put** command in the message box.

instance, if you put the "empty" value into the Message box, it is cleared of any other messages. You use the **Put** command for the job like this: type **put empty into the message box** and that does it.

Tip: You can type **put empty into field 1** to delete the contents of a field on a card. And you can command HyperCard to put numbers or letters into fields.

It and *Selection* as Containers

HyperCard also uses the words *It* and *Selection* as containers. The *It* variable contains information put there by one of several commands: **ask, ask password, answer, convert,** and **get**. You'll learn about the **Ask** and **Answer** commands in a later chapter. **Convert** is listed in Appendix B. For now, you'll learn how to use the **Get** command.

The Selection variable is used with the **Get** command to put any text you highlight into the variable *It*. For example, typing **get selection** will get a highlighted word and put that word into It. Then you can add a command that tells HyperCard what to do with the contents of It.

To get a better idea of how these commands and variables work, create a button that uses them in a script.

1. Go to the stack named HyperCard Tips if it isn't already displayed.

*2. Choose **NewButton** from the Objects menu. Double-click on the new button to display the Button Info dialog box. Type **Find** for the name of this button.*

3. Click on Script and type this script in the script window:

```
on mouseUp
  get selection
  find it
end mouseUp
```

4. Click OK.

5. Press ⌘-M to display the Message box. Then drag the Message box up so that it doesn't cover up the Find button.

*6. Type **tip** into the Message box and then highlight it, as in Figure 14.11, by dragging the insertion point through it.*

7. Click on the Find button. HyperCard finds and draws a box around the word tip.

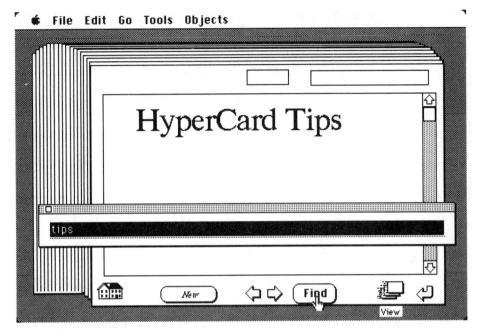

Figure 14.11 Highlight a word to find and click on the Find button.

*8. Press RETURN and you'll get an error message. Why? Because this script doesn't work the same way as choosing **Find** from the Go menu. With this script, you can find only the first occurrence of the selected word. So what good is it? Well, when used with other commands, a script like this can search several stacks until it finds the selected word or phrase. You'll learn about those other commands later in this chapter.*

To create a script that can search several stacks for one word, you'll need to know how to add variables and conditional statements to scripts. So take a moment now to learn about conditional statements.

Lesson 89: USING CONDITIONAL COMMANDS

Conditional Statements

"If you wash my car, then I'll give you $5.00" is a conditional statement. HyperCard understands conditional statements if you begin them with *if* and have a *then* somewhere in the statement like this:

```
if <the condition is true> then <do this>
```

Using **If** commands lets you control what HyperCard will do and when HyperCard will do it.

Using More than One Command with *If*

You can add an *else* statement after an **If-then** command to tell Hyper-Card what to do if the condition is not true, for example:

```
if field "category" = "Tip"
then put "It's a tip!" in the message box
else put "It's not a tip!" in the message box
```

You can also add more than one command following *else*. For instance, suppose you tell HyperCard to search through your address file to find the name "Colette." Well, you then have to tell HyperCard what to do: (1) if Colette is found and (2) if Colette isn't found. Here's a sample of the script with that conditional statement. Note that, if Colette isn't found, the message "not found" will appear *and* HyperCard goes to the first card in this stack.

```
if it is "Colette" then
  put "Found her!" in the message box
else
  put "not found" in the message box
  go to first card
end if
```

When you follow *then* or *else* with more than one command, you must include *end if* as the last line in this message; otherwise, the script won't work.

Using Functions with the If Statement

Using an If-Then statement, you can check for an error message by asking for **the result**. For instance, you might ask **if the result is empty** then do something else. This phrase, **the result**, is a HyperCard function. A **function** is a word or phrase that shows you either a number or a system variable, such as the time or the date. Functions provide information that you can use in commands or calculations, or display in a field, for example. You'll learn about different functions as you need them in the lessons in this book.

   The result function tells HyperCard whether there was an error with the command before it. If no error occurs, then the result is empty. So you can use this command to tell HyperCard to proceed if no errors have been made. For example, if you tell HyperCard to go to card 1000 and that card is not in the stack, nothing happens. To check for errors, you can write a script that tells HyperCard to display a **not found** message in the Message box when a specific card is not found. This particular script would look like this:

```
on mouseUp
  go card 1000
  if the result is not empty
  then put "not found" into the msg box
end mouseUp
```

Tip: You can press the Option and Return keys to extend a command to more than one line. The symbol that appears (¬) tells HyperCard to treat the next line as part of the previous command. You can connect as many lines as you like with this symbol. However, you cannot break a line in the middle of text enclosed in quotes.

Lesson 90: USING THE EXIT COMMAND

One command that's used often with **If** commands is **exit**. The **Exit** command tells HyperCard to exit the current script before reaching the End message. Use this command with a conditional command to stop executing the commands in a script under certain conditions. Doing so will speed up HyperCard because it can skip all the commands that follow the Exit message if the condition is true.

Example:

```
on mouseUp
    if card is "last one" then
      go to first card
      exit mouseUp
    else
      add prevtot to total
      go to next card
    end if
end mouseUp
```

Lesson 91: SEARCHING MORE THAN ONE STACK

Okay, now you can apply variables and conditionals to the button script to get it to search more than one stack:

Add a button to the HyperCard Tips stack that will search three stacks (the Tips stack, the Help stack, and the Address stack) for the word you highlight in any field.

*1. Choose **New Button** from the Objects menu.*

2. Double-click on the button. In the Button Info dialog box, name this button Search Stacks. Choose any button style you like. Then click Script. Type the script shown in Figure 14.12.

When you press Return, HyperCard indents the commands in the proper order. Note that each If statement has an associated *end if* with it only if there is more than one command following either *then* or *else*. If you forget an *end if* statement in this case, then your programming will contain an error. To check for enough *end if* statements, look at the alignment of the script text. **If** commands should be aligned with their associated *end if* statements. If they don't appear aligned, you may

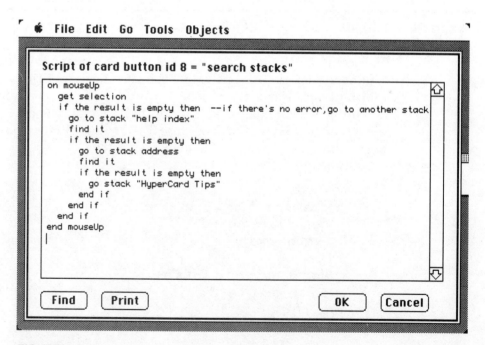

FIGURE 14.12 Script for Search Stacks button.

be missing an *end if* statement. You can tell at a glance if the script is not aligned and thus know if you've forgotten an *end if* statement.

Tip: While the script window is displayed, press the Tab key to align the commands.

---

3. Click OK.

*4. Press ⌘-Tab to choose the Browse tool. Then highlight a word to be found and click on the Search Stacks button. For practice, type the word **and** into the Message box, highlight it, and then click on the Search Stacks button. HyperCard will stop briefly on the first card with **and** in each stack listed in this script.*

This script is just one way to search stacks. You'll need to know a few more commands before you can write scripts that search more than one stack for every occurrence of the selected text. You'll learn how to do that in another chapter. As you learn other commands, you can add to or modify this script to meet your unique needs.

SUMMARY

You can write scripts for

- Stacks
- Backgrounds
- Cards
- Fields
- Buttons

Any object—a button, field, card, background, or stack—can have a script. A quick way to view or edit the script of a button or field is by choosing the appropriate tool (Button or Field tool), holding down the Shift key, and then double-clicking on the button or field.

To go directly to the script window of a card or background, display that card or background, hold down the Shift key, and choose **Card Info** or **Background Info** from the Objects menu. You can also go directly to a stack script by first opening the stack to edit, then holding down the Shift key and choosing **Stack Info** from the Objects menu.

HyperCard version 1.2 makes it even easier to display the scripts of objects. To see a button or field script, you simply hold down the Shift and Option keys and click once on the button or field of your choice. To see a card script, you press ⌘-Option-C. To see a background script, you press ⌘-Option-B. To see a stack script, you press ⌘-Option-S.

You learned how to create scripts that enable you to

- Create buttons for navigating through cards and between stacks.
- Add visual effects like **zoom open**.
- Find specific words or characters in one or more fields.
- Search more than one stack for a specific word.

You also learned how to use comment lines, variables and containers, functions, and conditional commands.

You can use the Message box to initiate a single HyperTalk command. But writing your own scripts gives you much greater control over Hyper-Card than using either the menu commands or the Message box. As you learn more commands, you'll see how to combine them with other commands to create more useful scripts.

15 What Goes Around, Comes Around

In this chapter, you'll learn how to make buttons flash, how to make check boxes work properly, and how to select one of a series of radio buttons. You'll also learn how to gain more control over when commands are executed and how to write scripts that can make decisions such as when to execute a command and when not to.

The lessons in this chapter show you how to

- Make cards flash to inverse video and back.
- Create flashing buttons.
- Add messages to open and close objects.
- Add messages to create or delete objects.
- Repeat commands several times.
- Pause for a few seconds between commands.
- Program check-box buttons.
- Program radio buttons.

with these commands:

flash
repeat
repeat until
repeat while
repeat with

     set

     wait

     open printing

     close printing

     doMenu

and these properties:

     textFont

     hilite

and these functions:

     number of cards

     the mouseClick

     the mouse

To complete the lessons in this chapter, you must set the user level to Scripting. Type **set the userlevel to 5** in the Message box to change the user level to Scripting.

Lesson 92: FLASHING CARDS

Go to your resume stack. You'll use it to practice the commands in this chapter. First, you'll learn how to make a card flash (that is, appear highlighted and then not highlighted several times).

There is a **Flash** command in HyperTalk. But it doesn't flash buttons, it only flashes cards. You can add the **Flash** command to any script and it will flash the card currently on the screen. Try it now.

1. Press ⌘-M to display the Message box.

*2. Type **flash 3** into the Message box and press RETURN. The card displayed on the screen will flash three times.*

You can also add this command to the stack script or card script to make the card flash automatically whenever you open the stack or display this card.

Flashing Only When the Stack Is First Opened

1. At the Resume stack, choose **Stack Info** *from the Objects menu.*

2. Click on the Script button to display the script window.

3. To make this card flash three times only when you open the stack, type the following into the stack script of your resume stack:

```
on openStack
   flash 3
end openStack
```

4. Click OK.

5. Now go to another stack, for example, go Home. Whenever you leave a stack, HyperCard closes it. So, going to the Home stack will close the Resume stack.

6. Choose **Go Back** *from the Go menu to open the Resume stack again so you can see the* **Flash** *command at work.*

Tip: It may seem natural to type the word *times* following the number in a Flash command, but do not do so or else this command won't work.

Flashing Each Time the Card Is Opened

1. Display the first card in your resume stack.

2. Choose **Card Info** *from the Objects menu.*

3. Click on the Script button to display the script window.

4. To make this card flash three times not only when you open the stack but each time you display this card, type the following into the card script of the first card in your resume stack:

```
on openCard
   flash 3
end openCard
```

5. Now click the Right Arrow button to go to another card. Then click the Left Arrow button to go back to the first card. The card flashes three times each time you open it.

You can use the **Flash** command only to flash cards. To make buttons flash, you don't use the **Flash** command or a visual effect. To make buttons flash, you use a HyperCard trick. The command you'll use is the **Set** command. You'll use it to set a button's highlight *property* to true or false (on or off). However, before getting to the actual script for the button-flashing trick, you need to know a few other things first.

What's a Property?

All objects in HyperCard have properties. A **property** is something the object owns. For example, each stack has a name, ID number, and script associated with it. These characteristics belong to the stack and therefore are the properties of that stack. When you choose **Stack Info** to look at information about a stack, each item listed is a property of that stack. The size of the stack and the free space (amount of space available but not being used in the stack) are also properties of that stack. (See Figure 15.1.)

Cards, backgrounds, fields, and buttons also have properties. Instead of covering every property now, you'll learn how setting a button property enables you to make buttons flash. You'll learn other properties as you go from lesson to lesson.

You've used the **Set** command before to change the textFont and textStyle of buttons in a previous chapter. You've also used the **Get** command to get highlighted text. You can use both of these commands to change the properties of an object.

Not all properties are listed on the information cards of each object. See the HyperCard Help Index stack for a list of object properties.

Using the **Set** Command with the Hilite Property to Flash Buttons

You'll use the **Set** command to change the value of a button's hilite property. Next, you'll make buttons flash:

- all the time
- a specific number of times
- when objects are opened, closed, created, or deleted

Each button has a name, ID number, order number, and script, as well as other properties that stacks and cards don't have: textStyle, textFont, textSize, style, location, hilite, and icon to name a few. These properties tell HyperCard what the button looks like.

The **hilite** property tells HyperCard whether the button is highlighted or not. You can set this property to true or false. Setting it to true tells

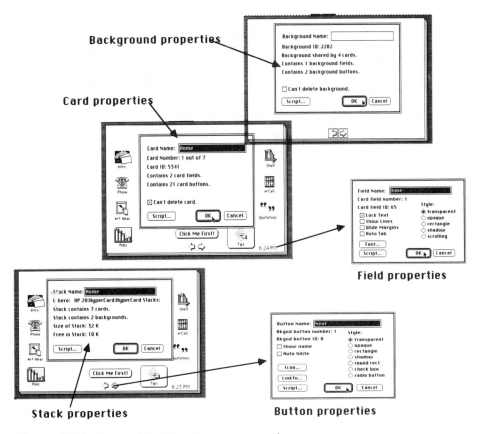

Figure 15.1   Every object has its own properties.

HyperCard that the button is highlighted. False means the button is not highlighted. Besides setting it to true or false, you can also change it to the opposite of its current highlight state. You'll use the hilite property to make the button appear to flash.

Auto hilite (Figure 15.2) is also a button property. You can set this property by choosing **Auto hilite** in the Button Info dialog box. Then the button will highlight each time you click it. You don't have to write a script for that button if that's all you want it to do.

Practice setting the hilite property of the background button named Next on your resume stack:

1. Press ⌘-M to display the Message box. Then move the Message box up and out of the way so it isn't covering up the buttons along the bottom of the card.

2. Type **set hilite of bkgnd button "Next" to true**. *Press RETURN. The button appears inverted (black with white letters).*

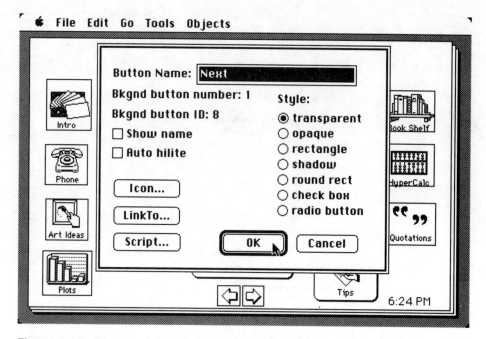

Figure 15.2 The auto hilite choice in the Button Info dialog box is a property.

3. Highlight the word true *and change it to* false. *Press RETURN. The button changes back to black letters on white.*

Instead of setting the button to true and then false, you can tell HyperCard to set the hilite property of a button to the opposite of its current state (that is, turn it on if it's off and turn it off if it's on). That way, you don't have to keep track of whether it's currently highlighted or not.

1. Choose the Button tool on the Tools menu.

2. Hold down the Shift key and double-click on the Right Arrow button to display its script window.

3. Position the insertion point after the command **go to next card** *and press RETURN to add a blank line. Then type the* **Set** *command as shown below:*

```
on mouseUp
  go to next card
  set the hilite of bkgnd button "Next" to not hilite of¬
    bkgnd button
"Next"
end mouseUp
```

4. Click OK. **Not** *tells HyperCard to turn the hilite property of the button off if it was on or on if it was off.*

5. Press ⌘-Tab to choose the Browse tool. Click on the button to highlight it. Click it on again to turn the highlighting off.

When Should HyperCard Set the Property?

Besides adding a **Set** command to a script, you must tell HyperCard *when to execute it.* For example, the **on mouseUp** message in the previous script tells HyperCard to set the hilite property when you click the right arrow button.

You don't always have to use the mouse to send messages to HyperCard. You can also tell HyperCard to execute commands whenever an object is opened or closed.

When Opening or Closing Objects

All objects (stacks, cards, backgrounds, and fields) *except buttons* can be *opened* or *closed*. Opening a stack, background, or card means showing it on the screen. Opening a field means moving the insertion point into it. When you open an object, HyperCard looks for a corresponding **openStack**, **openBackground**, **openCard**, or **openField** message. You've already used some of these messages in previous lessons. For example, you added this script to a card to make the card flash three times every time it was opened:

```
on openCard
  flash 3
end openCard
```

Closing a stack, card, or background means either quitting HyperCard or going to another stack, background, or card. Closing a field means moving the insertion point out of it after changing its contents.

Just before you go to another stack, HyperCard looks for a **closeStack** message. When you go to another card, HyperCard looks for a **closeCard** message. And, when you move the insertion point out of a field after changing its contents, HyperCard looks for a **closeField** message.

You can tell HyperCard to do something whenever an object is opened or closed by adding an Open or Close message to that script.

If you add this script to a card, the button named Next changes from highlighted to not highlighted or vice versa once each time the card is shown:

```
on openCard
  set hilite of button "Next" to not hilite of button
```

```
"Next"
end openCard
```

When Creating or Deleting Objects

Objects can also be created or deleted. And you can tell HyperCard to execute commands when an object is created or deleted. All the Open, Close, Create, and Delete messages are listed in Table 15.1.

Idle

Idle means that nothing is happening. Nothing is being clicked on, opened, closed, executed, etc. An Idle message tells HyperCard "when nothing is happening, I want you to do this." Idle messages are sent to a card only when no other message is being sent.

```
on idle
  put time into field "current time"
end idle
```

```
on idle
  wait 10 seconds
  go to first card
end idle
```

Tip: Keep in mind that Idle messages are sent to cards, not to buttons or fields. You can add Idle messages to card, background, or stack scripts only.

Stacks:	openStack, closeStack, newStack
Backgrounds:	openBackground, closeBackground, newBackground, deleteBackground
Cards:	openCard, closeCard, newCard, deleteCard
Fields:	openField, closeField, newField, deleteField
Buttons:	newButton, deleteButton

Table 15.1 Open, Close, New, and Delete messages.

So you've finally arrived at the message needed to use with the **Set** command to make buttons flash all the time—**on idle**!

Flashing All the Time

Since the Right Arrow button is a background button, you'll add the **on idle** message to the background script.

*1. Choose **Background Info** from the Objects menu.*

2. Click on Script.

3. Type this script in the window:

```
on idle
   set hilite of bkgnd button "Next" to not hilite of¬
      bkgnd button "Next"
end idle
```

4. Click OK.

This script tells HyperCard that, while nothing else is happening in the stack, turn the highlight property of the button named Next on and off.

The Right Arrow button is now blinking.

Flashing A Specific Number of Times

When you use conditional statements, HyperCard evaluates the condition to be either true or false. If it's true, then the commands that follow the condition are executed. If it's false, they are ignored. True and false are constants—values that never change.

You can set the hilite property to true or false. When you set the hilite of a button to true, it always means to highlight the button. False always means to unhighlight it.

Suppose you want the Right Arrow button to flash three times to draw attention when you first open the stack. To do so, you'd add these lines to the stack script:

```
on openStack
   set hilite of bkgnd button "Next" to true
   set hilite of bkgnd button "Next" to false
   set hilite of bkgnd button "Next" to true
   set hilite of bkgnd button "Next" to false
   set hilite of bkgnd button "Next" to true
   set hilite of bkgnd button "Next" to false
end openStack
```

What if you wanted the button to flash 10 times? You could type **set hilite of bkgnd button "Next" to true** 10 times as well as setting it to false 10 times. But, as with other programming languages, there is a more efficient method for doing this—the **Repeat** command.

You can use the **Repeat** command to repeat a command or group of commands several times. You'll do that next.

Lesson 93: REPEATING COMMANDS IN A SCRIPT

You can either repeat commands a specific number of times, or you can repeat them while some condition is true. The **Repeat** command has four different formats you can use:

- Repeat for
- Repeat while
- Repeat until
- Repeat with

Repeat For

This command lets you choose how many times you want the commands repeated.

For example, if you want to repeat a flashing procedure 10 times, you could use this Repeat command instead of typing the commands 10 times:

```
on openCard
  repeat for 10 times
    set hilite of bkgnd button "Next" to true
    set hilite of bkgnd button "Next" to false
  end repeat
end openCard
```

You don't have to use the word *for* in this kind of loop. **Repeat 10 times** will work just as well. Or just **repeat 10**. Figure 15.3 illustrates the mechanics of a repeat loop.

Tip: Using the **Repeat** command saves you time when writing scripts. It also makes it easier to read scripts because you won't have as many lines to read. And, because HyperCard won't have as many lines to read and interpret, it speeds up the execution of a script.

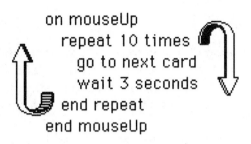

```
on mouseUp
   repeat 10 times
      go to next card
      wait 3 seconds
   end repeat
end mouseUp
```

Figure 15.3 A repeat loop.

Creating a Browse Button

Here is the script attached to a Browse or View button:

```
on mouseUp
   show all cards
end mouseUp
```

This button script tells HyperCard to flip through all the cards in the stack once, showing each card for about 1 second.

Suppose you want to show each card every 5 seconds. You can use the **Repeat** command to specify how many cards HyperCard is to show and for how long. All you need to do is add **number of cards times** following the **Repeat** command. The phrase **number of cards** is another HyperTalk function. As you recall from the previous chapter, functions are words or phrases that provide information. This function keeps track of how many cards are in a stack. Instead of counting the cards yourself, you can retrieve this information by typing **number of cards** into a script or even into the Message box.

To create a Browse button that shows each card in a stack for five seconds, add this to its button script:

```
on mouseUp
   repeat number of cards times
      show card
      wait 5 seconds
   end repeat
end mouseUp
```

Tip: In version 1.2, you can get the number of cards in a specific background instead of asking for all cards in a stack. For example, you can type **number of cards of background 1** to show or print all cards with that background only.

Repeat With

The **Repeat With** command is followed by a variable that changes in value each time the repeat procedure goes from an **end repeat** back to a **repeat**. This variable is usually used in place of a specific card number or field number. Each time the command is repeated, HyperCard adds 1 to the variable.

Suppose you have a stack with several fields full of outdated information. You want to enter new information into those fields without taking the time to delete the contents of each field one at a time. You can write a simple script that clears all the fields for you by using a **Repeat** command. For example, this button script will empty the contents of each background field on every card with the current background:

```
on mouseUp
  repeat with x = 1 to the number of bkgnd fields
    put empty into bkgnd field x
  end repeat
end mouseUp
```

The variable **x** begins with a value of 1. The **Put** command then empties the contents of background field 1. Then HyperCard adds 1 to **x** and **x** becomes 2. The **Put** command then empties the contents of background field 2. This process continues until the last background field has been emptied.

When using this repeat structure, you'll normally refer to objects by number so that, as the variable changes, the commands affect a different object.

The difference between using a **Repeat** command and not using a **Repeat** command is apparent in the following two scripts. Each script gives you the same result. Example 2, however, is faster and more efficient than example 1.

Example 1:

```
on openCard
  set hilite of button 1 to true
  set hilite of button 2 to true
  set hilite of button 3 to true
  set hilite of button 4 to true
  set hilite of button 5 to true
end openCard
```

Example 2:

```
on openCard
  repeat with i = 1 to 5
```

```
      set hilite of button i to true
    end repeat
  end openCard
```

In addition to incrementing the value of the variable by 1, you can reduce or *decrement* the value of the variable by 1. Suppose you want a field to show a countdown from 10 to 1. To do so, add this script to a card:

```
on openCard
  repeat with x = 10 downTo 1
    put x into field 1
    wait 2 seconds
  end repeat
  go to next card
end openCard
```

Besides repeating one or more commands a specific number of times, you can also repeat them while a certain condition is true or until a certain condition is false. You'll do that next.

One thing you must be sure of when using these kinds of repeat loops is that the condition will eventually be true or false so HyperCard will stop repeating the commands. Otherwise, you'll end up with what's called an **infinite loop**. It repeats the commands forever or until you press ⌘-. (period) to stop the script.

Tip: If you use **repeat** by itself, the commands between **on repeat** and **end repeat** will keep on repeating until you either press ⌘-. or you quit HyperCard. This situation is known affectionately in programming as an infinite loop.

Repeat Until

Another variation on the **Repeat** command lets you specify a condition under which HyperCard is to stop repeating the commands between **repeat** and **end repeat**.

This kind of repeat loop is used when you want the commands to be repeated until something happens—for example, until you click the mouse or press a key.

To indicate to HyperCard whether the mouse button has been pressed, you'll need to add a function named the **mouseClick** to the

Repeat command. This script tells HyperCard to show each card in the stack until you click the mouse:

```
on openStack
  repeat until the mouseClick
    show all cards
  end repeat
  go demo B
end openStack
```

This script could be used to display a sales demo that ran continually until someone clicked the mouse. Then, when the mouse was clicked, HyperCard would go to the stack named demo B.

Repeat While

This command does just the opposite of the **Repeat Until** command. It repeats these commands as long as the condition is true. The condition could be that the mouse is being held down, or it could be that a variable is not equal to 100, for example.

The mouse is a function, like the mouseClick. The mouse function tells HyperCard whether the mouse is up or down, depending on whether you're holding the mouse button down or not.

To indicate to HyperCard whether the mouse button is being pressed, you'll need to add the function **the mouse** to the Repeat command. This script tells HyperCard to display the words "Let go!" in the Message box while the mouse button is being held down:

```
on mouseDown
  repeat while the mouse is down
    show message box
    put "Let go!" into msg box
    wait 2 seconds
    put empty into msg box
  end repeat
end mouseDown
```

Lesson 94:   WAITING FOR SOMETHING TO HAPPEN

The **Wait** command tells HyperCard to pause before executing the command that follows **Wait**. You can add a **Wait** command anywhere you like in a script. You can follow the **Wait** command by a number of seconds or ticks and the word **seconds** or **ticks**. A tick is approximately 1/60 of a second, but this varies depending on whether you're using a Macintosh Plus, Macintosh SE, or Macintosh II. If you don't add **seconds** or **ticks** following the number, HyperTalk assumes you mean **ticks**.

You can also follow **Wait** with either **while** or **until** to tell HyperCard to wait while some condition is true or until some condition is true. For example, this script waits until someone presses down on the mouse button before executing the commands that follow **Wait**:

```
wait until the mouse is down
```

Conversely, this script pauses while you hold down the mouse button and continues after you've released the mouse button:

```
wait while the mouse is down
```

Usually, you'll use the **Wait** command to slow down some process. In the following script, the **Wait** command makes HyperCard pause for 3 seconds before showing the next card:

```
on mouseUp
  repeat with i = 1 to the number of cards
    show card i
    wait 3 seconds
  end repeat
end mouseUp
```

When automating cards one after the other, as in the script of a Browse button or in an animated sequence, you'll want to control how quickly one card is displayed after another. The **Wait** command gives you that control.

Tip: In versions 1.0.1 and 1.1, HyperCard could not understand the word *second*. It only understood the plural of this word—seconds. So, if you wanted HyperCard to wait 1 second, you had to type **wait 1 seconds**. This bug has been corrected in version 1.2, so now you can type **wait 1 second**.

Lesson 95: TURNING CHECK-BOX BUTTONS ON AND OFF

A Check-Box button is a button style that contains a box that you can click in to select it. You can tell when the button is selected because an

x appears within its box. When you click in it again, the **x** disappears, indicating the button is unselected.

Check boxes (Figure 15.4) are used to select more than one choice at a time. Radio buttons are used when you can have one choice or the other, but not both. For example, in the Button Info dialog box, the Radio button is for choosing only one button style, but the Check box is for choosing either or both of the options: Auto hilite and Show name.

Choosing **Auto hilite** in the Button Info dialog box is all you need to do to make Check-box buttons work properly. Remember, if you want to highlight these buttons from anywhere other than in the button script, you'll need to know how to change the hilite property of the buttons. So, instead of just choosing Auto hilite, you'll learn how to write scripts that control Check-box buttons.

To make the **x** appear, set the hilite property of a Check-box button to true. To make the **x** disappear, set its hilite property to false. (See Figure 15.5.)

You've already learned a more efficient way to write a script that turns a button on when it's off and off when it's on—set hilite of button <name or number> to not hilite of button <name or number>. Next you'll learn a variation of that script.

Me

HyperCard has a special variable named **me** that you can use in place of a button's name or number when writing a button script. **Me** refers

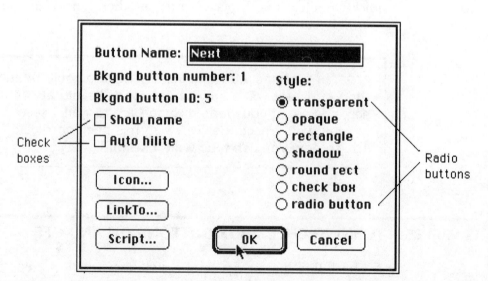

Figure 15.4 Check boxes turn features on and off. Radio buttons give you choices.

to the name of the object to which the script is attached. So, **me** in a button's script is the name of that button, whereas **me** in a card's script is the name of that card. Using **me** is quicker and easier because you don't have to remember the name or number of the object as well as whether it's a background or card object.

> *Tip:* In version 1.2, **Me** can also refer to a container such as a field.

You'll use **me** in the script of a check-box button. To create a check box, follow these steps:

*1. Choose **New Button** from the Objects menu.*

2. Double-click on the new button.

*3. Choose **check box** for the button style.*

4. Click on Script. Then type this script:

```
on mouseUp
   set the hilite of me to not the hilite of me
end mouseUp
```

5. Click OK.

6. Switch to the Browse tool and click on the check box to see the effect.

Because Check-box buttons are used to toggle features on and off, you can follow the **Set** command with a conditional command that tells HyperCard what to do if the box is checked (toggled on) and what to do if it's not checked (toggled off). For example, this script tells HyperCard to go to card 3 if the box is checked (true) or go to card 10 if it's unchecked (false):

```
on mouseUp
   set the hilite of me to not the hilite of me
```

☒ **True**

☐ **False**

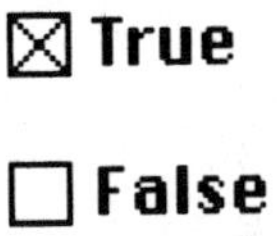

Figure 15.5 If the hilite property is true, an **x** appears in the check box. If it is false, the **x** does not appear.

```
      if it is true then go card 3
      if it is false then go card 10
   end mouseUp
```

Lesson 96: SELECTING FROM RADIO BUTTONS

Use Radio buttons to select one of a number of buttons. You can choose **Auto hilite** in a button's Button Info dialog box to make a black spot appear in the center of the button when it has been selected. But clicking on one Radio button does not automatically unselect the others. You have to tell HyperCard to do the "unselecting."

Thus, highlighting one Radio button while unhighlighting all the other Radio buttons in a set requires some scripting. If you have three Radio buttons on a background card (numbered from 1 to 3), adding this script to the first button highlights the first button when you click on it (see Figure 15.6) and unhighlights the other two:

```
on mouseUp
   set hilite of bkgnd button 1 to true
   set hilite of bkgnd button 2 to false
   set hilite of bkgnd button 3 to false
   go to card 3
end mouseUp
```

You'll also need to write a script for the second (Figure 15.7) and third (Figure 15.8) buttons to tell HyperCard what to do when you click on either one of them. The second button would have this script:

```
on mouseUp
   set hilite of bkgnd button 1 to false
   set hilite of bkgnd button 2 to true
   set hilite of bkgnd button 3 to false
   go to card 4
end mouseUp
```

The third button would have this script:

```
on mouseUp
   set hilite of bkgnd button 1 to false
   set hilite of bkgnd button 2 to false
   set hilite of bkgnd button 3 to true
   go to card 5
end mouseUp
```

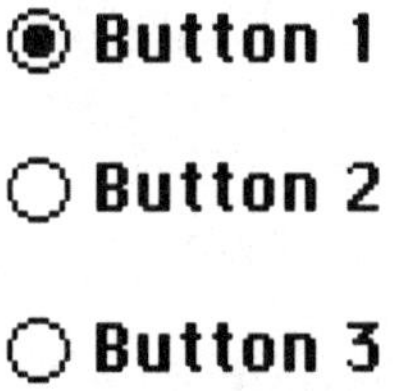

◉ **Button 1**

○ **Button 2**

○ **Button 3**

Figure 15.6 The result of clicking on the first Radio button.

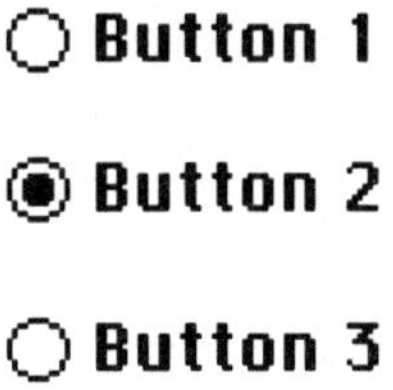

○ **Button 1**

◉ **Button 2**

○ **Button 3**

Figure 15.7 The result of choosing Button 2.

○ **Button 1**

○ **Button 2**

◉ **Button 3**

Figure 15.8 The result of choosing Button 3.

SUMMARY

In this chapter, you learned how to make objects flash. You also learned about properties and how to set them. Properties are characteristics that identify an object. Each object has different kinds of properties associated with it.

The hilite property is a button property. No other object has a hilite property. You can use the **Set** command to make a button appear highlighted or unhighlighted. Using an **idle** message with the **Set** command and hilite property enables you to create flashing buttons.

Using a **Repeat** command, you can write a script that executes commands a number of times. The **Repeat** command has four different formats from which to choose. You learned how and when to use each form. **Repeat** commands save you time by repeating instructions a specific number of times or under certain conditions. Now that you know how to use this command, the lessons that follow will take advantage of your knowledge.

You also learned about the **Wait** command. This command is often used with the **Repeat** command to pause so many seconds before continuing with the commands in a repeat loop.

Finally, you learned how easy it is to program Check-box and Radio buttons.

In the next chapter, you'll learn how to automate other tasks with HyperCard and how to make objects appear and disappear.

16 Now You See it, Now You Don't

In this chapter, you'll learn how to write scripts commonly associated with fields.

The lessons in this chapter show you how to

- Display the current time in a field.
- Put the current date into an updated field.
- Renumber cards when new cards are added.
- Make HyperCard respond to the location of the pointer.
- Show and hide buttons, fields, and pictures.
- Create pop-up fields.

You'll learn how to use these commands:

pass
show
hide

and these properties:

visible
lockscreen

and these functions:

the time
the date

To complete the lessons in this chapter, you must set the user level to Scripting. Type **set the userlevel to 5** in the Message box to change the user level to Scripting.

Lesson 97:   DISPLAYING THE CURRENT TIME IN A FIELD

You can write a script that puts the current time into a field continuously or only when something else has happened, such as when you've clicked on a button.

Looking at the Card Script for the Home Card

A field on your Home card displays the current time continuously. The script that puts the time in that field is a card script. Look at that script now.

1. Choose **Home** *from the Go menu. You'll look at the script created for the Home card.*

2. Choose **Card Info...** *from the Objects menu.*

3. Click on **Script...** *to see the script for this card. This script tells HyperCard to display the current time in the field named Time when this card is displayed and nothing else is happening.*

```
on idle
   put the time into card field "time"
   pass idle
end idle
```

The Time is a function. It returns the current time as shown on your Macintosh internal clock. To set this clock, choose the Alarm Clock desk accessory from the menu. Then click once on the switch to the right of the AM/PM. Click on the clock, then click on the numbers for the current hour. Up and down arrows appear to the right of the time. Click on the up arrow to set the time ahead one hour, or click on the down arrow to set the time back one hour. Do the same for the minutes and seconds if necessary.

The **Pass** command in this script tells HyperCard that, besides the card script, there may also be an Idle message tracked by this stack script.

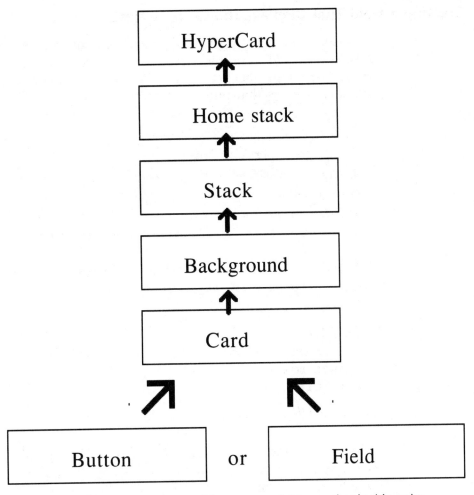

Figure 16.1 Messages are passed from one script to another in this order.

HyperTalk commands are automatically passed from a button or field to a card, then to a background, stack, the Home stack, and then to HyperCard itself, as in Figure 16.1.

Once the message is received, however, the commands following it are executed but HyperCard looks no further for any more of the same kind of messages. For example, once HyperCard does the **on idle** message in the card script, it won't look in any other script for another **on idle** message unless it sees a **Pass idle** command. So, if you did have an **on idle** message in your stack script as well, HyperCard would never see it.

4. Click OK.

Creating a Field That Displays the Current Time

To display the current time in a card field, all you need to do is create a field and add a simple script to the card. For practice, go to the HyperCard Tips stack, create a field named Time on the first card, and add a card script that puts the current time into the Time field.

1. Press ⌘-M to display the Message box.

2. Type **go HyperCard Tips** *and press Return.*

3. Create a new field on the first card in this stack. Choose **shadow** *for the field style, and name this field Time. Click OK.*

4. Resize this field so that it has only one line. Move this field to an out-of-the-way location on your card. For example, move it to the upper left corner of the card.

5. Hold down the Shift key and choose **Card Info...** *from the Objects menu to go directly to the script window for the current card.*

6. Type this script into the window:

```
on idle
  put the time into card field "time"
  pass idle
end idle
```

7. Click OK.

The current time, as determined by the setting on the Macintosh internal clock, appears in the new field (see Figure 16.2). Since you added this field to the card and not its background, the time will be shown only on the first card.

Keeping Track of Time Spent on the Telephone

To put the time into a field only under certain conditions, specify those conditions using an **If** command. Next, you'll create a stack you can use to keep track of each telephone conversation you have.

1. Go to the Home card. Choose **New Stack** *from the File menu. You'll copy the background of the Home stack for this new stack. Name this stack Phone Calls.*

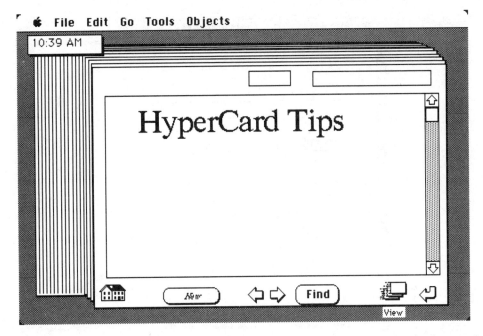

Figure 16.2 You can display the current time in a field on any card or background.

2. Press ⌘-B to display the background. Create two fields on this background. Name one field Start Time. Choose **Rectangle** *for the field style. Name the other field Stop Time. Resize and position these fields on the background.*

3. Create two buttons on the background. Name the first button Start and the second button Stop. Resize and position the start button below the field named Start Time. Resize and position the stop button below the field named Stop Time.

Figure 16.3 shows background fields and buttons for the start and stop times.

4. Add this script to the button named Start:

```
on mouseUp
    put the time into background field "start time"
end mouseUp
```

5. Click OK. Now, when you click on the button named Start, HyperCard will put the current time into the background field named Start Time.

6. Add this script to the Stop button:

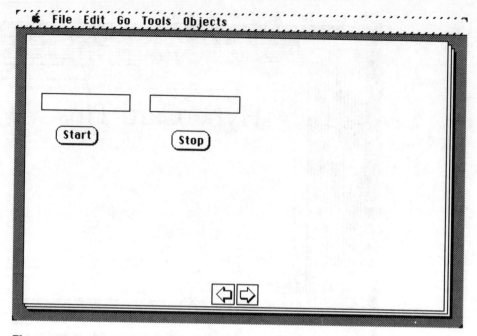

Figure 16.3 Add background fields and buttons for the start and stop times.

```
on mouseUp
  put the time into background field "stop time"
end mouseUp
```

7. Click OK.

8. Now test it by clicking on the Start button. Wait at least one minute and then click on the stop button. That's it!

These buttons, as Figure 16.4 shows, help you keep track of the time you spend on the telephone.

This script is useful for recording when you start and stop a telephone conversation with a client. If you charge an hourly rate, it helps you accurately record how much time to bill to each client.

Tip: If you created these fields on a card instead of its background, be sure to type **card field** instead of **background field** or these scripts won't work. For example, you'd type **put the time into card field "start time"**.

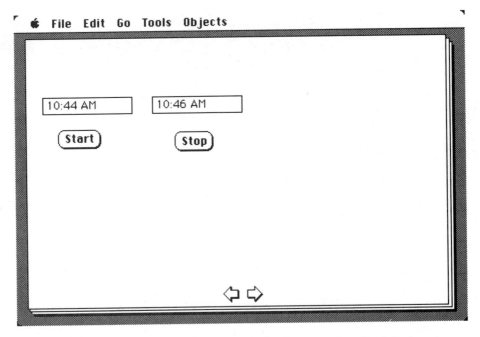

Figure 16.4 These buttons help you track the time spent on the telephone.

Lesson 98: PUTTING TODAY'S DATE IN UPDATED CARDS

In this lesson, you'll create a new background field in the HyperCard Tips stack. Then you'll write a script that tells HyperCard to put today's date in that field only when the card has been updated.

1. Type **go to HyperCard tips** *into the Message box, and press Return.*

2. Press ⌘-B to display the background. You'll add a field to this background.

3. Choose **New field** *from the Objects menu. Press ⌘-M to close the Message box so it's not in the way.*

4. Double-click on this field to see the Field Info dialog box. Type **date** *for the name of this field, and choose* **opaque** *for the field style. Then click OK.*

5. Resize the field and drag it to the bottom center of the card as shown in Figure 16.5.

Since this field is on the background, you'll add a background script that tells HyperCard to put today's date in the background field "date" whenever a card is updated. Whenever you make a change in any field

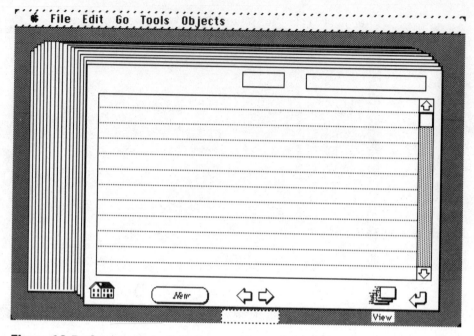

Figure 16.5 Create a Date field on your HyperCard Tips stack.

on any card with this background, HyperCard puts the current date, as
set in the Macintosh internal clock, into that field.

*6. Choose **Bkgnd Info...** from the Objects menu. Then click on Script to display
the script window.*

7. Type the following script:

```
on closeField
  put the date into field "date"
end closeField
```

This script tells HyperCard to change the date in the Date field whenever the contents of any field on this card has been changed. (The **close-
Field** message is sent to a field when you move the insertion point out
of a field after changing its contents.)

8. Click OK.

*9. Press ⌘-Tab to choose the Browse tool. Click on the Right Arrow button
once to go to the next card. Then type information in any field on any card in
this stack. (In Figure 16.6, the second paragraph is new information added to
the Description field.)*

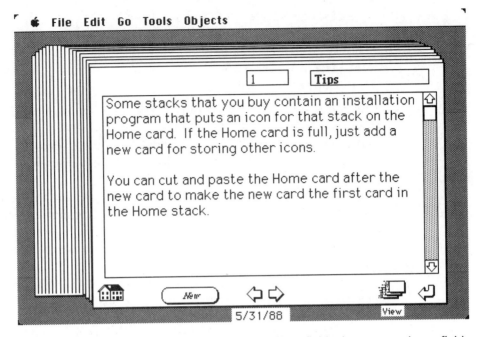

Figure 16.6 The current date appears in the Date field when you update a field.

10. Now press the Tab key to move to another field. Notice that today's date appeared in the date field.

Lesson 99: NUMBERING CARDS AUTOMATICALLY

Looking at a Script That Assigns a Number to Each New Card

The script for the button named New in the HyperCard Tips stack you created earlier shows one way to number each card added to a stack. Look at this script now.

1. Choose the Button tool.

2. Hold down the Shift key and double-click on the New button. It's script looks like this:

```
on mouseUp
   set lockscreen to true
   go to last card
   get field "Index Number"
   doMenu "New Card"
```

```
set lockscreen to false
put it + 1 into field "Index Number"
choose browse tool
click at 100,100
end mouseUp
```

Lockscreen is a card property. You can set this property to either true or false. When you set it to true, the card shown is locked or frozen on the screen while other commands are being executed. When you set **lockscreen** to false, the card is unlocked from the screen, enabling other cards to be displayed.

Use the lockscreen property to freeze a card on the screen so other commands can be done "behind the scenes." **Lockscreen** makes activities invisible to prevent those who use your stack from becoming confused or distracted by cards appearing and disappearing on the screen as a series of commands is executed.

So, while you're looking at a single card "frozen" on the screen, here's what that card script will do: go to the last card, put the number in the Index Number field into the variable It, add a new card following the last card, and then unlock the screen. After unlocking the screen, HyperCard adds 1 to It and puts that number in the Index Number field of the new card, then the insertion point is put into the next field, which has a location of 100,100 on the card. (You'll learn about the **Choose** and **Click** commands later.)

This script does not renumber cards. It only adds a new card after the last card in the stack and adds a number to the Index field that is 1 greater than the card before it. So, if you deleted a card anywhere in this stack, the numbering scheme would be all wrong. To correct this problem, next you'll learn how to write a script that automatically renumbers all cards whenever a new card is added or an existing card is deleted from this stack.

3. Since you'll be creating a new script that renumbers these cards for you, you won't need this script to do that. Delete all but the commands shown in Figure 16.7 from the button script:

4. Click OK.

Tip: HyperCard version 1.2 has two new commands you can use to lock and unlock the screen. They are simply "lock screen" and "unlock screen." You can use these commands instead of setting the lockScreen card property to true and then false.

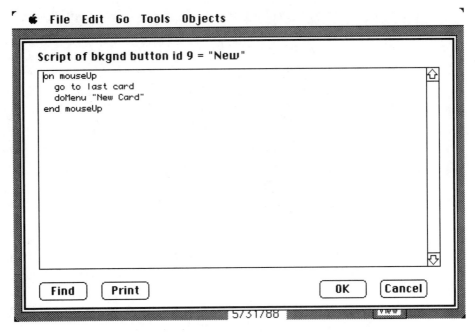

Figure 16.7 Revised script for the button named New.

Lock Screen is equivalent to setting lockScreen to true. Unlock Screen is equivalent to setting lockScreen to false. Each Lock Screen command must have a corresponding Unlock Screen command. In addition, you can add one visual effect after the Unlock Screen command as follows: unlock screen with visual dissolve.

Write a Script that Automatically Renumbers All Cards in a Stack

You'll add one more background field to the HyperCard Tips stack, next to the Index Number field. The Index Number field will contain the order number of the card as it appears in the stack. The new field will contain the total number of cards in this stack. You'll also add the word "card" before the Index Number field and the word "of" between that field and the new field.

*1. Choose **Background** from the Edit menu.*

2. Double-click on the Text tool in the Tools menu to choose the Text tool and *go directly to the Text Style dialog box. Choose **Bold**, **Times**, and **12 point** for the text. Then click OK.*

*3. Position the insertion point in the upper left corner of the card and type **Card**. Press the space bar 10 times to insert 10 spaces, then type **of**.*

*4. Choose the Field tool and click once on the Index Number field to select it. Then drag it between the words **Card** and **of** which you just typed. Resize that field so it fits between the words as shown in Figure 16.8.*

*5. Choose **New field** from the Objects menu. Resize the field and drag it to the right of the word "of" as in Figure 16.9.*

*6. Choose **Field Info...** from the Objects menu. Type **total** for the name of this field. Then click OK.*

Next you'll write a stack script that tells HyperCard to put the total number of cards into the new field "total" and then renumber all the cards in the stack each time you add a card to this stack.

*7. Choose **Stack Info...** from the Objects menu. Click on **Script...** in the Stack Info box to see the script window.*

*8. Add the script in Figure 16.10 below the **end openStack** message.*

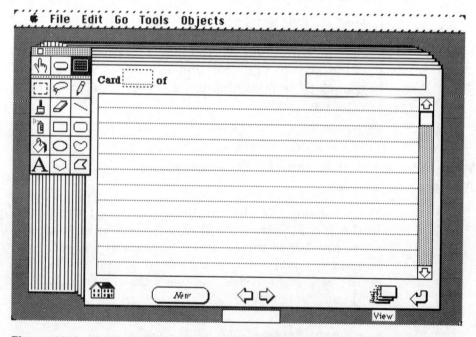

Figure 16.8 Move the Index Number field between the words you typed.

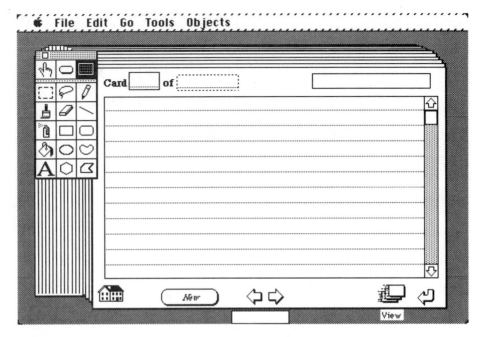

Figure 16.9 Create a field in which to display the total number of cards.

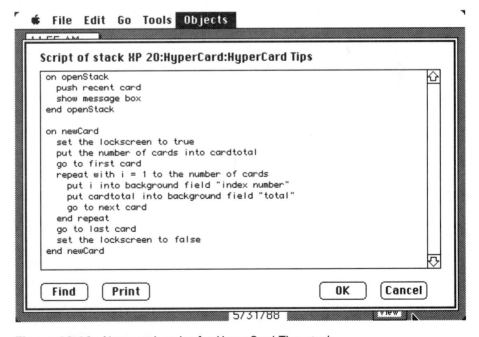

Figure 16.10 New stack script for HyperCard Tips stack.

9. Click once on the button named New to add a new card to this stack. Notice that HyperCard automatically numbers every card in this stack.

This script automatically renumbers every card in this stack whenever a new card has been added. Whether you choose **New Card** from the Edit menu or click on the New button, HyperCard adds a new card to the stack. Then it looks for a **newCard** message. The script beginning **on newCard** is then executed.

You would think that the **deleteCard** message works the same way. But it doesn't. In fact, it works the opposite way. When you choose **Delete Card** from the Edit menu, HyperCard first looks for a **deleteCard** message, executes the commands following it, and then deletes the card.

So, adding a similar script using **deleteCard** instead of **newCard** will renumber the cards *before* the card has been deleted. All the numbering would be wrong then. The following script is the trick you need in order to have HyperCard renumber the cards *after* a card has been deleted. You can either add a new card and then delete that new card, or create a background button with this script:

```
on mouseUp
  set lockscreen to true
  doMenu Delete Card  -- delete the card shown on the
    screen
  go to last card  -- go to the last card in this stack
  doMenu New Card  -- add a new card to trigger the
    script
  doMenu Delete Card  -- delete the new card
  set lockscreen to false
end mouseUp
```

Instead of choosing **Delete Card** from the Edit menu to delete a card, click on this button both to delete a card and consequently renumber the cards. This script works only if you also add the stack script with **on newCard** in the previous example.

How to Get Information from a Field

Each word you type into a field is referred to as a *word* in HyperTalk. You can get any word from any field by noting its position in the field. Is it the first word, fifth word, or last word?

*1. Type **This is just an example of "programming with HyperCard."** into the description field of the HyperCard Tips stack.*

2. Press ⌘-M to display the Message box.

3. To get the fifth word in this field, type **get word 5 of field "description"** *into the Message box and press Return. HyperCard puts word 5 into the variable named It. To see the result, type* **put it into msg box** *and press Return.*

4. The word **example** *appears in the Message box.*

5. Type **get word 7 of field "description"** *into the Message box and press Return. To see the result, type* **put it into msg box** *and press Return.*

*6. Instead of the seventh word (***programming***), the words* **programming with HyperCard** *appear in the Message box! That's because text between quotes is treated as one word in HyperCard (see Figure 16.11).*

Tip: Remember that text you get with the **Get** command is automatically put into the variable named It. In a script, you'll almost always follow a **Get** command with a **Put** command that tells HyperCard where to put the contents of It.

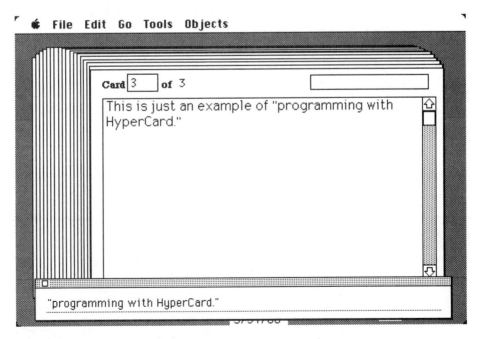

Figure 16.11 Text between quotation marks is treated as one word.

Words that are separated by commas are known as **items**. For example, the following field has three lines of text, but only two items.

100 Park Street
Anywhere, USA
99999

Let's call this field Address for this example. Item 1 in this field is **100 Park Street Anywhere**. Item 2 is **USA 99999**.

You can ask HyperCard to get the contents of the first line of this field by typing **get line 1 of field "address"**. To see the result, type **put it into message box** and press Return. Result: **100 Park Street**.

If the field has more than one line of text and you want to get the second word from the second line, include the line number as well as the word: **get word 2 of line 2 of field "address"**. Result: **USA**.

You can also get one character of a word. For example, to get a 0, type the following to get the third character of the first word in the first line of "address": **get character 3 of word 1 of line 1 of field "address"**. Result: **0**.

You can also ask for a range of characters to get. For example, type the following to get the first three characters of word 4, **Anywhere**, from the Address field: **get character 1 to 3 of word 4 of field "address"**. Result: **Any**.

Tip: Do not use the plural **characters** when specifying a range. HyperCard understands **character** but not **characters**. This is a bug.

Lesson 100: BUILDING A BETTER MOUSETRAP

By adding **mouseUp** messages to buttons, you control what happens when someone clicks on those buttons. HyperCard follows the commands between **on mouseUp** and **end mouseUp** when you click the mouse.

Besides using **on mouseUp** messages to trap the mouse, you can use five other mouse messages:

```
on mouseDown
on mouseStillDown
on mouseEnter
on mouseWithin
on mouseLeave
```

The MouseDown Message

When you press the mouse button, HyperCard sends a **mouseDown** message to the object you clicked on. If that object has a **mouseDown** message in its script, then HyperCard executes the commands that follow **on mouseDown**. Otherwise, the **mouseDown** message is passed—from the button or field to the card to the background to the stack to the Home stack to HyperCard—until HyperCard finds a **mouseDown** message in one of those scripts. If that message is not found, nothing happens.

When you release the mouse while still pointing to the object that got the **mouseDown** message, HyperCard sends a **mouseUp** message to that object. The whole process of passing messages is then repeated. If you move the mouse outside of the object before releasing the mouse button, then HyperCard does not send a **mouseUp** message anywhere.

Use the **mouseDown** message to tell HyperCard to do something as soon as someone presses the mouse button down. For example, adding this script to a button tells HyperCard to hide field 1 when you click on the button:

```
on mouseDown
  hide field 1
end mouseDown
```

The MouseStillDown Message

For as long as you are holding the mouse button down, HyperCard sends a **mouseStillDown** message to the object you clicked on.

Use this message to tell HyperCard to keep executing the commands following it for as long as the mouse button is held down. HyperCard keeps sending this message even when you move the mouse away from the object—as long as the mouse button is still held down.

The minute you release the mouse button, HyperCard stops executing the commands following **mouseStillDown**.

1. Create a new button on any card to practice using mouse messages. You can delete this button when you're through.

2. Add the following script to this button:

```
on mouseStillDown
  wait 3 seconds
  put "release the mouse button" into message box
  wait 3 seconds
  put "Let go of me!" into the message box
end mouseStillDown
```

This script tells HyperCard to put a different message into the Message box every three seconds or until the mouse button is released. **MouseStillDown** messages are commonly used to display hidden fields as long as the mouse is down. When you release the mouse button, the fields disappear again.

3. Choose the Browse tool. Then move the Browse hand over the button and hold down the mouse button until you see **"Let go of me!"** *appear in the Message box.*

Important Note: In a text field, HyperCard understands **mouseUp**, **mouseDown**, and **mouseStillDown** messages only if the field contains locked text. To lock the text, choose **Lock Text** in the Field Info dialog box. If you don't lock the text, HyperCard ignores any mouse messages in that field's script.

The next three mouse messages keep track of where the mouse pointer is on the screen.

The MouseEnter Message

When you point to a button, HyperCard sends a **mouseEnter** message to that button. If that button's script has an **on mouseEnter** message in it, HyperCard executes the commands following that message. For example, this button script tells HyperCard to show all invisible fields when you simply point to that button:

```
on mouseEnter
  show all fields
end mouseEnter
```

The MouseWithin Message

This message is similar to **mouseEnter**. The difference between **mouseEnter** and **mouseWithin** is the same as the difference between **mouseDown** and **mouseStillDown**. HyperCard sends **mouseWithin** messages as long as the pointer remains within the boundaries of the button or field to which it is pointing. And, if that object has a **mouseWithin** message in its script, then HyperCard continuously executes the commands that follow it.

The MouseLeave Message

This message is sent to a button or field as soon as the pointer moves outside of that button or field.

Important: The **mouseUp**, **mouseDown**, and **mouseStillDown** messages can be used in button, field, card, background, and stack scripts. The **mouseEnter**, **mouseWithin**, and **mouseLeave** messages can be used only in button and field scripts.

You'll use these mouse messages next in button and field scripts to control when fields and buttons disappear and reappear.

Lesson 101: MAKING OBJECTS DISAPPEAR AND REAPPEAR

You can make the following objects disappear with the **Hide** command and reappear with the **Show** command:

- The menubar
- The message box
- The tool window
- The pattern window
- Card and background pictures (version 1.2 only)
- Fields
- Buttons

The **Hide** and **Show** commands give you greater control over when different objects are shown on the screen.

Hiding and Showing the Menu Bar

Putting the **hide menubar** command in the stack script hides the menu bar right before the stack is open. Add this stack script to any stack to hide the menu bar when you open the stack:

```
on openStack
   hide menubar
end openStack
```

> *Tip:* Even if you use this script to hide the menu bar, pressing the ⌘ and Spacebar keys will make the menu bar reappear.

When you create stacks such as sales demos, you'll want to control the way people navigate through your stack so they won't get lost. Hiding the menu bar prevents others from navigating with the commands on the Go menu as well as from making changes to an unprotected stack.

Hiding the menu bar also gives you one additional line of card space to work with.

Hiding and Showing the Message Box

When you display the Message box, it stays on the screen until you either click in its close box or press ⌘-M. To "clean up" your card or put away the Message box if it was left out before the stack was closed, you can add a **hide message box** command to a stack script. You can add this command anywhere you like, but most often it is put in the stack script.

```
on openStack
   hide message box
end openStack
```

Displaying Instructions in the Message Box

Since the message box is a container, you can use it to display instructions, error messages, or any other message you like. To do so, use the **Put** command followed by the message you want to appear in the message box as follows:

```
on openStack
   show message box
   put "Click on one of the buttons on the right." into
     message box
end openStack
```

You can either hide this message after the mouse is clicked by adding **hide message box** to the card script or you can replace that message with another message by using another **Put** command. When HyperCard sees another **Put** command, for example, **Put "Press the Return key" in message box**, it replaces the current message with the new one.

Hiding and Showing the Tool and Patterns Menus

You can put the Tools Menu or **window** on a card with this command: **show tool window**. And put it back with this command: **hide tool window**.

Likewise, you can put the Patterns Menu on a card with this command: **show pattern window**. And put it back with this command: **hide pattern window**.

> *Important:* You must use **window** and not **menu** when refer-ring to the Tools and Patterns menus in a HyperCard script. Also, you must use the singular "tool" or "pattern" instead of "tools" or "patterns."

Hiding and Showing Fields

Cards that are crowded with lots of buttons and fields are hard to read. By creating fields that are hidden when not needed, you can both provide information and prevent screen clutter. Here's how to create a pop-up field:

1. Go to the HyperCard Tips stack. You'll create a pop-up field on the Title card.
2. Create a card field with a shadow style. Name this field Help Text. Put this field anywhere on the card.
3. Press ⌘-Tab to choose the Browse tool. Type some information into this field that explains how to use this stack, as in Figure 16.12.
4. You'll make this field appear and disappear by clicking on a button. Choose **New Button** from the Objects menu to create a card button. Name this button Show. Choose **transparent** for the button style, uncheck Show Name, and click on Icon.
5. Scroll to the bottom of the Icon window until you see icons that look like question marks. Choose one of those icons for the Show button. Click OK.

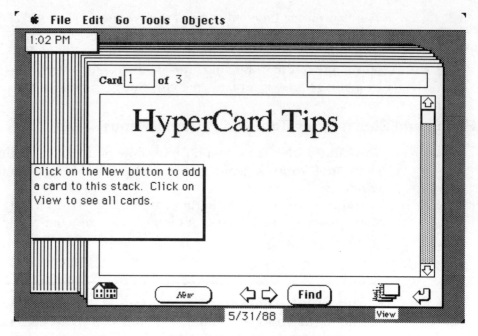

Figure 16.12   Create a card field to contain help text.

6. Double-click on the Show button to see its Button Info dialog box again.
7. Click on Script and type the script from Figure 16.13 into the script window.
8. Click OK. Then press ⌘-Tab to choose the Browse tool and click on the button to test it. The Help Text field should alternately disappear and reappear each time you click on the Show button.

Another way to hide this field is by clicking on it. But before you can do that, you must add a Hide command to the field script. You already learned that you can add mouse messages to fields as long as the field has locked text.

1. Display the Help Text field. Choose the Field tool.

2. Double click on that field and click on the Script button.

3. Before locking the field, add this script to the Help Text field:

```
on mouseUp
   hide card field "help text"
```

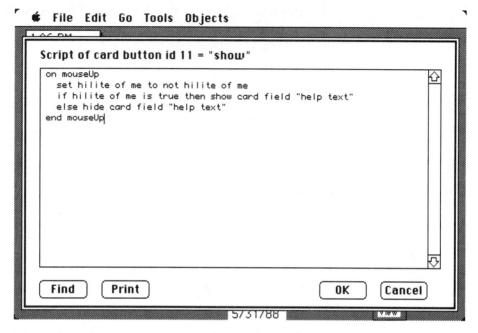

Figure 16.13 Script for a pop-up field.

```
set hilite of card button "show" to false
end mouseUp
```

4. Click OK. Then display the Field Info dialog box again and check the box for Lock Text.

Now you can hide the Help Text field by clicking on the field itself as well as the Show button.

Tip: Some stacks have hidden fields that contain information such as the version number of the stack or credits listing the names of those who created a particular stack. These fields are usually displayed when you click on a button with a question mark icon.

Besides hiding and showing fields, you can hide and show buttons in the same way and often for the same reasons. Some stacks have hidden fields that include an OK button that you click on to put away the field (hide it). For example, Figure 16.14 below shows a field that appears when you click on the Search button.

The script for the button looks like this:

```
on mouseUp
  show card field "search info"
  show card button 21
end mouseUp
```

When you click on this button, you see the field in Figure 16.15.

Here's the trick involved: The OK button is not part of the field. It just looks as if it is. It's actually lying on top of the field. When you click on OK, it hides itself as well as the field. The script that hides both is in the OK button. It looks like this:

```
on mouseUp
  hide card button 21
  hide card field "search info"
end mouseUp
```

Clicking on OK hides *both* the button you clicked on *and* the field.

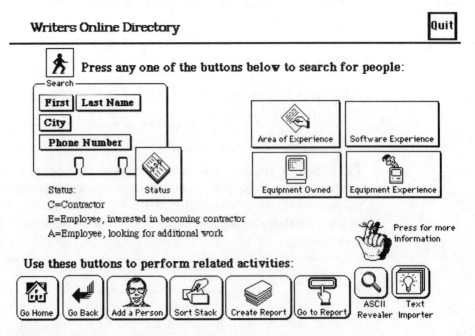

Figure 16.14 Writers Online Stack by Cynthia Kolnick.

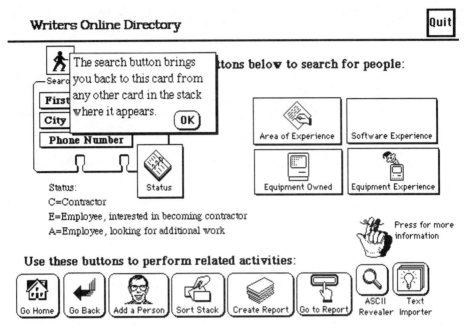

Figure 16.15 The OK button was created on top of the field.

Lesson 102: HIDING PICTURES

You can hide and show fields and buttons by putting the **Hide** and **Show** commands in scripts. But what if you want to hide a drawing you made and have it appear when you click on a button?

In HyperCard version 1.2, you now have commands that enable you to hide and show card and background pictures. These commands are **show picture** and **hide picture**. These commands affect all the pictures on the card or background, whichever you specify.

To hide all pictures on a card, you'd add **hide card picture** to a script. To hide all pictures on a background, you'd add **hide background picture** to a script. To show a hidden picture, you'd add **show card picture** or **show background picture** to a script. HyperCard treats all graphics on a card as one picture, so you can't hide just one graphic on a card with this command.

To hide one particular drawing requires a trick that you'll learn next. This trick involves using opaque fields and buttons. An opaque object covers up whatever is under it. And opaque fields and buttons have no visible borders. The catch is that the card must be white because opaque objects are white. Otherwise, the opaque objects will stand out.

Using Opaque Buttons and Fields to Hide Drawings

Put an opaque button or field on top of a picture to hide it. Then, to reveal the hidden picture, hide the opaque buttons or fields. (You show an opaque field to cover up what's beneath it and then hide the opaque field to reveal what's under it.)

So opaque fields and opaque buttons can be used as a sort of veil—to cover up pictures or other buttons or fields.

1. To practice using opaque objects to hide parts of a picture, create a new stack and draw a card with a flowchart similar to the one in Figure 16.16.

2. Then create three opaque buttons, one to cover each box in the flowchart. Next you'll write a card script that hides and shows these buttons to reveal what's under them, as Figure 16.17 illustrates.

You cannot see these buttons because the background card is white. These same buttons on a nonwhite background would be obvious as in Figure 16.18.

To reveal parts of the flowchart that are covered by these buttons,

Figure 16.16   Create a simple flowchart similar to this.

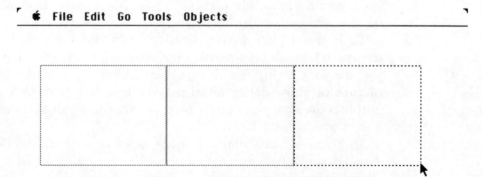

Figure 16.17   Use opaque buttons to hide parts of a picture on a card.

Figure 16.18 Opaque objects that are not on a white background.

you'll hide one opaque button every three seconds. By hiding the opaque button, you reveal one box of the flowchart.

3. To achieve this effect, add the following script to the card:

```
on openCard
  wait 3 seconds
  hide card button 1
  wait 3 seconds
  hide card button 2
  wait 3 seconds
  hide card button 3
end openCard

on closeCard
  repeat with x = 1 to 3
  show card button x
  end repeat
end closeCard
```

This script reveals a box of the flowchart each 3 seconds. When you leave this card either by going to another card or by closing this stack, the **closeCard** message tells HyperCard to make the opaque buttons reappear to cover up the flowchart.

4. Add a new card to this stack so you can see the effect of closing and opening this card. Choose **New Card** *from the Edit menu. Then go back to the first card and watch what happens.*

When using opaque fields and buttons, you must remember to *use the* **Show** *command to hide a picture* or object, and *use the* **Hide** *command to show it.* That's because, to hide a picture, you must show an opaque button or field so it covers up what's under it.

Lesson 103: CREATING A TUTORIAL ON THE SOLAR SYSTEM

Another good use for pop-up fields is to display information about different objects drawn on a card. For example, you can create a stack about the solar system by first drawing all the planets as in Figure 16.19, and

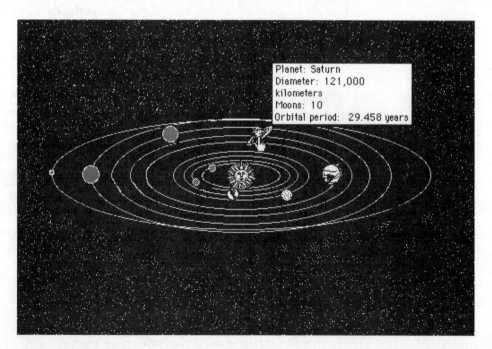

Figure 16.19 The solar system on a stack.

then creating buttons and fields that work together to provide you with more information about each planet.

A Lesson in Astronomy

To create a stack like the one in Figure 16.19, follow these steps:

*1. Choose **New Stack** from the File menu.*

*2. Uncheck the box next to **Copy current background** since you don't want to copy a background card.*

*3. Type **Astronomy** for the name of this stack and press Return to start building a new stack. You should see a blank white screen.*

You can create a night time sky like the one in Figure 16.20 very easily. Here's how:

4. Choose one of the paint tools on the Tools menu.

*5. Choose **Select All** from the Paint menu. Click on black in the Patterns menu. Then choose **Fill** from the Paint menu. The entire card will be black. Now choose **Lighten** from the Paint menu. Your night sky fills with stars!*

Now add your planets. (Figure 16.21 provides an illustration.)

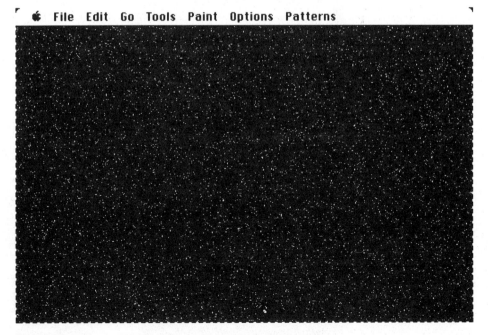

Figure 16.20 A quick and easy night sky filled with stars.

Figure 16.21 Add some planets.

6. Go to the Art Ideas stack and find the card with stars, moons, and planets. (It's on the second index card in this stack.) Copy a planet and then paste it on your Astronomy card. Or draw your own planets using the tools in the Tools menu. Then copy and paste them onto the card with the night sky.

Tip: To draw a white line on the black card, first draw the line in black and then choose **Invert** from the Paint menu.

---

7. Create an invisible button over each planet. (See Figure 16.22.)

Tip: For the fastest way to create invisible buttons, choose the Button tool and then hold down the ⌘ key and drag until the button is the size you want it.

---

8. Create a field next to each planet—with information about that planet such as name, diameter, number of moons, and time it takes to orbit the sun as shown in Figure 16-23. It's okay if the fields overlap each other. Table 16.1 lists information about each planet.

Figure 16.22 Add some invisible buttons.

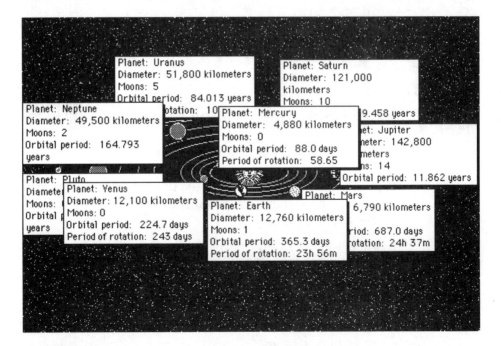

Figure 16.23 Fields with information about each planet.

Planet Name	Diameter (in kilometers)	Moons	Orbital Period	Period of rotation
Mercury		0	88.0 days	58.65 days
Venus	12,100	0	224.7 days	243 days
Earth	12,760	1	365.3 days	23 hours 56 minutes
Mars		2	687.0 days	24 hours 37 minutes
Jupiter	142,800	14	11.862 years	9 hours 50 minutes
Saturn	121,000	10	29.458 years	10 hours 14 minutes
Uranus	51,800	5	84.013 years	10 hours 49 minutes
Neptune	49,500	2	164.793 years	16 hours 0 minutes
Pluto		0	247.686 years	6.39 days

Table 16.1 Field information for each planet

Now you're ready to script. The first thing you want to do is hide all the fields.

9. Hold down the Shift key and choose **Stack Info** *from the Objects menu to go to the script window for the stack. Type this script into the script window:*

```
on openStack
  repeat with i = 1 to the number of card fields
    hide card field i
  end repeat
end openStack
```

10. Click OK.

To make a field appear only when you point to its corresponding planet, you'll need to add a script to each button. For example, to show the field you named "Earth" while the pointer is within the button named Earth and hide that field when the pointer moves away, add this script to the Earth button:

```
on mouseWithin
  show card field "Earth"
end mouseWithin

on mouseLeave
  hide card field "Earth"
end mouseLeave
```

This script tells HyperCard to show the field with information about the Earth while the pointer is within the Earth button and to put away the field when the pointer moves away. (Copy and paste this script into the script window of each button, replacing the field name with the appropriate name.)

Besides using **Hide** and **Show** commands to make objects appear and disappear, there's another way to make objects appear and disappear— by using the **Set** command with a property called **the visible**. If you recall, you use the **Set** command to change an object's properties.

The Visible Property

You can write a script that checks to see if an object is visible. If it isn't, you can make it visible. If it is, you can make it invisible. This visibility or invisibility is another one of the many properties that an object owns. When the visible property is set to true, the object is visible. When the visible property is set to false, the object is invisible.

```
set the visible of button 1 to true   -- show the button
set the visible of button 1 to false   -- hide the button
```

So, using the **Show** command is the same as setting an object's visible property to true. And using the **Hide** command is the same as setting the visible property to false.

The difference is that, with the visible property, you can use the **Get** command to find out if the object is currently visible. You can then add conditional commands that tell HyperCard what to do if the visible of the object is true and what to do if it is false. When you use **Hide** and **Show** commands, you can't do that.

For example, adding this button script to the Earth button has the same result as the previous script you wrote for this same button:

```
on mouseEnter
  set the visible of field 3 to true
end mouseEnter
```

However, with the visible property you can also create button scripts like this:

```
on mouseEnter
  if the visible of field 3 is true then go card 5
  else
  set the visible of field 3 to true
end mouseEnter
```

If you'll be hiding and showing lots of fields and buttons, it's a good idea to clean up your card before going to another card. Add this card script to the Astronomy card to hide fields on this card upon leaving it to go to another card:

```
on closeCard
   repeat with i = 1 to the number of fields
      set the visible of card field i to false
   end repeat
end closeCard
```

This tutorial would not be complete without a series of cards explaining more about the solar system. You can add several cards to this stack containing more information in any order you like. The next card in the stack could be a menu of topics that are linked to other cards as in Figure 16.24.

Or you could create nine cards, each one describing a different planet in more depth. Then you could use the Button Info dialog box to link each button to the appropriate card. If you do so, HyperCard will add a "mouseUp" message at the beginning of the script as in Figure 16.25.

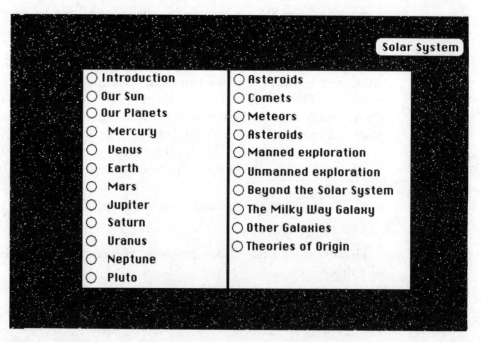

Figure 16.24 You can add a card listing topics to choose from.

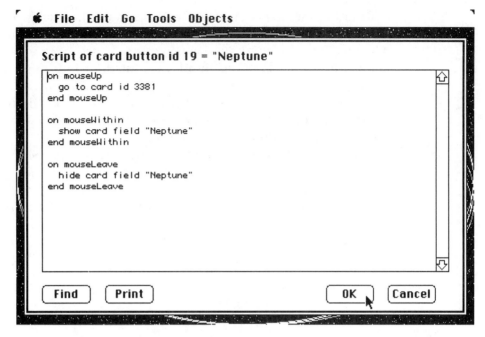

Figure 16.25 A mouseUp message is automatically added to the beginning of a script when you link a button to a card.

Tip: If fields and buttons are on a background card, make sure to type **background field** in place of **card field** or else you'll get an error message.

HyperCard makes it easy to create tutorials the way you teach. Students can follow along as you lecture or you can create self-study stacks they can use to learn at their own pace.

SUMMARY

In this chapter, you learned how to display the current time and date on cards, hide and show fields, create pop-up fields, and hide and show artwork. You also learned how to trap the mouse—that is, tell HyperCard whether the mouse button is up or down and where the cursor is located.

You can hide and show fields, buttons, card and background pictures, the menu bar, the Message box, and the Tool and Pattern window. Whenever you hide any object, make sure it has a corresponding **Show** command in a stack, background, card, field, or button script.

To hide and show one of several graphics on a card or background, cover them up with opaque buttons or fields. For this to work, you need to put your artwork on a white background; otherwise, the opaque buttons will show up as a white object.

Use the visible property instead of the **Hide** and **Show** commands when you want to tell HyperCard to do something besides just hide or show an object.

In the next chapter, you'll learn how to perform simple arithmetic and put the results into fields.

17 Simple Mathematics

In this chapter, you'll learn how to write scripts that perform calculations in fields. Once you know how to do that, you can create fields that automatically subtotal other fields. These fields are referred to as **running totals**.

The lessons in this chapter show you how to

- Add, subtract, multiply, and divide numbers in fields.
- Assign a format to a field for displaying numbers.
- Create fields that keep running totals.
- Join words and pieces of text.
- Compare the values in two or more fields.
- Evaluate two or more expressions at the same time.

You'll learn how to use these commands:

add
subtract
divide
multiply

and these operators:

$+, -, *, /, \wedge, <, >, < =, > =, =, <>$
and
or
not

and these constants:

quote

return

space

tab

formFeed

lineFeed

and this property:

the numberFormat

To complete the lessons in this chapter, you must set the user level to Scripting. Type **set the userlevel to 5** in the Message box to change the user level to Scripting.

HyperCard can add, subtract, multiply, and divide; it can also perform complicated calculations. But, because this is not a book about programming but about using simple HyperTalk commands, you'll stick with simple arithmetic.

There are a couple of ways to perform calculations in HyperTalk. One way is to use the **Add**, **Subtract**, **Multiply**, and **Divide** commands. Another way is to use operators. **Operators** are the symbols that define an operation or action to be performed such as addition, subtraction, multiplication, and division. HyperCard uses several kinds operators:

Arithmetic Operators

+	Add
−	Subtract
*	Multiply
/	Divide
^	Raise to an exponent

Comparison Operators

<	Less than
>	Greater than
< =	Less than or equal to
> =	Greater than or equal to
<>	Not equal to
=	Equal to

String Operators

| & | Combine words or characters without adding a space between them |
| && | Combine words or characters, adding a space between them |

Logical operators

AND	Returns a value of true or false
OR	Returns a value of true or false
NOT	Returns a value of true or false

These operators are explained in this chapter.

Lesson 104: USING THE ADD COMMAND

In this lesson, you'll create a new stack you can use to practice writing scripts that use the **Add** command to total numbers in fields. This stack will be a simple ledger for keeping track of tax deductible expenses.

*1. Choose **New Stack** from the File menu. Uncheck the **Copy current background** box. You'll create a stack with a plain white background.*

2. Name this stack Deductions and press Return.

3. Press ⌘-B to display the background. Then create nine background fields in the order shown in Figure 17.1.

Each line in the first field will contain the names of credit cards. The second field will contain the annual interest paid on each card. The third field will contain the names of charities you've given to. The fourth field will contain the amount donated to each charity. The fifth field will contain the names of institutions from which you borrowed money. And the sixth field will contain the annual interest paid to each institution. The last three fields will contain the totals of the lines in fields 2, 4, and 6, respectively.

4. Use the Text tool to create headers above the fields. Then fill in the blanks so the first card looks like Figure 17.2.

Next you'll learn how to use the **Add** command in button scripts to total the amounts in these fields.

File Edit Go Tools Objects

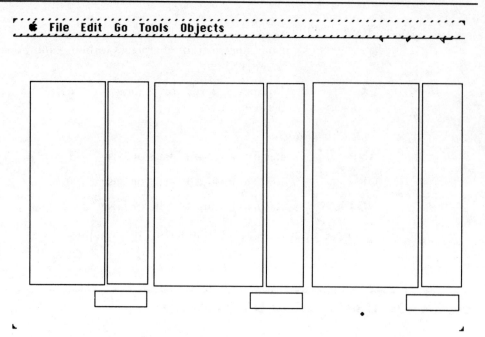

Figure 17.1 Background fields for the Deductions stack. (These numbers don't actually appear on the screen.)

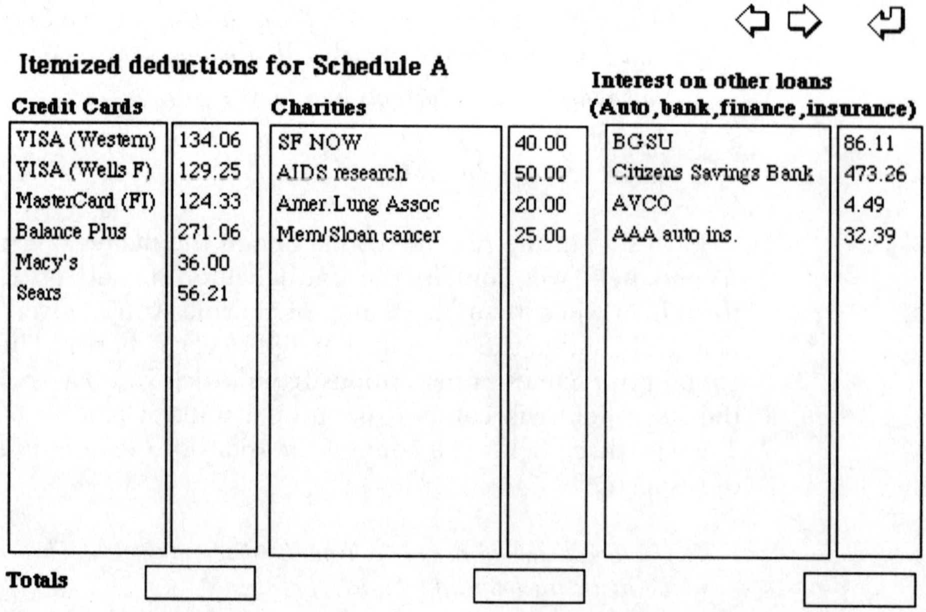

Itemized deductions for Schedule A
Credit Cards
VISA (Western) 134.06
VISA (Wells F) 129.25
MasterCard (FI) 124.33
Balance Plus 271.06
Macy's 36.00
Sears 56.21
Charities
SF NOW 40.00
AIDS research 50.00
Amer.Lung Assoc 20.00
Mem/Sloan cancer 25.00
Interest on other loans
(Auto,bank,finance,insurance)
BGSU 86.11
Citizens Savings Bank 473.26
AVCO 4.49
AAA auto ins. 32.39
Totals

Figure 17.2 Contents of the first card in the Deductions stack.

Adding Two Fields

To add the contents of one field to the contents of another field so that the second field contains the result, use the **Add** command.

1. Create a new button named Calc.

2. Add this script to the button:

```
on mouseUp
   add line 1 of field 2 to field 7
end mouseUp
```

3. Click OK.

4. Choose the Browse tool and click on this button.

When you clicked on this button, it put the contents of line 1 of field 2 into field 7. The result, if you used the amounts shown in Figure 17.2, should be 134.06. Click on Calc again and it adds the contents of line 1 again to the new total in field 7 for a result of 268.12.

But that's not exactly what you want to do in this stack. You want to add the numbers on each line and put that total into background field 7. Of course, there are several ways to do this. One of the easiest ways, however, is by putting 0 into field 7 to clear a previous total, then adding the numbers again, and putting the result into field 7.

Next you'll create a script that does that.

5. Open the script window of the Calc button and type this script in place of its current script:

```
on mouseUp
   put 0 into field 7
   repeat with i = 1 to 14
     add line i of field 2 to field 7
   end repeat
end mouseUp
```

6. Click OK.

Since there are 14 lines in field 2, using a repeat loop is a fast way to add them all. Figure 17.3 shows the results of this procedure.

> *Tip:* The field that is to contain the result must not be empty. Otherwise, you'll get an error message. A field that contains 0 is not an empty field.

Using the numberFormat property

When working with numbers in monetary units, you need to align the decimal points properly. To control how many decimal places numbers have, use the **numberFormat** property. This property affects all numbers produced by mathematical calculations.

Unless you set this property, HyperCard will regard all numbers as whole numbers, that is, numbers without decimal points. When HyperCard is idle, the numberFormat property automatically resets itself.

You can set or change this property by using zeroes (0) and decimal points (.) as you want the numbers to appear. You can use either a zero or the number sign (#) for each number to the right of the decimal. (# displays a number when it is not zero.)

For monetary values, use this format: **"0.00"**. If your calculations need to be very precise, use a format like this: **"0.########"**.

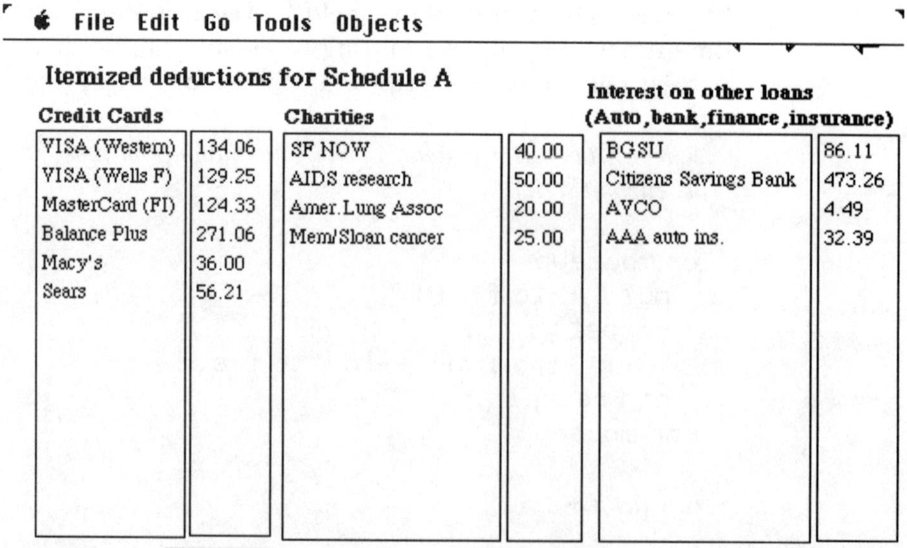

 File   Edit   Go   Tools   Objects

Itemized deductions for Schedule A

Interest on other loans (Auto, bank, finance, insurance)

Credit Cards		Charities		Interest on other loans	
VISA (Western)	134.06	SF NOW	40.00	BGSU	86.11
VISA (Wells F)	129.25	AIDS research	50.00	Citizens Savings Bank	473.26
MasterCard (FI)	124.33	Amer. Lung Assoc	20.00	AVCO	4.49
Balance Plus	271.06	Mem/Sloan cancer	25.00	AAA auto ins.	32.39
Macy's	36.00				
Sears	56.21				

Totals 750.91

(Calc)

Figure 17.3 The Calc button now totals the contents of field 2.

Next you'll set the numberFormat property in the Calc button script for monetary amounts.

1. Choose the Button tool. Hold down the Shift key and double-click on the Calc button to see its script.

*2. Position the insertion point after **on mouseUp** and press Return to insert a blank line. Then type **set the numberFormat to "0.00"** and click OK. Your script should look like this:*

```
on mouseUp
  set the numberFormat to "0.00"
  put 0 into field 7
  repeat with i = 1 to 14
    add line i of field 2 to field 7
  end repeat
end mouseUp
```

*3. To total the contents of fields 4 and 6, highlight the lines after **on mouseUp** and before **end mouseUp**. Then press ⌘-C to copy them. Position the insertion point just before **end mouseUp** and press ⌘-V to paste it. Then change **field 2 to field 4** and **field 7 to field 8**. Repeat this procedure to add the contents of field 6 to field 9.*

Figure 17.4 shows the script for calculating all three fields.

Besides adding the contents of fields to each other, you can also add a specific number to a field. For example: **add 20 to field 7**. Another way to add the contents of fields to each other is by using the plus (+) operator. You'll do that next.

Lesson 105: USING ARITHMETIC OPERATORS

Arithmetic operators are the ones you're already familiar with. The operator for addition is the plus sign (+), and the operator for subtraction is the minus sign (−). However, the operator for multiplication is the asterisk (*) instead of the x, and the operator for division is the slash (/) instead of . . . of . . . . It's not even on your keyboard! Another operator that you probably won't use often is the carat (^), which symbolizes exponentiation; for example, 4^2 means 4 raised to the power of 2, which equals 16.

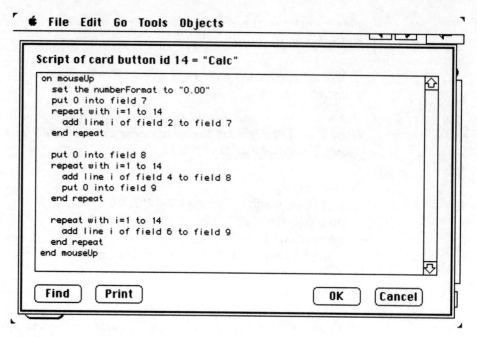

Figure 17.4 Script for calculating totals in all three fields.

When you combine fields or numbers with operators, you create what is known as an expression. **Expressions** consist of two or more values that are evaluated and operated upon. For example, $2 + 2$ is an expression.

Adding More than Two Fields

You've been adding the contents of one field to the contents of another. But what if you want to add the contents of two fields and put the result in a third field? If you used the **Add** command, the contents of the third field would automatically be added as well. If you don't want to add the contents of the third field to the final result, then you'll need to use the + operator instead of the **Add** command to do the arithmetic. Besides that, you'll need to tell HyperCard where to put the result. In the following example, the contents of fields 1, 2, and 3 are added and the result is put into field 4, replacing its previous contents.

```
on mouseUp
  put field 1 + field 2 + field 3 into field 4
end mouseUp
```

You can put the result into any field, including one of the fields in the equation. For example, you can type:

```
put field 1 + field 2 + field 3 into field 3
```

You can also put the result into a variable for temporary storage until you're ready to add it to some other value. This example adds fields 1, 2, and 3 and puts the result into a variable named **temp**:

```
put field 1 + field 2 + field 3 into temp
```

Subtraction

To subtract the contents of one field from another, use either the **Subtract** command or the minus operator ($-$).

For example, this script subtracts the contents of field 1 from the contents of field 3 and puts the result in field 3 each time the insertion point enters a field with this script:

```
on openField
   subtract field 1 from field 3
end openField
```

This script, on the other hand, subtracts the contents of field 3 from field 1 and puts the result in field 8:

```
on openField
   put field 1 - field 3 into field 8
end openField
```

Division

To divide the contents of one field by those of another, use the **Divide** command or the division operator (/).

Examples:

```
divide field 1 by field 3
```

```
put field 1 / field 3 into field 8
```

Multiplication

To multiply the contents of one field with another, use the **Multiply** command or the multiply operator (*).

Examples:

```
multiply field 1 and field 3
```

```
put field 1 * field 3 into field 8
```

A good example of multiplying fields is available in Stack Ideas.

1. Go to the Home card. Click on Stack Ideas.

2. Find the picture named Sales Form (Figure 17.5) and click on it.

The script of the Amount field shows how to multiply the contents of the Quantity field with the contents of the corresponding line in the Price field (see Figure 17.6). The result is put into the Amount field. This script also shows how to keep a running total of the amounts in the Total field.

Next you'll learn how to write scripts that keep running totals.

Lesson 106: CREATING AN INVOICE WITH RUNNING TOTALS

In this lesson, you'll put together a stack to help you keep track of the amount billed to clients each month as well as a running total of the amount billed so far this year.

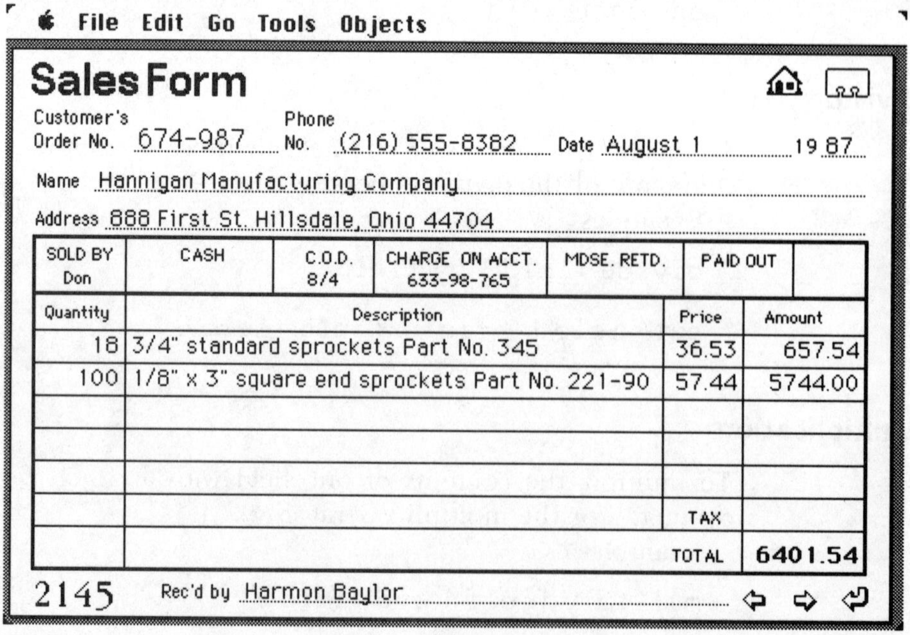

Figure 17.5 The sales form in Stack Ideas multiplies the contents of two fields.

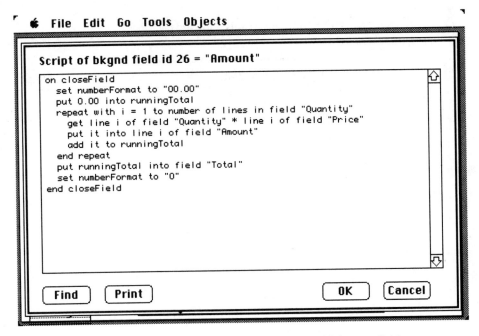

Figure 17.6 Script of amount field shows how to multiply two fields.

Creating a Simple Invoice Stack

1. Choose **New Stack** *from the File menu. Uncheck* **Copy current background***. Name this stack Invoice and press Return.*

2. Create a background like the one shown in Figure 17.7.

3. Name the last two fields This Month and Yearly Total, respectively.

4. Fill in the blanks as shown in Figure 17.8.

5. Notice that the numbers in the fields were automatically left aligned. You can right align them from the Field Info dialog box. Choose the Field tool and double-click on the Amount field. Click on Font. Then click on the Radio button labeled **right***, which is below* **Align***.*

6. Create a background button named Calc with the script in Figure 17.9.

7. Add a new card to this stack. Enter some data into the Amount fields. Then click on Calc to see the result. (Figure 17.10)

This button script automatically totals the amounts for the month, putting the total into the field named This Month. Then the contents of This Month are added to the Yearly Total field.

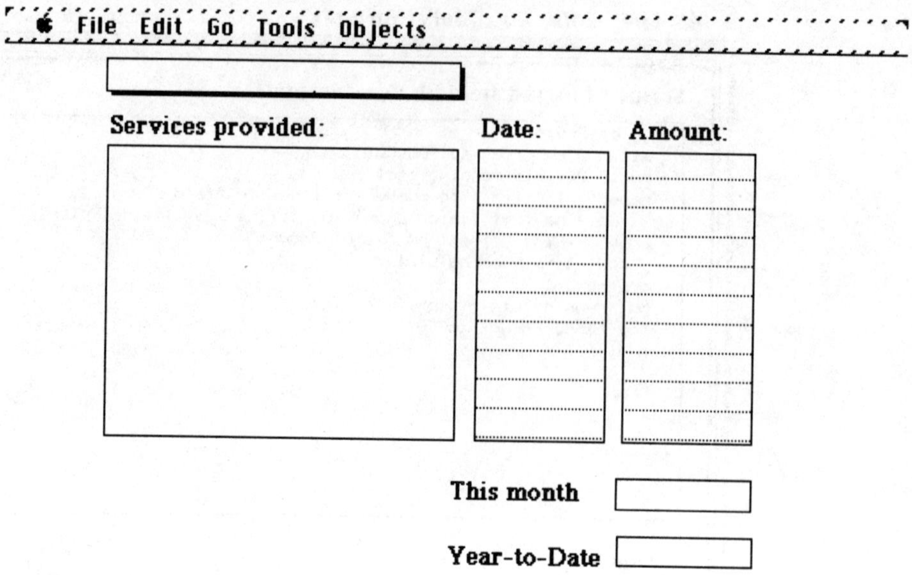

```
  File   Edit   Go   Tools   Objects
```

Services provided: **Date:**   **Amount:**

This month [   ]

Year-to-Date [   ]

Figure 17.7   An invoice with running totals.

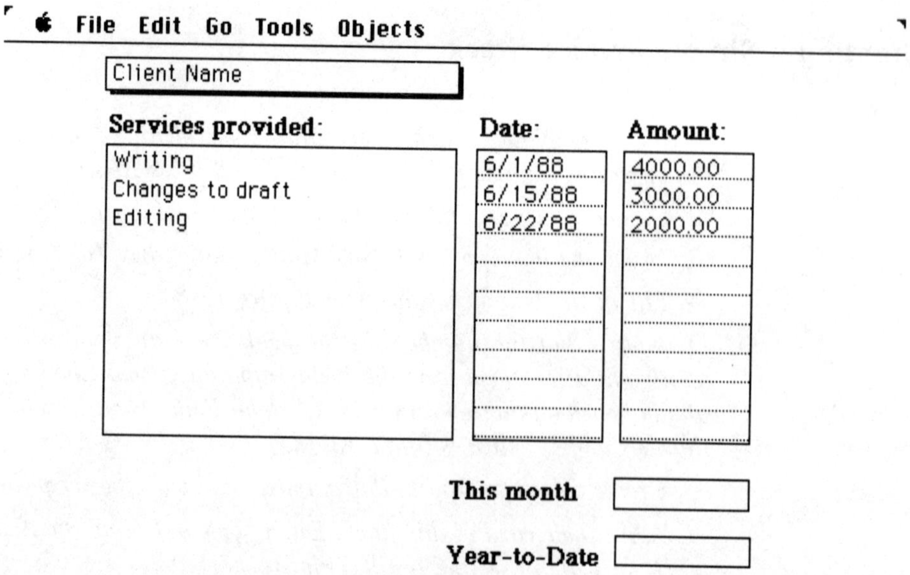

```
  File   Edit   Go   Tools   Objects
```

Client Name

Services provided: **Date:**   **Amount:**

Writing   6/1/88   4000.00
Changes to draft   6/15/88   3000.00
Editing   6/22/88   2000.00

This month [   ]

Year-to-Date [   ]

Figure 17.8   Adding sample data to the fields.

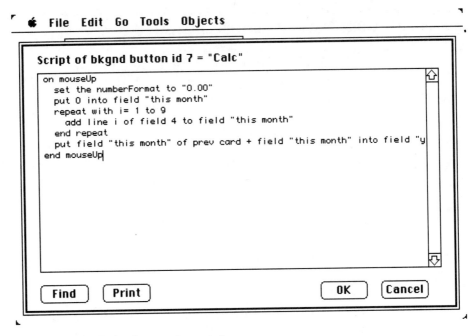

```
 ¢  File  Edit  Go  Tools  Objects

Script of bkgnd button id 7 = "Calc"

on mouseUp
  set the numberFormat to "0.00"
  put 0 into field "this month"
  repeat with i= 1 to 9
    add line i of field 4 to field "this month"
  end repeat
  put field "this month" of prev card + field "this month" into field "y
end mouseUp

 Find    Print                              OK    Cancel
```

Figure 17.9 Script for running totals.

```
 ¢  File  Edit  Go  Tools  Objects

Client Name

Services provided:        Date:       Amount:
Second draft              7/2/88        3000.00








                          This month    3000.00

      Calc                Year-to-Date  12000.00
```

Figure 17.10 Adding a new card and some more sample data to test the button script.

Lesson 107: USING COMPARISON OPERATORS

Comparison operators are symbols used to compare two values to see if they are equal or if one is greater or less than the other. These symbols are:

<	Less than
>	Greater than
< =	Less than or equal to
> =	Greater than or equal to
<>	Not equal to
=	Equal to

Use these operators to compare two expressions in an **If** command.

This button script compares the contents of a total field to determine whether to print a card. If the contents of the total are greater than 1,000, the card is printed. If not, it isn't.

```
on mouseUp
  repeat with i = 1 to the number of cards
    if card field "total" > 1000 then
      doMenu print card
    end if
    go next card
  end repeat
end mouseUp
```

You'll use comparison operators most often with **If** commands.

Lesson 108: USING STRING OPERATORS

The ampersand (&) is a string operator. One or more characters is known as a **string**. A word is a string of characters. In HyperCard jargon, words are strings and numbers are values. Combining two or more pieces of text (or strings) together is called **concatenation**.

Use ampersands to concatenate the words, the contents of fields, the Message box, and variables and put the result in a field or other container.

One ampersand puts strings together with no space between them. For example, if field 1 contains the word *Phoebe* then this script

```
put field 1 & "Beebe" into field 3
```

results in field 3 looking like this: **PhoebeBeebe**

When you want a space between two words, use two ampersands like this:

```
put field 1 && "Beebe" into field 3
```

Result: **Phoebe Beebe**

Constants Used with Concatenation

Remember that the words *true*, *false*, and *empty* are constants in HyperTalk. HyperTalk also has special constants you can use when concatenating text in scripts. They are:

```
quote
return
space
tab
formFeed
lineFeed
```

Use **quote** when you want to add a quotation mark around text. Otherwise, if you add the quotation symbol ("), HyperTalk will think it marks the beginning or end of a string.

Use **return** to insert a carriage return. Each carriage return will move the insertion point down one line in a field.

Use **space** to insert a space. (Using the two ampersands (&&) does the same thing.)

Use **tab** to advance the insertion point to the next field.

Use **formFeed** to push one sheet of paper out of the printer.

Use **lineFeed** to push the paper in the printer up one line.

For example, Figure 17.11 shows a script using some of these constants.

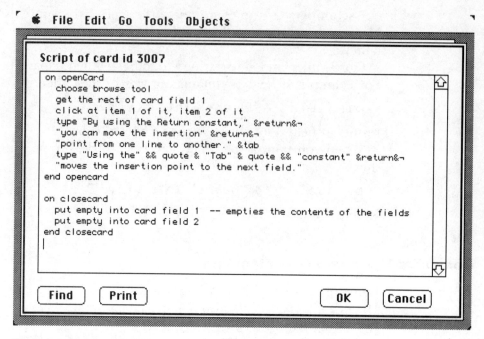

Figure 17.11 A script using constants.

Lesson 109: USING LOGICAL OPERATORS

Logical operators are used to test two or more expressions or conditions to see if they are true or false. **And**, **Or**, and **Not** are logical operators. They return a value of either true or false. The And operator returns a value of true only when both of the expressions connected with And are true. The Or operator returns a value of true when either of the expressions are true. Not returns a value of true only if both expressions are false.

Use these operators to test several conditions in the same script. You'll use them often when scripting check-box buttons. For example, the following button script tests whether an **X** appears in both check boxes or in one of them. If an **X** appears in both button 1 and button 2, then the next card is shown. If an **X** appears in button 1 only, card 10 is shown. If an **X** appears in button 2 only, card 12 is shown.

```
on mouseUp
  if hilite of button 1 is true and hilite of button
    2 is true
```

```
    then go to next card
    if hilite of button 1 is true and hilite of button ¬
      2 is false
    then go to card 10
    if hilite of button 1 is false and hilite of ¬
      button 2 is true
    then go to card 12
  end mouseUp
```

SUMMARY

In this chapter, you learned how to perform calculations with Hyper-Card, create fields with running totals, compare values in one or more fields, and concatenate words.

Whether to use commands such as **Add**, **Subtract**, **Divide**, or **Multiply** or operators (for example, $+$, $*$, $-$, $/$, $<$, $>$, and, or, not) depends on the result you want. To add the contents of two or more fields and store the result in another field, you'll have to use an operator instead of an arithmetic command.

Arithmetic commands store their results in the last field in that command; for example, **add field 1 to field 2** stores the result in field 2. When using **Add**, **Subtract**, **Multiply**, or **Divide** commands, make sure the field in which you put the result is not empty or else you'll get an error message.

In the next chapter, you'll learn how to create dialog boxes with the **Ask** and **Answer** commands.

18 Creating Dialog Boxes

In this chapter, you'll see how to create and use two different kinds of dialog boxes with the **Ask** and **Answer** commands. Besides creating all kinds of buttons that use dialog boxes, you'll add a quiz card to the Astronomy stack that you created in Chapter 16.

The lessons in this chapter show you how to

- Write scripts to create dialog boxes.
- Sort cards by different fields.
- Search several stacks for every occurrence of a word.
- Create buttons that print selected cards.
- Create tests or quizzes.
- Protect stack with passwords.

with these commands:

ask

answer

sort

protect

ask password

print

open printing

close printing

To complete the lessons in this chapter, you must set the user level to Scripting. Type **set the userlevel to 5** in the Message box to change the user level to Scripting if necessary.

HyperCard's **Ask** and **Answer** commands enable you to create two different kinds of dialog boxes. You'll use the **Ask** command to create dialog boxes that request you to enter information (Figure 18.1).

You'll use the **Answer** command to create dialog boxes with buttons to click on in response to a question or instruction (Figure 18.2).

Lesson 110: REQUESTING INFORMATION WITH ASK

The **Ask** command displays a dialog box with a question, a field for entering information, and two buttons—OK and Cancel. To create this dialog box, you simply add the **Ask** command to a script. The **Ask** command must be followed by a sentence enclosed in quotations, usually a question or instruction. You can type up to 40 characters in this question.

In this lesson, you'll add an **Ask** command to the stack script of the Invoice stack you created earlier.

1. Open the stack named Invoice.

*2. Hold the Shift key and choose **Stack Info** from the Objects menu to see the script window. Type the script shown in Figure 18.3.*

3. Click OK.

The only time you'll see this dialog box is the first time you open a stack. Here's a quick way to close a stack and re-open it: go to the Home card (or any other stack) to close the Invoice stack, and then press the tilde (~) or esc key to come back to it.

4. As soon as you open the stack, it asks you to enter your name in the dialog box. (See Figure 18.4.)

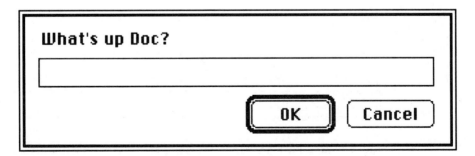

Figure 18.1 A dialog box created with the **Ask** command.

Figure 18.2 A dialog box created with the **Answer** command.

5. After typing your name, you must click on either the OK or Cancel button.

If you click on OK, then the words you typed into this dialog box are put into the variable It. So you can then put It in a field or do whatever you like with It. This script puts the name you typed into the Ask dialog box into the Message box following the text enclosed in quotes ("Good morning,"). You'll see a message like the one in Figure 18.5.

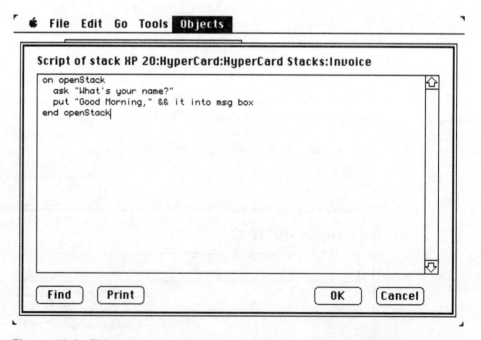

Figure 18.3 This stack script displays a dialog box asking you to enter your name. Then it puts your name following "Good morning," into the Message box.

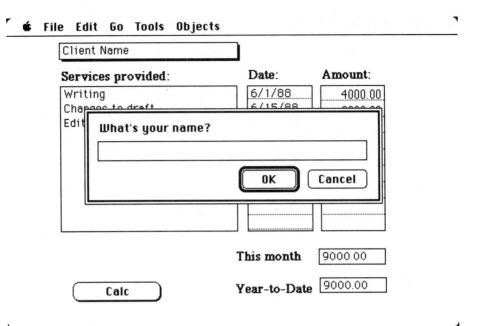

Figure 18.4 The stack script you just created displays this dialog box only when the stack is first opened.

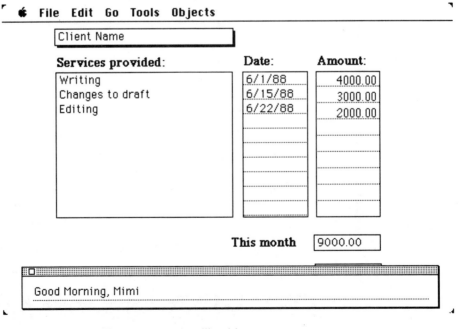

Figure 18.5 You'll see a message like this.

Using a Default Answer with the Ask Command

One of the main tricks used with the **Ask** command is to put a default answer in the field (Figure 18.6). For example:

```
ask "Print how many?" with "1"
```

If the usual reply is 1, then providing the 1 already in the field makes it unnecessary for you to type a 1 in this field every time. All you need to do is click OK.

Lesson 111: GIVING CHOICES WITH THE ANSWER COMMAND

The **Answer** command displays a dialog box with a question, and gives you buttons to click on in response to that question.

Sort buttons usually contain a script with an **Answer** command. The **Answer** command displays a dialog box (Figure 18.7) asking you which of two or three fields you want to sort by. For example, the following button script asks whether you want to sort the cards by name or phone:

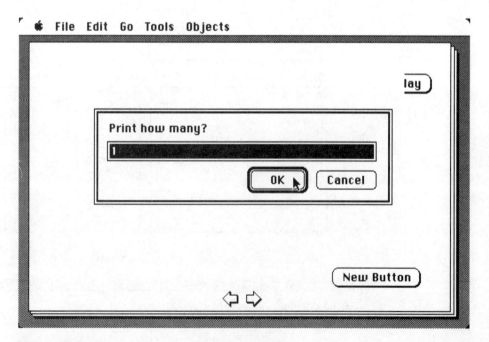

Figure 18.6 You can supply a default answer.

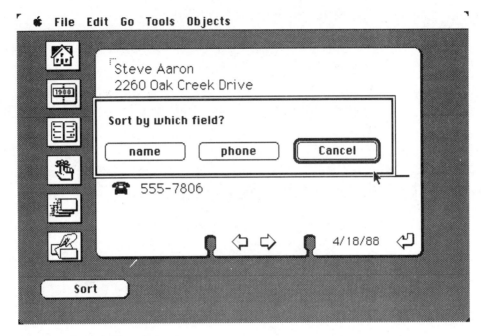

Figure 18.7 A Sort dialog box.

```
on mouseUp
   answer "Sort by which field?" with "name" or
"phone" or "Cancel"
end mouseUp
```

Like the **Ask** command, the **Answer** command must be followed by a sentence enclosed in quotations. This sentence can be up to 40 characters long. Optionally, you can follow this sentence with the word **with** and two or three words that you want to appear in buttons. The words that appear inside of buttons are centered automatically and must be short (11 or 12 characters) or they won't fit within the buttons. These buttons are always the same size and can't be changed. Each of these words must be separated by the word **or**. The format of this command is

```
answer "question" with "this" or "that" or "cancel"
```

The button you click on is put into the variable It. So you can use conditional statements with It to determine what HyperCard should do when you click on each button. For example, this script tells HyperCard to go to the Home card when you click on the Yes button:

```
on mouseUp
   answer "Go Home?" with "yes" or "no"
      if it is "yes" then go Home
```

```
        else
           go next card
        end if
     end mouseUp
```

A big time-saving trick: It's almost always easier to modify existing scripts and buttons than to create new ones. In this next lesson, you'll do just that.

Lesson 112: SORTING CARDS BY DIFFERENT FIELDS

In this lesson, you'll copy the Sort button from the Address stack to your HyperCard Tips stack. Then you'll modify the script of that Sort button so that it sorts by index number and category instead of by name and phone number.

Copying the Sort Button from the Address Stack

*1. Press ⌘-M to display the Message box. Type **go address** and press Return to go to the Address stack.*

2. Choose the Button tool on the Tools menu.

3. Click on the Sort button to choose it. (It's the last one on the Address card.) A moving dotted line appears around it.

*4. Choose **Copy Button** (or press ⌘-C) from the Edit menu.*

5. Go to the HyperCard Tips stack. (Use either the Recent card or the Message box.)

*6. Choose **Background** from the Edit menu.*

*7. Choose **Paste Button** (or press ⌘-V) from the Edit menu.*

8. Drag the button to the lower right of the card, next to the View button (Figure 18.8).

9. Hold down the Shift key and double-click on the Sort button to get to the script window. The script looks like this:

```
on mouseUp
  answer "Sort all cards of this stack according to:" ¬
  with "First Name" or "Last Name" or "Cancel"
  if it is "First Name"
  then sort by first word of first line of field¬
  "Name and Address"
else if it is "Last Name"
```

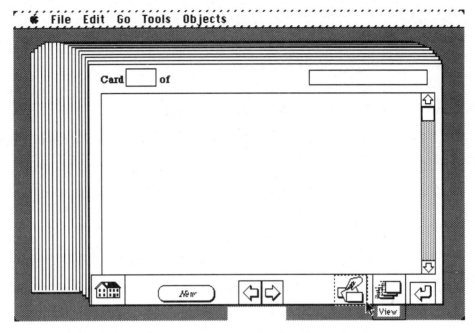

Figure 18.8 Drag the Sort button next to the View button.

```
then sort by last word of first line of field "Name
   and Address"
end mouseUp
```

You'll change this script by replacing the words **"First Name"** and **"Last Name"** with **"Index number"** and **"Category"**. Also, replace **"Name and Address"** with the appropriate field name to sort by.

*10. To sort by the index number field instead of **"First Name"**, highlight the word **"name"** and type **"Index Number"** in its place.*

*11. To sort by the category field, change **"Last Name"** to **"Category"**.*

*12. You also need to change what happens if you choose **"Index Number"** or **"Category"**. Your edited script should look like this when done:*

```
on mouseUp
   answer "Sort all cards of this stack according to:"¬
   with "Index Number" or "Category" or "Cancel"
   if it is "Index Number"
   then sort by field "Index Number"
   else if it is "Category"
   then sort by field "Category"
end mouseUp
```

13. That's it! Click OK.

14. Choose the Browse tool in the Tools menu so you can test the button. Click on the Sort button. Your new dialog box should look like the one in Figure 18.9.

Sorting Cards Alphabetically and Numerically

You don't have to use an Answer dialog with the **Sort** command. If you want to sort by a particular field, for example, field 1, type **sort by field 1** into the Message box and press Return.

The Sort command sorts cards alphabetically in ascending order (from *a* to *z*) unless you specify descending (from *z* to *a*) as follows:

`sort descending by field 1`

If the field contains numbers instead of letters, use this format:

`sort numeric by field 2`

To sort numbers in descending order, use this format:

`sort descending numeric by field 2`

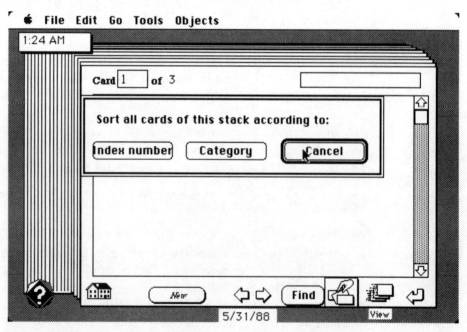

Figure 18.9 Your new Sort dialog box.

> *Tip:* If the field you're sorting by contains letters as well as numbers, HyperCard treats that field as text.

Sorting Cards By More than One Field

It's important to note that you can sort by more than one field when you use the & operator as follows:

```
sort by field "State" & field "city" & field "last name"
```

This **Sort** command is useful for sorting mailings alphabetically by city within each state and by last name within each city.

Sorting Cards by Date or Time

To sort cards by fields that contain a date or time, you must use this format:

```
sort dateTime by field "date"
sort dateTime by field "time"
```

Lesson 113: SEARCHING STACKS FOR ALL MATCHES

As promised in a previous chapter, you now know enough to write a script that searches several stacks not for just one occurrence of a word, but each occurrence of that word.

Why "Find It" Won't Find It More than Once

When you use **get selection** and **find it** to search fields for a highlighted word, the found word appears with a box around it. But, for some reason, these commands work only once. Pressing Return doesn't find the next occurrence of the word. Instead, you get an error message. If the message box is empty, HyperCard displays **unexpected end of line**. Otherwise, HyperCard displays **can't understand <whatever's in the message box>**. This kind of feedback can be maddening. Apparently, what happens is that, after the word is found, HyperCard empties the variable named It, which contained the selected word. Is there a way around this problem? Of course. But it requires a trick to outsmart HyperCard.

Outsmarting HyperCard

You can outsmart HyperCard by putting the selected text into another variable. That way, before HyperCard dumps the selected word out of the variable It, you will have copied the selected word to a different variable. Or you can write a script that simulates the **Find** command in the Go menu:

```
on mouseUp
  get selection
  type "Find" && quote & it & quote & return
end mouseUp
```

But you'll need to add more commands to this script to find words in more than one stack. You'll also need to use the **Repeat** commands so that HyperCard is told to search the stack more than once. And you'll need an **Answer** command to tell HyperCard when to keep searching and when to stop. If you'll recall, only certain commands put their results into the It variable. One of these commands is **Answer** (others are **Ask**, **Ask password**, **Convert**, and **Get**).

Writing the Search Script

Okay, now let's apply what we know about **Answer** and **Repeat** commands to create a button script that searches more than one stack for a word. Instead of selecting a word, you'll use the Ask command to prompt you for a word to find.

Add a button to the Address stack that will search an unlimited number of stacks for the word you enter in the Ask dialog box.

*1. Go to the Address stack by typing **go address** into the Message box. Press Return.*

*2. Choose **New Button** from the Objects menu.*

3. Double-click on the button. In the Button Info dialog box, name this button Search All. Choose any button style you like. Then click Script. Type the following script:

```
on mouseUp
  push card
  put "yes" into it
  repeat until it is "no"
```

```
ask "Enter the words you want to find."
type "find" && quote & it & quote & return
put it into tempword
repeat until it is "no"
  answer "Find next occurrence?" with "yes" or "no"
  if it is "yes" then returnKey
  if it is "no" then
    answer "Search another stack?" with "yes" ¬
        or "no"
    if it is "yes" then
      ask "which stack?"
      put it into stackname
      go stackname
    end if
  end if
end repeat
answer "Find a different word?" with "yes" or "no"
end repeat
pop card
end mouseUp
```

4. Click OK.

5. Press the Tab key to choose the Browse tool. Add a name to the Address stack. Add that same name on several pages of the Datebook stack so you can test this button. Then click on the Search All button and type that name into the Ask dialog box.

Lesson 114: PRINTING SELECTED CARDS

Way back in Chapter 4, you learned how to print stacks by using the **Print** commands on the File menu and the Message box. Instead of typing lots of commands into the Message box, you can add these commands to a button script to create a button that saves you time by executing all of those commands automatically.

In this lesson, you'll create buttons that print selected cards from the HyperCard Tips stack.

Creating a Button That Prints Selected Cards

Here's how to create a button script that prints only cards that match specific criteria in the HyperCard Tips stack.

1. Open the HyperCard Tips stack.

*2. Choose **New Button** from the Objects menu. Hold down the Shift key and double-click on the new button to get to its script.*

3. The following script prints only cards with "Tips" in the category field.

```
on mouseUp
  open printing
  repeat for the number of cards
    if field "Category" is "Tips" then print card
    go next card
  end repeat
  close printing
end mouseUp
```

Writing Scripts That Print Cards in a Different Order

Without writing a script, you can choose to print cards in different sizes, but they are always printed in the order in which they are organized in the stack. Of course, you can manually cut and paste cards in a stack to put them in another order and then print them. But, by writing a script, you can print cards in any order you like without manual cutting and pasting. Instead, you'll copy the stack, open that copy, and then delete the cards that you don't want included in the printout. Here's how:

1. Go to the stack with the cards you want to print.

2. Create a background button named Print Selected Cards.

3. The following button script will copy the original stack and prompt you to open that copy. Then it asks you to select which cards you want to print and deletes those that you don't. After that, you choose whether you want to print the stack or a report listing only the information on those cards.

```
on mouseUp
  push card
  doMenu "Save a Copy..."
  doMenu open stack...   --open the copy you just created
  repeat for number of cards
    answer "Delete this card or keep it" with
        "delete it" or "keep it" or "cancel"
    if it is "cancel" then exit mouseUp
    if it is "delete it" then doMenu delete card
```

```
        if it is "keep it" then go to next card
      end repeat
      answer "what do you want to print?" with "Stack"¬
         or "Report"
      if it is "stack" then doMenu "print stack..."
      if it is "report" then doMenu "print report..."
      doMenu delete stack...
      answer "return to original stack" with "ok"
      pop card
    end mouseUp
```

Lesson 115: CREATING A MULTIPLE CHOICE TEST

This lesson shows how to create a test or quiz that provides immediate feedback and one that waits until all questions are answered before showing the test score. First you'll create a multiple choice test that tells you whether each answer is correct or incorrect. Then you'll create a multiple choice test that waits until all questions on the card have been answered before responding with a score.

The steps you use here can be applied to any stack to create a test or quiz on any subject. First you'll create a quiz (Figure 18.10) to go with the Astronomy stack you created earlier.

Providing Immediate Responses

Follow these steps to create a multiple choice quiz that immediately responds to your answer.

*1. Choose **New stack** from the File menu to create a stack for the quiz.*

2. Create one field for each question you want to ask. Then type the questions into the fields. See Figure 18.10 for an example.

3. Create three Radio buttons below each field. For each button, type the answer that you want to appear in the button for the button's name. Click on Script.

4. Adding the following script turns off the highlighting in the other two buttons (if one was previously chosen) and displays a dialog box reponding that you answered correctly. The correct answer to the first question shown in Figure 18.10 is button number 3. Add a script similar to the following one to each button with the correct answer:

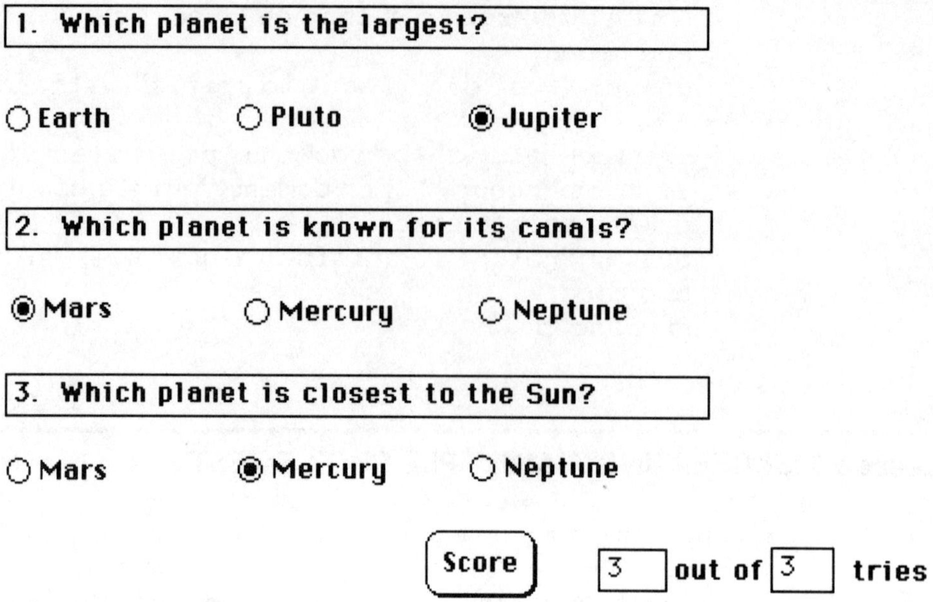

Figure 18.10 A quiz in astronomy.

```
on mouseUp
   set the hilite of me to true
   set the hilite of button 1 to false
   set the hilite of button 2 to false
   answer "Correct!"
   add 1 to card field "total tries"
end mouseUp
```

5. Add a script similar to this for each button with an incorrect answer:

```
on mouseUp
   set the hilite of me to true
   set the hilite of button 2 to false
   set the hilite of button 3 to false
   answer "That is not correct."
   add 1 to card field "total tries"
end mouseUp
```

6. Create two card fields. Name the first field "total correct." Name the other field "total tries." Each time any one of the buttons are clicked on, 1 is added to the "total tries" field to keep track of how many attempts were made.

7. Create a button named "score." Add this script to the Score button:

```
on mouseUp
   put 0 into yourscore
   if the hilite of button 3 is true
   then add 1 to your score
   if the hilite of button 4 is true
   then add 1 to yourscore
   if the hilite of button 8 is true
   then add 1 to yourscore
   put yourscore into card field "total correct"
end mouseUp
```

Keeping Score

Most likely, you'll create a test that doesn't show the results until all the questions have been answered. You can record how many answers were correct by writing another kind of script. Please keep in mind that there are countless ways to program scripts. Here you'll learn one way to see how you scored. First create a new card with fields as in Figure 18.11

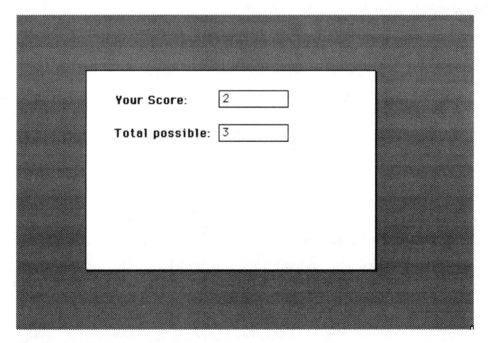

Figure 18.11 A score card.

below. Name the first new field **score** and the other field **total** in the Field Info dialog box for each. Type **3** into the Total field for the total number of correct answers possible.

To see how many questions were answered correctly on the previous card, add this script to the card:

```
on openCard
  put 0 into card field "score"
  if the hilite of button 3 of prev card is true
  then add 1 to card field "score"
  if the hilite of button 4 of prev card is true
  then add 1 to card field "score"
  if the hilite of button 8 of prev card is true
  then add 1 to card field "score"
end openCard
```

In this script, buttons 3, 4, and 8 on the previous card were the correct answers. When you open this card, HyperCard checks your answers in the previous card and displays the number correct in the field named **score**.

Branching to Other Cards

When creating interactive tutorials, you'll often find it necessary to branch to other cards depending on how someone responds to the dialog boxes.

You can create dialog boxes that ask users whether they want to know more about a subject or whether they want to go on to a new topic. The following button script shows one way to use branching in a tutorial:

```
on mouseUp
  answer "Do you want more information?" with "yes" or
    "no" or "cancel"
  if it is "yes" then go to next card
  if it is "no" then go to card "topic 2"
end mouseUp
```

Attach this kind of script to a button on the last card in a series of cards on one topic to give the person using the stack more control over the learning process. When you're learning about a subject, you know how much information you want. You don't want to be forced to look at more cards than you're interested in. Neither does anyone else. Writing scripts that provide choices is what HyperCard is all about.

Lesson 116: ASSIGNING PASSWORDS TO STACKS

You can protect a stack from being altered by someone else by choosing **Protect Stack** from the File menu if you are at user level 5. You'll see the dialog box in Figure 18.12.

You can choose the user level that this stack will have when someone opens it. To protect your artwork, fields, and buttons from changes, set the user level to Typing. To prevent just fields and buttons from being altered or removed, set the user level to Painting. To prevent anyone from looking at or changing your scripts, set the user level to Authoring.

Checking **Private Access** prevents just anyone from opening this stack. It presents a dialog box asking for the password before it will open the stack. Once you choose **Private Access**, you can't open this stack unless you first enter the password.

Checking **No Delete** prevents anyone from deleting this stack from the disk.

Whatever you type into the dialog box will be the password that you must enter to access a user level greater than the one this stack is set for in the Protect Stack dialog box. For example, if you set the user level to 4 and then chose **Protect Stack**, you would not be able to see any of the scripts in this stack unless you first entered the password. To enter the password, you again choose **Protect Stack** from the File menu. HyperCard then automatically asks you for your password.

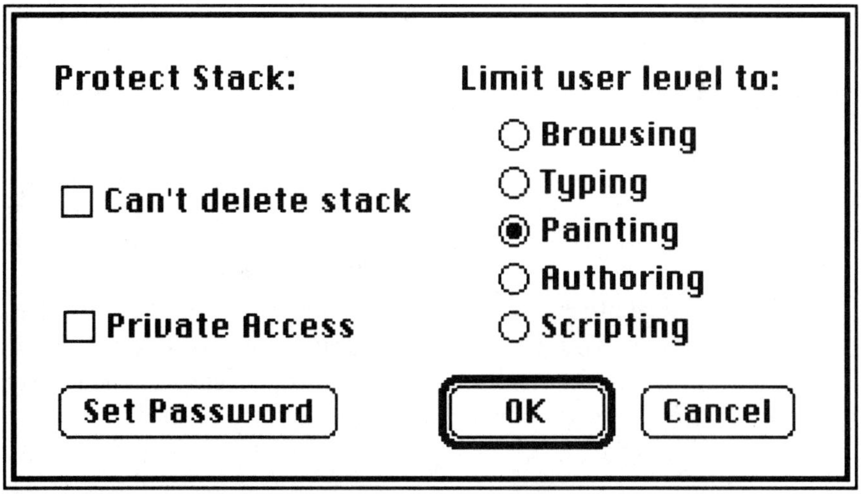

Figure 18.12   Protect Stack dialog box.

Figure 18.13   Password information window.

Tip: If the userlevel is set to Typing or Browsing, hold down the ⌘ key before pulling down the File menu to see the **Protect Stack** choice in the menu.

When you click OK, you'll see a dialog box (Figure 18.13) asking you to set your password. Type the password again for verification. Then click OK.

SUMMARY

In this chapter, you learned how to create two kinds of dialog boxes: Ask dialogs and Answer dialogs. Ask dialogs presented you with a question requiring you to type a response. Answer dialogs presented you with a question requiring you to click on a button in response. Then you used these dialog boxes to create different kinds of Sort, Search, and Print buttons. You also added dialog boxes to a card script to create a quiz stack. Finally, you learned how to protect your stack scripts from others by requiring a password to get to user level 5.

19 Creating Sound Effects

In this chapter, you'll write scripts that make sounds and produce music. You'll also learn how to create digitized sounds, store them in HyperCard stacks, and add them to scripts.

The lessons in this chapter show you how to

- Control and play the Macintosh beep sound.
- Use the HyperTalk **Play** command.
- Play and modify built-in sounds: boing and harpsichord.
- Create and play digitized sounds.

To complete the lessons in this chapter, you must set the user level to Scripting. Type **set the userlevel to 5** in the Message box to change the user level to Scripting if necessary.

Lesson 117: CONTROLLING THE BEEP

HyperCard understands the word *beep* as the Macintosh beep, so if you type **beep** into the Message box and press Return, you'll hear the beep sound. Do that now.

1. Press ⌘-M to display the Message box.

*2. Type **beep** and press Return to hear one beep.*

*3. Type **beep 3** and press Return to hear 3 beeps.*

You can control when the Macintosh beeps by adding this command to a script. Use the **Beep** command in a script to call attention to something like a dialog box or an error. For practice, follow these steps to create a button with the **Beep** command in the button script:

1. Go to any stack and add a new card. You'll practice programming sounds using this card.

*2. Choose **New Button** from the Objects menu. You'll program this button so it plays a sound when you click on it.*

3. Hold down the Shift key and double-click on the button to display the script window.

4. Type the following in the script window:

```
on mouseUp
   answer "How many beeps do you want to hear?" with¬
      1 or 2 or Cancel
      if it is 1 then beep
      if it is 2 then beep 2
      if it is "Cancel" then exit mouseUp
end mouseUp
```

4. Click OK.

5. Press ⌘-Tab once. Then click on the new button to see the result.

This script beeps 1 or 2 times depending on which button you click in the Answer dialog box that appears. If you click on Cancel, the dialog box goes away and you won't hear a beep. Note that the numbers in the If statements did not require quotation marks, but the word **cancel** did. You must enclose text strings in quotes so HyperCard knows they aren't variables.

Lesson 118: PLAYING BOING AND HARPSICHORD

Besides Beep and a telephone dial tone, Boing and Harpsichord are the only other sounds built into HyperCard. You can hear these sounds by using the **Play** command. A sound following the **Play** command is known as a **voice**. Boing and Harpsichord are both voices in HyperCard.

1. Display the Message box.

*2. Type **Play "boing"** and press Return to hear the boing sound.*

*3. Highlight the word **"boing"** and type **"harpsichord"** in its place. Then press Return to hear the harpsichord sound.*

You can add the **Play** command followed by either **"boing"** or **"harpsichord"** to any script. For example, this button script plays boing:

```
on mouseUp
   play "boing"
end mouseUp
```

You can also modify sounds within a script—you don't have to, but, if you like, you can follow each sound with a tempo, notes to play, and the length of each note. Here is the format to use:

```
play "voice" tempo <tempo speed> <notes>
```

For example:

```
play "boing" tempo 180 "a b c"
```

The number following the word **tempo** indicates the speed at which the notes are to be played. You can specify a tempo from 1 to about 800. The higher the number, the faster the tempo. The standard tempo in HyperCard is 200. Tempo 200 is not the same as 200 beats per minute, however. HyperCard has its own unique tempo rhythm. So, when using the **Play** command, vary the tempo until you find one that works best for you.

Assigning Notes

Assign notes using the letters of the scale: a, b, c, d, e, f, and g.

Notes can be natural, sharp or flat. To indicate a sharp note, simply follow that note with a pound sign (#); for example, c# means c sharp. To indicate a flat note, follow it with a b; for example, cb means c flat.

Octaves

There are three octaves to choose from: 3, 4, or 5. Specify the octave as part of a note. Unless you specify an octave as part of the first note in the **Play** command, HyperCard plays a quarter note in the middle octave (c). The octave you specify stays in effect for the notes that follow it until HyperCard sees another octave. For example, **a5 bh c d4 e f** plays a, b, and c in the fifth octave followed by d, e, and f in the fourth octave.

Note Duration

How long is the note? For example, is it a whole note or a half note? You can assign one of the following times to each note:

w   Whole note
h   Half note
q   Quarter note
e   Eighth note
s   Sixteenth note
t   Thirty-second note
x   Sixty-fourth note

You must separate each note with a space so HyperCard knows what goes with what.

For example, **play "harpsichord" "a#w gs de ge bbq cw"** means

play a sharp as a whole note,

play g as a sixteenth note,

play d as an eighth note,

play g as an eighth note,

play b flat as a quarter note,

and play c as a whole note.

Finally, you can add an extension to specify a dotted or triplet note. Follow the note with a period to specify a dotted note; follow the note with a 3 to specify a triplet note. A dotted note plays 1 1/2 times as long as a non-dotted one. A triplet note plays three times as long.

Tip: A script continues running while a sound is played. So you can create background music as you flip through cards.

Playing "Happy Birthday"

Create a birthday card and then add this card script to play "Happy Birthday" with harpsichord when the card is first opened:

```
on openCard
   play "harpsichord" "ge ge aq gq e5q b4h ge ge aq gq ¬
      d5q ch g4e ge g5q ce ce b4q aq f5e fe eq cq dq ch"
end openCard
```

Be sure to type all the notes on the same line. Normally, you can press the Option and Return keys to extend a command to more than one line. The symbol that appears (¬) tells HyperCard to treat the next line as part of the previous command. However, you can't break a line in the middle of text enclosed within quotation marks. Here's a trick for seeing what you're typing: Go ahead and type some of the notes on the second line so you can see what you're typing. When you're done, position the insertion point before the first letter on the second line and press the Backspace key until the second line moves up to the end of the first line.

Tip: In HyperCard version 1.2, you don't need to enclose voices or notes in quotations. However, HyperCard still thinks of a group of notes as text within quotations. Therefore, it won't play notes on a line following a ¬ symbol. There are only two times when you can't break a line: (1) when listing notes in a **Play** command, and (2) in the middle of text enclosed in quotes.

The Play Stop Command

When you use a command such as **play "boing,"** HyperCard plays Boing just once. However, if you have a stack script like the following, Boing will continue to play forever or until you close this stack:

```
on openStack
   repeat
   play "boing"
end openStack
```

To stop a sound from playing before the stack is closed, use the **Play Stop** command. This command tells HyperCard to stop playing whatever sound it is currently playing. So you could create a script that tells HyperCard to stop playing the sound only under certain conditions such as when you click on a button to go to another card or stack. For example, this script tells HyperCard to stop any sound that's playing, and then go to the next card:

```
on mouseUp
  play stop
  go to next card
end mouseUp
```

Lesson 119: BEYOND BOING AND HARPSICHORD

Besides making beeps and playing Boing and Harpsichord, you can add sounds from other sources such as your television. To do that, you must have a hardware device known as a **sound digitizer**. A sound digitizer converts sounds from sources such as a television, tape, album, or voice into files that can be played back with the program packaged with your digitizer. You can hear sounds through the audio port on the Macintosh.

You must convert the digitized sound into an SND resource (SND is short for "sound") before you can play it in a HyperCard stack.

MacRecorder by Farallon Computing is a digitizer with a built-in microphone that you can use to record your own voice as well as sounds from audio devices. MacRecorder comes with a stack called HyperSound. You can use this stack to play back digitized sounds, alter those sounds, and store them as an SND resource directly into a stack.

Some digitizers store digitized sound in SoundCap files, as shown in Figure 19.1.

Other digitizers create SoundWave files, as shown in Figure 19.2.

The Impulse Audio Digitizer enables you to digitize sounds in Sound-

StarTrek Alert   Scream   HAL   vulcan mind

Figure 19.1 Soundcap files look like this.

I do I do I do I do   I'll get you my pretty   You're the best friends

Figure 19.2 SoundWave files look like this.

Wave format. To use SoundWave sounds in a HyperCard stack, you need to use a utility program to store them in a stack.

A HyperCard stack named ResCopier written by Steve Maller of Apple Computer provides you with a quick and easy way to copy sounds from one stack to another, see which sounds are present in a stack, and delete sounds from a stack. Of course, sounds are just one kind of resource in a stack. You can also use this stack to see, copy, move, or delete other resources such as icons. Figure 19.3 shows the first screen of the ResCopier stack.

ResCopier is easy to use. (See Figure 19.4.) You just click on the name of a resource listed in the left window. Open the stack to copy it to. The resources in this stack will appear in the window on the right. Then click on the button named Copy, which is located between the two windows. This stack works almost exactly like the Font/DA Mover.

How to Play Digitized Sounds

To play a digitized sound in HyperCard, you must copy the sound file into a stack using one of the special stacks mentioned, such as ResCopier. This kind of stack translates the digitized sound into a sound resource recognizable by HyperCard.

The digitized sound is then referred to as a **voice**. You can play this voice with the **Play** command. For example, suppose you digitized the theme to a cartoon and named it Cartoon. Then you copied the cartoon sound into a stack using ResCopier. To play that theme, all you need to do is add **play "cartoon"** to any script in that stack. You can even test it by typing **play "cartoon"** into the Message box and pressing Return.

You can play any sound that exists in one of the following:

the current stack open

the Home stack

the HyperCard application

the System file

Figure 19.3 The first screen of the ResCopier stack.

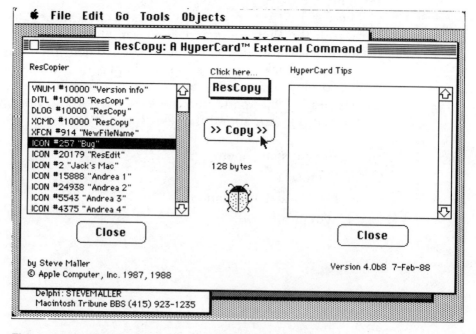

Figure 19.4 Use ResCopier to copy sound files into stacks.

SUMMARY

In this chapter, you learned how to make beep sounds, play built-in sounds like Harpsichord and Boing, and create and play back your own digitized sounds.

When working with sounds, keep these points in mind:

- Each note must be separated by a space.
- Any sound, except Beep, can have a tempo, notes, and octave associated with it.
- You can stop a sound from playing at any time with the **Play Stop** command.
- You can copy sounds from one stack to another using a stack such as ResCopier or a utility program such as ResEdit.
- To play a digitized sound in HyperCard, it must be stored as an SND resource in either the System file, the HyperCard application, the Home stack, or in the stack that also contains the **Play** command for that sound.

In the next chapter, you'll learn how to animate pictures and objects.

20 Animation and Other Magic Tricks

In this chapter, you'll learn how to use commands to work magic. You'll animate pictures—make a globe spin and a ball bounce—and may even have fun doing it. You'll also learn how to make HyperCard type text into fields and paint text onto cards automatically.

The lessons in this chapter show you how to

- Make motion pictures.
- Speed up the animation.
- Change the cursor icon.
- Make HyperCard do the typing.
- Draw a ball and make it bounce.

with these commands:

choose

click

drag

type

and these functions:

location

the mouseLoc

and these properties: **cursor**

dragSpeed

and this constant: **return**

To complete the lessons in this chapter, you must set the user level to Scripting. Type **set the userlevel to 5** in the Message box to change the user level to Scripting if necessary.

> *Tip:* One word about graphics in HyperCard: Keep in mind that the more graphics you use, the more disk space and memory in RAM the stacks will take up.

Lesson 120: MAKING "MOTION PICTURES"

The easy way to animate cards with HyperCard is by first creating a series of cards, each with the same picture in a slightly different location on the card. By adding a **Show** command to a script, you can flip through all the cards. This makes the object appear to move. For practice create a new stack and name it Pictures. Then follow these steps:

1. Draw a long rectangle on the first card.

2. Choose **Copy card** *from the Edit menu. You now have two copies of the same card.*

3. Choose the Lasso tool on the Tools menu and drag around the rectangle to select it. Then choose **Rotate Right** *from the Paint menu.*

4. Choose **Copy card**, **Paste card** *and* **Rotate** *the rectangle again.*

5. Repeat step 4 until you have several cards with rectangles in different positions.

6. Create a new button with the following script:

```
on mouseUp
     Show All Cards
end mouseUp
```

7. Click on the button to set the rectangle in motion.

Lesson 121: SPEEDING UP THE SHOW COMMAND

When you use the **Show** command, HyperCard shows the cards one at at time. But, before showing a card, HyperCard reads the card into memory. It reads one card, shows it, gets the next card, reads it, shows it, and so on.

Reading cards takes a little time, so your animation may not appear as fast as you'd like. Here's the trick for speeding up this process. To make the cards appear slightly faster, tell HyperCard to read all the cards into memory first and then show them one at a time. Before you do this, freeze the screen so you won't have to watch HyperCard do this each time you open the stack. To speed up the showing of cards, add this script to your stack:

```
on openStack
   set lockscreen to true
   show all cards
   set lockscreen to false
end openStack
```

This script reads all the cards into memory. When HyperCard finds a **Show Card** command in a script, it shows that card more quickly.

Lesson 122: MAKING THE WORLD GO ROUND

Using the knowledge gained from the previous two lessons, you can now create a spinning globe.

*1. Choose **New Stack** from the File menu. You'll create a new stack and add three cards to it. Each card will have a picture of the Earth viewed from a slightly different angle. Name this stack "globe."*

2. Copy the picture of the Earth from the Art Ideas stack. Paste the copied picture on the first card in the stack named "globe." Or draw it yourself using the drawing tools in the Tools menu.

3. Choose the Lasso tool. Hold down the Shift key while you lasso the Earth so you select only the picture and no white space around it. Press ⌘-C to copy this picture (Figure 20.1).

4. Add a new card. Then press ⌘-V to paste the copied picture on this card (see Figure 20.2) (The picture will appear in the exact same location on the new card.)

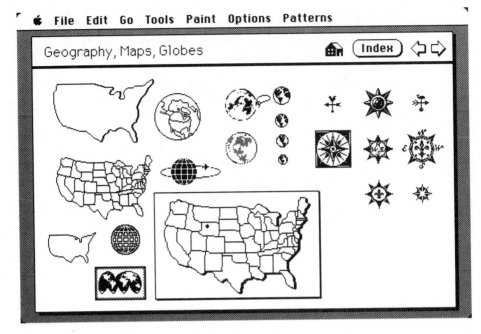

Figure 20.1 Click the button to see the card move.

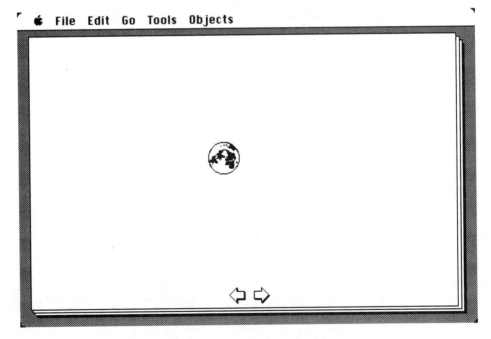

Figure 20.2 Copy the picture of the Earth from Art Ideas.

5. Use the paint tools to alter this picture so it looks like Figure 20.3.

6. Repeat steps 3 and 4 for the third card. Alter the third card so it looks like Figure 20.4.

7. Add this stack script to the stack so that, when you open the stack, the cards are shown continuously, making it appear as though the picture is actually spinning.

```
on openStack
  set lockscreen to true
  show all cards
  set lockscreen to false
  repeat until the mouseclick
    go to next card
  end repeat
end openStack
```

The command **repeat until the mouseclick** enables you to stop this animation at any time by clicking the mouse.

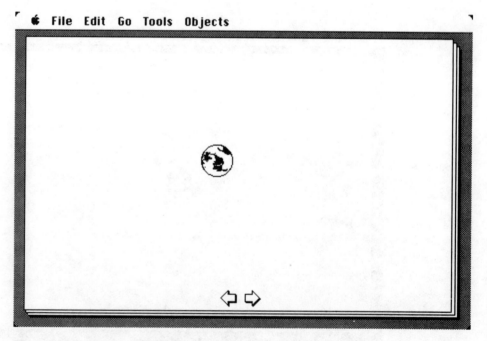

Figure 20.3 Second card in the stack.

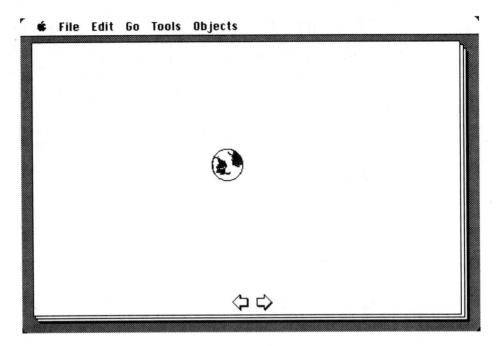

Figure 20.4 Third card in the globe stack.

Lesson 123: CHANGING THE CURSOR TO A WATCH

You can use the **Set** command to change the cursor into one of four icons, from an insertion point to a watch for example. To do this, if you're using version 1.0.1 or 1.1, you need to know which number corresponds to which icon.

Figure 20.5 shows which number corresponds to each cursor style.

Set cursor to 4 turns the cursor into a watch. If the commands in a script are going to take longer than a second or two, you'll want to change the cursor to a watch until the commands are finished. For example, if you are going back and forth from one card to another or one stack to

Figure 20.5 HyperCard cursor styles.

another, copying fields or cards, you'll want to display the watch icon instead of leaving the insertion point on the screen. Otherwise, someone else using your stack might think something's wrong with it as it will appear frozen until HyperCard is done executing the commands. You can then set the cursor back to its original style. If you don't, HyperCard will eventually reset it for you anyway.

If you have HyperCard version 1.2, you can refer to cursors by name instead of number. This version also gives you eight kinds of cursors to choose from—including the beach ball! To change the cursor, use one of these commands:

```
set cursor to I-beam
set cursor to cross
set cursor to plus
set cursor to watch
set cursor to arrow
set cursor to hand
set cursor to none
set cursor to busy
```

Table 20.1 illustrates the cursors available in HyperCard version 1.2. Setting the cursor to **none** hides it.

Cursor name	What it looks like
I-beam	I
Cross	+
Plus	✛
Watch	⌚
Arrow	➤
Hand	☝
None	
Busy	✪

Table 20.1 Cursors available in HyperCard Version 1.2.

> *Tip:* In version 1.2, the cursor, menu bar, Tools menu, and Patterns menu are frozen when the screen is locked. That is, you won't see them change while a script is working as long as the script includes **set lockscreen to true**.

Lesson 124: MAGIC TYPING

Before going any further, create a new stack and give it a name, such as Animation. You'll practice animation techniques using this new stack.

1. Choose **New Stack** from the File menu. Name it Animation. Press Return.
2. Add a few fields to the background of this stack. Also add two card fields.

You can write scripts that make HyperCard type words into fields or on a card, one character at a time. You do this with the **Type** command. Like many other HyperTalk commands, type doesn't work alone. To make words appear within fields or on cards, you'll need to know two other commands: **Choose** and **Click**. And you'll need to learn about another property: **location**.

Before you can type text *onto a card*, you must choose the Text tool. So, if you want HyperCard to type text for you, you must tell HyperCard to choose the Text tool. That's where the **Choose** command comes in.

Use the **Choose** command to tell HyperCard which tool to choose. If you want text typed into a *field*, add this command to your script:

```
choose browse tool
```

If you want text typed onto a *card*, add this command to your script:

```
choose text tool
```

You can choose any tool from the Tools menu with the **Choose** command. To do so, make sure you use the correct names for the tools you want to use as listed in Figure 20.6.

After you choose the appropriate tool, you need to tell HyperCard where to begin typing—either in a field or on a card. You already know

browse tool	button tool	field tool
select tool	lasso tool	pencil tool
brush tool	eraser tool	line tool
spray tool	rectangle tool	round rect tool
bucket tool	oval tool	curve tool
text tool	regular polygon tool	polygon tool

Figure 20.6 You can choose a tool from the Tools menu by using the appropriate tool name as listed here.

which field HyperCard will type into, but you most likely don't know its exact location on the card.

> *Tip:* To tell HyperCard to begin typing on the first line in a field, you can use **send Tab to field** <**number or name**> to move the insertion point into a specific field instead of getting its location.

Cards can be 512 dots wide and 342 dots long. The upper left corner of the card has a location of 0,0. The lower right corner has a location of 512, 342. These locations are referred to as **coordinates**. (See Figure 20.7.)

Don't worry—you won't have to count pixels! HyperCard doesn't expect you to figure out the exact coordinates of a field on a card. Instead, each field has a property called **rect**. Rect is short for rectangle. This property controls the size and location of the field. When you ask HyperCard to get the rect of a field, rect will contain the coordinates of the upper left and lower right corners of a field.

Getting the rect
Ask HyperCard to get the location of the field for you by adding this command to the script:

get rect of field 1

Then you need to tell HyperCard where to click in the field.

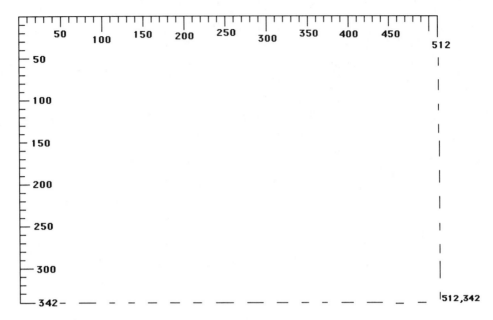

Figure 20.7 Each card has an invisible grid.

As you know, information typed into fields and separated by commas are known as **items**.

To find the location of the top left corner so you can click at it, tell HyperCard to get item 1 of the rect. Item 1 is the first line of a blank field. The location retrieved with the **Get** command is put into the variable It. So, by adding **click at item 1 of it** to your script, you can position the pointer in the upper left corner of the field.

Tip: In version 1.2, you no longer have to **get the rect** of a field. Fields, buttons, and windows have four new properties: top, left, bottom, and right. For example, to position the insertion point in field 1, add **click at the top left of field1** to your script.

Now you can create a script that tells HyperCard to type something in a field.

*1. While any card is displayed, hold down the Shift key and choose **Card Info** from the Objects menu to get to the script window of the card.*

2. Add this script to the card:

```
on openCard
  choose browse tool
  get the rect of card field 1
  click at item 1 of it
  type "Do you believe in magic?"
end openCard
```

3. Click OK.

4. Go to another card and then come back to this card. When you open this card, HyperCard types "Do you believe in magic?" into field 1.

Shortcut: If using version 1.2, use this script instead of the previous one:

```
on openCard
  choose browse tool
  get the rect of card field 1
  click at item 1 of it
  type "Do you believe in magic?"
  wait 3 seconds
end openCard
```

To make HyperCard continue typing on the second line, add **& return** at the end of the first line to be typed:

```
on openCard
  choose browse tool
  get the rect of card field 1
  click at item 1 of it
  type "Do you believe in magic?" & return
  wait 3 seconds
  type "I do."
end openCard
```

If you want HyperCard to type those words into this field each time you open this card, then add a **closeCard** command to erase the contents of the field before going to another card. Add this handler following **"end openCard"** in the card script:

```
on closecard
  put empty into card field 1
end closecard
```

Writing a script that automatically types text into fields is easy when you use the rect property and **Type** command.

Automatic Typing with the Text Tool

To type text on a card with the Text tool, you must tell HyperCard where to begin typing. Finding the coordinates of a location is just as easy as typing into a field when you use the mouse and a function called **the mouseLoc**.

Using the mouseLoc

1. Point anywhere on the card.

*2. Display the Message box. Type **the mouseLoc** and press Return. The numbers that appear in the Message box are the exact coordinates of the position of the pointer on the card. Write down those numbers. You'll need them to write the script.*

3. Now add this script to a card, substituting your coordinates for the ones listed below:

```
on openCard
  choose text tool
  click at 100,100
  set the textFont to Geneva
  set the textStyle to bold
  set the textSize to 14
  type "That wasn't so bad."
end openCard
```

Tip: You can also use buttons and fields as reference points and then use addition or subtraction to determine an approximate location on the card. For example, you can type **get loc of field 1** followed by **add 10 to it**. Typing **click at it** after that would position the cursor 10 spaces to the right of the field.

Lesson 125: ANIMATING A BOUNCING BALL

To make an object move without the flipping of cards, use the **Choose** command and the Select tool to select the drawing. Then use the **Drag** command to move the picture to another location.

The **Drag** command moves a picture that you selected with either the Selection tool or Lasso tool to the location (exact coordinates) you specify in a script. So you'll need to use the mouseLoc function to locate pictures.

When you use the **Drag** command, you can tell HyperCard how fast to drag an object by setting the property named **dragSpeed**. DragSpeed determines how many pixels per second HyperCard will drag the object. The fastest dragSpeed setting is 0. The slowest is 1. You'll play with different dragSpeed settings next.

In this lesson, you'll make a ball bounce.

1. Add a new card to your animation stack.

*2. Draw a circle using the oval tool on the Tools menu. You can draw a filled circle by first choosing **Draw Filled** from the Options menu.*

Find out the approximate coordinates of the ball.

*3. Point to the ball. Type **the mouseLoc** into the Message box and press Return. Write down the coordinates. Move the mouse to the top of the screen where you want the ball to bounce to. Type **the mouseLoc** into the Message box again and press Return. Write down the coordinates. In the Message box, the first coordinate is the horizontal location of the ball on the card, and the second coordinate is the vertical location.*

4. Then create a button with this script, using your coordinates in place of the ones in this example:

```
on mouseUp
  choose lasso tool
  repeat 10 times
    click at 100,100 with commandKey
    set dragspeed to 800
    drag from 100,100 to 100,300
    click at 100,300 with commandKey
    drag from 100,300 to 100,100
  end repeat
end mouseUp
```

> *Tip:* Adding **with commandKey** to a **Click** command tells HyperCard to hold down the ⌘ key while clicking with the lasso to select an object.

5. Click OK. Click on the button to set the ball in motion.

6. Create a button named Faster and add the following script to it. This script bounces the ball up and down 10 times. Then it bounces the ball off the sides of the card. Instead of knowing the coordinates of the ball, this time you'll tell HyperCard to select the last object selected.

```
on mouseUp
  choose lasso tool
  doMenu Select
  set dragspeed to 3000
  repeat 10 times
    drag from 240,235 to 240,57--horizontal by vertical
    drag from 240,57 to 240,235
  end repeat
  repeat 10 times
    drag from 240,235 to 321,63
    drag from 321,63 to 501,275
    drag from 501, 275 to 377,318
    drag from 377,318 to 12,233
    drag from 12, 233 to 11,27
    drag from 11,27 to 239,235
  end repeat
  doMenu ''Revert''
  choose browse tool
end mouseUp
```

Play with different dragSpeeds to see how fast or slow you can make the ball bounce.

> *Tip:* To animate more than one picture, use **doMenu Select All** instead of **doMenu Select**. You can then drag all of the pictures on the card.

SUMMARY

In this chapter, you learned how to animate pictures, change the cursor, and automate typing. You also learned how to use three new commands: **Click**, **Choose**, and **Drag**. You'll use these commands most often when creating scripts for animation.

The next chapter shows you how to create your own command words.

21 On Your Own

In this chapter, you'll learn how to create your own commands and how to edit scripts. As in previous chapters in this section, make sure the user level is set to Scripting.

Lesson 126: CREATING YOUR OWN COMMANDS

You can create commands by typing **on** followed by any word that is not a HyperCard reserved word such as the names of commands, functions, and properties. Of course, you then type what you want to happen when you use that command word. Then type **end** followed by that same word.

For example, to create a command named **ClearFields**, type the following into the stack script window:

```
on ClearFields
  repeat with i = 1 to the number of fields
    put empty into field i
  end repeat
end ClearFields
```

This script empties the contents of all background fields on a card.

Add this command to the stack script. Then HyperCard will recognize it from within any script in that stack. For example, you could then add a button with this script:

```
on mouseUp
  clearFields
end mouseUp
```

Opening Files from Other Programs

Use the **Open** command to open other programs such as MicroSoft Word or files created with other programs. You already learned how to create buttons that open applications in Chapter 13. You created a new button and then added this script:

```
on mouseUp
  open "MicroSoft Word"
end mouseUp
```

You can also open applications by creating a command word that opens an application whenever you type that word from the keyboard. To do this, define any letter or combination of letters that are not recognized as a command or other word in HyperTalk by simply adding the word **on** before the letter(s). For example, to define **ex** as a command that opens the Excel application whenever you type **ex** into the Message box, create a stack script with this handler:

```
on Ex
  open "Excel"
end Ex
```

If you check the Blind typing option on the user preferences card, typing **x** without the Message box displayed also opens the Excel application.

Lesson 127: EDITING SCRIPTS

Sometimes you may find that you'll create a script that you can't open for one reason or another because of the way you've written that script. If this happens, there's a trick for using the Message box to go directly to the script window of a stack, background, card, field, or button.

Of course, you must know the name, number, or ID of the object whose stack you want to access. All you need to do is type **edit script of** <**object**> into the Message box and press Return. The script window of the named object will appear. Here are some examples of the **Edit Script** command:

```
edit script of stack "clip art"
edit script of background 3
edit script of card 1
```

```
edit script of field ID 890
edit script of button "next"
```

The user level must be set to Scripting, or this command won't work.

SUMMARY

Congratulations! You have learned all the commands you need to know to script most HyperCard stacks.

Here are the commands you've learned how to use in Section Three:

add	find	print
answer	flash	push
ask	get	put
beep	go	repeat
choose	hide	set
click	if	show
close printing	multiply	sort
divide	open	subtract
doMenu	open printing	type
drag	pass	visual
edit script	play	wait
exit	pop	

You can now create your own stacks to keep track of the myriad of information thrown at you every day. Good luck!

APPENDIX A HYPERCARD 1.2 SPECIFICATIONS

HyperCard runs on a Macintosh Plus, Macintosh SE, and Macintosh II with either a hard disk or two 800K disk drives. A hard disk is recommended because all the stacks will be more easily accessible from a hard disk than from two floppy disk drives. With two floppy disk drives, you'll need to do a lot of disk swapping.

System and Finder

Which version of the System and Finder you should be using depends on which of those computers you are using:

Macintosh Plus: System 3.2 or higher, Finder 5.3 or higher, LaserWriter 4.0
Macintosh SE: System 4.0 or higher, Finder 5.4 or higher, LaserWriter 4.0
Macintosh II: System 4.1 or higher, Finder 5.5 or higher, LaserWriter 4.0

It's always best to use the latest System and Finder available. At this time, the latest versions are System 6.0 and Finder 6.1.

Memory Requirements

You must have at least 1 megabyte of RAM to use HyperCard. HyperCard version 1.1 uses about 750K of RAM. HyperCard version 1.2 uses about 700K of RAM.

For faster HyperCard performance, set the RAM cache in the Control Panel to off. HyperCard has its own way of caching information in and out of memory, so turning off the Macintosh RAM cache speeds up HyperCard. To turn off the RAM cache, choose Control Panel from the menu. Click the Off button.

HyperCard with MultiFinder

If you're using HyperCard with MultiFinder, your computer should have at least 2 megabytes of RAM. Set HyperCard's "Application Memory Size" in the Get Info box to at least 750K for HyperCard version 1.1 or 700K for HyperCard version 1.2. Set it to 1 megabyte to get top HyperCard performance.

386

HyperCard Limits

This table lists the maximum sizes of each HyperCard component.

Component	**Size or Number**
Stacks	Maximum size of stack: 4096 megabytes
number of cards per stack	As many as will fit on your disk.
number of backgrounds per stack	As many as will fit on your disk.
name of stack	Up to 253 characters
Backgrounds	
number of cards per background	As many as will fit on your disk.
name of background	Up to 253 characters
Cards	Maximum:
size of a card	512 horizontal by 342 vertical pixels
number of fields per card	Unlimited
number of buttons per card	Unlimited
number of links per card	Unlimited
name of card	Up to 253 characters
Fields:	Maximum:
number of characters per field	32,767
name of field	Up to 253 characters
Buttons:	
name of button	Up to 253 characters
Scripts	Maximum:
number of characters per script	30,000

HyperCard 1.2 New Features:

Auto Tab

An Auto Tab field property has been added to the Field Info dialog box. Checking this option enables you to press Return instead of the Tab key to go from one field to another. (Pressing Return still takes you to the next line in a multi-line field if the insertion point is not on the last line. When the insertion point is on the last line of a field, pressing Return moves the insertion point to the next field in tab order.)

Changing Between Tools

⌘-Tab chooses the Browse tool.
⌘-Tab-Tab chooses the Button tool.
⌘-Tab-Tab-Tab chooses the Field tool.

Peeking at Scripts

Now you don't have to choose the Button or Field tool first to look at a button or field script. Just hold down the Shift, ⌘, and Option keys and click once on the button or field of your choice to get to its script. Also, you can now look at the script of a card by pressing ⌘-Option-C. Look at a background script by pressing ⌘-Option-B. And look at a stack script by pressing ⌘-Option-S.

Other Highlights:

- HyperCard 1.2 runs in 700K of RAM
- Over 200 bug fixes.
- Faster searching of large stacks
- Faster changing between the Browse, Button, and Field tools.
- Stacks on an AppleShare file server can be viewed by any number of users.
- You can add visual effects to the "unlock screen" command.
- Four new cursors are now available: arrow, hand, none, beachball.
- New commands enable you to hide and show background and card pictures.
- The menubar, Tools menu, Patterns menu, and cursor will be frozen when the screen is locked.
- When printing cards, you can choose to hide the backgrounds.

Locked Stacks

Locking a stack means that no one can make changes to it. You can lock stacks in many ways. CD-ROM players only enable you to look at stacks; therefore, stacks on CD-ROM disks are always considered "locked".

You can lock a stack on a 3.5-inch disk by pushing the little black square in the upper-right corner of the disk up. You can lock a stack on any disk in the Finder by clicking once on the stack to select it, choosing Get Info from the File menu, and checking the box named "Locked." Stacks on a file server are locked if they are in a folder with Read Only access privileges. You must lock a stack on a file server if you want more than one person to be able to access that stack.

Locked stacks are write protected. You cannot make changes to stacks that are write protected. But you can view and copy HyperCard stacks that are write-protected. If a stack is write-protected, you'll see a padlock icon on the menu bar. Locked stacks are always write-protected. You can also write-protect a stack by checking the "Can't Modify Stack" box in the Protect Stack dialog box or by setting the "cantModify" stack property to TRUE in the stack script. To unprotect a locked stack, you must first unlock it.

HyperCard 1.2 and AppleShare

Stacks can now be opened from volumes on an AppleShare file server.

- Any number of users can look at a stack (Read Only) on an AppleShare file server if the stack is locked. If it's not locked, only one user at a time can look at the stack.

- Only one user at a time can add or change information in a stack on a file server.

- You can lock a stack on a file server by putting the stack in a folder with Read Only access privileges.

For more about additions and changes in HyperCard version 1.2, click on the "Click Me First!" button on the Home card.

THE HYPERTALK SCRIPTING LANGUAGE

This appendix lists all HyperTalk commands, properties, functions, variables, messages, and operators that were covered in this book plus others that were not. HyperCard objects are also listed. However, optional words that can be used with commands are not listed separately but with their appropriate commands.

HyperTalk words added to version 1.2 are preceded by an asterisk (*). In the Format column, square brackets ([ ]) indicate an optional word you can include, the symbols < > indicate that you must type something. Slashes (/) within square brackets indicate that you can use one or the other, but not both. Slashes within < > indicate that you must type one of the choices.

Use this appendix as a quick reference guide when scripting with HyperTalk. Commands are not case-sensitive, therefore; it doesn't matter whether you capitalize one letter or all letters or no letters.

Note: The more esoteric HyperTalk words were not included. To fully understand how to use those words, it is necessary to either take a class or read a book on HyperTalk programming.

Key Word	Description	Format	Examples
abs	This function returns the absolute value of a number, which is always a postive value. The absolute value of -23 is 23.	the abs of <container or value> abs(container or value)	get the abs of field 10 put abs(field 20) into varx
add	This command adds numbers together and puts the result into the last field listed.	add <source> to <container>	add field 1 to field 2 add 10 to card field 3
and	This logical operator joins two or more expressions. It is used with the If command and returns a value of true if both expressions are true, or false if one expression is false.	<exp> and <exp	If x = 9 and "Yes" is in field 1 then print card

Key Word	Description	Format	Examples
annuity	This function computes your monthly payments on a loan. The rate is the interest rate per month, year, or other time period. You must divide the annuity by the amount of the loan to get the amount to be paid per time period, for example, per month.	annuity (\<rate\>,\<period\>)	put 2000 / annuity (.12,4) into msg box (the above formula computes the monthly payments on $2000 at 12% annually for four years and displays that amount in the message box.
answer	This command displays a dialog box with buttons.	answer "\<question\>" with "\<reply\>" or "\<reply\>" or"\<reply\>"	answer "Do you want to continue?" with "yes" or "no" or "cancel"
arrowKey	This message is sent to a card when an arrow key (up, down left, or right) is pressed. Use the If command to tell HyperCard what to do when a particular arrow key is pressed.	arrowKey up/down/left/right	if arrowKey is "up" then go to next card of background 1
ask	This command displays a dialog box that includes one line into which you can type. Adding "with" followed by an answer will put that answer in the line. You can then either change it or press Return to accept it.	ask "\<question\>" ask "\<question\>" with "\<answer\>"	ask "What's your name?" ask "How many?" with "1"
ask password	This command displays a dialog box in which you must enter a password. The text typed within quotes appears in the dialog box.	ask password "\<question\>"	ask password "Enter password"
autoHilite	This button property makes a button appear highlighted while the mouse button is down. Set it to false if you don't want the button to be highlighted when the mouse is down. You can set this button property to true or false in a script as well as in the Button Info dialog box.		set autoHilite of btn 1 to true
*autoTab	This field property moves the insertion point to the next field when you press the Return key and the insertion point is in the last line of that field. You can set this field property to true or false in a script as well as in the Field Info dialog box.		set autoTab to true

Key Word	Description	Format	Examples
average	This function gives you the average of a list of numbers.	average (numbers)	average (4,6,9,12)
background	This word refers to a HyperCard object. Refer to a background by its name, order number, or unique ID number. You don't have to spell it out. Its abbreviated form is "bkgnd." In version 1.2, you can also abbreviate it as "bg" and "bgs."	background bkgnd bg bgs	
beep	Beep is the sound you hear when you've made a mistake or when the Macintosh wants to alert you for some reason, for example, when the printer is out of paper or a search is complete. You can control when the Macintosh beeps by adding the Beep command to a script.	beep <number> beep 3	beep
blindTyping	You can set this HyperCard property to true (on) or false (off). BlindTyping lets you type commands from the keyboard without using the Message box. (You won't see what you type, but the command(s) will be executed.)		set blindTyping to true set blindTyping to false
*bottom	This property applies to fields, buttons, and windows. It refers to the current vertical coordinate of the bottom of the object. You can get or set this property. Use this property to move an object up or down on a card or to move the insertion point within a field.		get bottom of card field 1 set bottom of field 9 to 200 set bottom of tool window to 300 set bottom of msg box to x*10
*bottomRight	This property applies to fields, buttons, and windows. It refers to the horizontal and vertical coordinates of the bottom-right corner of an object. You can get or set this property. Use this property to move an object to a new position on the card or to move the insertion point within a field.		get bottomRight of btn 1 set bottomRight of btn 1 to 9, 9 click at bottomRight of field 1
brush	This paint property tells HyperCard to select the size of the brush. Choose a number between 1 and 32.	set brush to <number>	set brush to 1 set brush to 12 set brush to 32

Key Word	Description	Format	Examples
button	A HyperCard object. Refer to a button by name, order number, or unique ID number. In version 1.2 you can use the abbreviation "btn". Precede the button specified with "bkgnd" if it's a background button. Otherwise, HyperCard assumes you're referring to a card button.	button btn	set textStyle of button to plain get the mouseloc of btn 8 show bkgnd button "Ok"
*cantDelete	This property applies to cards, backgrounds, and stacks. You can get or set this property. Setting this property to true prevents you from deleting the named object.		set cantDelete of card to true get cantDelete of this stack
*cantModify	This stack property can be set to true or false. When true, no one can make any changes to this stack. Note: If the userModify property is set to true, you can temporarily use the paint tools and make changes to field text; however, those changes are not saved. When you close the card, it reverts back to the way it was.		set cantModify of this stack to true
card	A HyperCard object. Refer to a card by name, order number, or unique ID number. In version 1.2 you can use the abbreviation "cd" and "cds".	card cd cards cds	go to card 5 go to card ID 7890 go to card "main menu" show all cards
centered	Set this paint property to true or false, depending on where you want HyperCard to start drawing. To draw a shape from its center out, set centered to true. To begin drawing from the top-left corner of the object, set centered to false.		set centered to true set centered to false
choose	This command tells HyperCard which tool in the Tools menu to select.	choose <tool name> tool	choose button tool choose lasso tool choose select tool
click	This command positions the pointer or insertion point at a specific location on the card. The first number is the horizontal coordinate. The second number is its vertical coordinate. To type with paint text, first choose the Text tool.	click at <horiz.>,<vert.> [with ShiftKey/OptionKey/ CommandKey]	click at the loc of btn 1 click at the topLeft of field 1 choose text tool click at 300,300 type "magic typing."

Key Word	Description	Format	Examples
*clickH	This function gives you only the horizontal coordinate of the last mouse click.	the clickH	put the clickH into msg box
*clickV	This function gives you only the vertical coordinate of the last mouse click.	the clickV	put the clickV into msg box
clickLoc	This function gives you the location of the mouse pointer where it was last clicked. The value returned is the horizontal and vertical location of the pointer on the screen (h,v).	the clickLoc	get the clickLoc put the clickLoc into it
close file	This command closes a file after reading from it or writing to it. This command is used only for importing or exporting text. If the file to be closed is inside a folder, you must name the folder in which it is located as well as the name of the file.	close file "name of file"	close file "budget" close file ":Finances: Budget"
close printing	This command tells HyperCard when to stop printing cards. Used with the Open Printing command.	close printing	open printing repeat with x = 1 to 12 print card go next card end repeat close printing
closeBack-ground	This message is sent to a background as soon as you either press Command-B, choose Background from the Edit menu to leave the current background shown, or exit HyperCard.		on closeBackground doMenu revert reset paint end close Background
closeCard	This message is sent to a card as soon as you go to another card or stack or exit HyperCard.		on closeCard hide button 3 end closeCard
closeField	This message tells HyperCard what to do when the insertion point leaves a field whose contents have been changed.		on closeField put the date into field "date" end closeField
closeStack	This message is sent when this stack is closed.		on closeStack show menubar hide field 2 end closeStack
commandKey	This function tells you whether the command key is up or down.	the commandKey the cmdKey	get the commandKey if the command Key is down then show card field 4

Key Word	Description	Format	Examples
compound	This function computes the interest gained on the principal and interest of a specified amount. Enter the interest rate and time period that rate corresponds to. For example, if you specified the interest rate per year, then the period must be specified in years. The result is the amount earned per period (month or year) specified.	compound (<rate>,<period>)	put 2000 * compound (.06,30) (The above example computes the value of a $2000 investment earning 6% interest compounded annually for 30 years. At the end of 30 years, the original $2000 will have grown to $11,486.98.)
contains	This operator returns a value of true or false.	<container> contains <value>	if field 1 contains 101 then print card
convert	This command changes a time or date from its current format into the format specified.

Acceptable formats: short date, long date, abbr date, short time, long time, abbr time, seconds, dateItems.

When converted into seconds, you can perform calculations which can then be converted back into another time/date format.

The DateItems format converts the date into numbers separated by commas. These numbers represent the year, month, day, hour, minute, second, and day of the week, in that order. For days of the week, Sunday is 1, Monday is 2, etc. | convert <container> to <format> | convert time to seconds convert date to short date |
| cursor | You can set the property to a number that corresponds to a cursor resource. You can choose a number between 1 and 5 to change the cursor to an I-beam, a plus sign, a cross, a watch, or a pointer arrow, respectively.

If you have installed other cursor resources in your stack, you can change the cursor to the name or number that corresponds to the one you want. | | set cursor to 1 set cursor to 2 set cursor to 3 set cursor to 4 set cursor to 5 |

394

Key Word	Description	Format	Examples
*cursor	In version 1.2, you can refer to cursors by name. There are also three additional cursor properties: hand, none, busy. Hand is the browse tool. None makes the cursor disappear. Busy is the beach ball.	set cursor to <name>	set cursor to I-beam set cursor to cross set cursor to plus set cursor to watch set cursor to arrow set cursor to hand set cursor to none set cursor to busy
date	This function gives you the current date. This date is the one determined by your internal Macintosh clock. the date: same format as the short date the short date: 07/27/88 the long date: Friday, October 20, 1988 the abbr date: Fri, Oct 20, 1988	the date the short date the long date the abbr date	get the date put the date into field "date"
delete	This command erases the chunk of text in the named field.	delete <chunk> of card <name>	delete char 1 to 3 of field 3 delete word 2 of field 1
delete-Background	This message tells HyperCard what to do before deleting a background card.		on delete Background answer "Are you sure?" with "yes" or "cancel" end delete Background
deleteButton	This message tells Hypercard what to do before deleting a button.		on deleteButton answer "Are you sure?" with "yes" or "cancel" end deleteButton

deleteCard	This message tells HyperCard what to do before deleting the card currently shown.		on deleteCard
			  global temp
			  put field "name" into temp
			end deleteCard

deleteField	This message tells HyperCard what to do before deleting this field.		on deleteField add field 4 to field 9 end deleteField
deleteStack	This message tells HyperCard what to do before deleting this stack.		on deleteStack doMenu Save a Copy... end deleteStack

Key Word	Description	Format	Examples
dial	This command dials a telephone number. Be sure the Macintosh is connected to your telephone with the appropriate hardware before using this command. Include "with modem" if using a modem.	dial <phone number> dial <phone number> with modem	
diskSpace	This function tells you how much storage space is left on the disk you're currently using.	the diskSpace	put the diskSpace into msg box
divide	This command divides the value of the container by the number listed. The container must contain a number or you'll get an error message.	divide <container> by <number>	divide field 5 by field 3 divide card field 4 by 12
do	This command executes the commands in a container. The information in the container must be a HyperTalk command. (You cannot use the Do command from within the message box. You must type it into a script.)	do <container>	do field 1 do it
doMenu	This command selects a command from a pull-down menu. You must spell the menu command exactly as it appears on the pull-down menu for this command to work. Also, the command must be available at the current user level setting.	doMenu <menu choice>	doMenu Delete Card doMenu Open Stack...
down	This constant is the value of the mouse button or a key on the keyboard when it is pressed down.		if the mouse is down then show card field 9
drag	This command moves selected objects from one place on a card to another. You can also use it to draw by first choosing one of the paint tools for drawing.	drag from <x,y> to <x,y>	choose select tool drag from 0,0 to 0,300 choose oval tool drag from 10,15 to 54,80
dragSpeed	This property is used to set the speed at which a tool is dragged with the Drag command. Set the dragspeed to 0 for the fastest possible performance. A normal speed is 400. A slow speed is 1. (The speed is measured in pixels per second.)		set dragSpeed to 0 set dragSpeed to 400

Key Word	Description	Format	Examples
edit script of	This command displays the script of the named object. This command comes in handy when you need to get to a card's script but can't because of mistakes made in other scripts. Make sure the user level is set to Scripting or this command won't work.	edit script of <object name>	edit script of card 1 edit script of btn 10 edit script of field "calc"
empty	This constant when used with the Put command empties the contents of a field or other container.		put empty into It put empty into field 1
end	Signals the end of a handler. Tells HyperCard to stop executing instructions.	end <message>	on mouseUp go to next card end mouseUp

enterInField	This message tells HyperCard if the Enter key is pressed while the insertion point or a selection is within a field.		on enterInField
			  put line 1 + line 2
			    into line 3
			end enterInField

exit	This command tells HyperCard to stop executing the commands in this handler.	exit <message>	on mouseUp
			  if hilite of button 1 is
			    false
			     then exit mouseUp
			    else go next card
			end mouseUp

exit repeat	This command stops executing commands in a repeat loop on some condition.	exit repeat	repeat with x = 1 to 100
			  go to card x
			  if field 1>100
			    then exit repeat
			  print card x
			end repeat

exit to HyperCard	This command stops executing all handlers in a script. The message box will not recognize this command. You must type it into a script.	exit to HyperCard	if commandKey is down
			  then exit to Hyper-
			    Card

false	False is a constant. Some properties have a value of either true or false. Setting a property to false is the same as turning a feature off.
	
	You can set up conditional commands that tell HyperCard what to do when a property is true and what to do when it is false.
	
	It is also useful at times to assign a value of true or false to a variable.
			set hilite of button 1 to
			  false
			set the visible of field 1
			  to false
			set bindTyping to false
			
			if the hilite of button 1
			  is false
			  then show card field 4
			
			set tempflag to false

Key Word	Description	Format	Examples
field	A HyperCard object. Refer to a field by its name, order number, or unique ID number. Precede the field specified with "card" if it's a card field. Otherwise, HyperCard assumes you're referring to a background field. In version 1.2 you can use the abbreviation "fld" and "flds".	field fields fld flds	go to field 8 put it into card field ID 45
filled	A paint property you can set to true or false. When true, shapes drawn are filled with the current pattern selected. When false, shapes drawn are unfilled.		set filled to true set filled to false
find	This command finds a word, number, or group of characters in one or more fields.	find chars "<characters>" find word "<word>" find "<text>" in field <name>	find chars "ed" find word "hello" find "hello" in field 3
*find	In version 1.2, you can now use "whole" and "string" in a Find command. Searches include spaces.	find whole "<word or phrase>" find string "<word or phrase>"	find "John Doe" find "26AB"
flash	This command turns a card from white to black and white again. The current card shown will invert the number of times specified.	flash	flash 3
formFeed	This constant is used to advance the paper in the printer to the top of the next page.		print card & formFeed
*foundChunk	This function shows where the chunk expression was found. For example, if the found text is characters 3 to 5 of card field 9, the value returned is "char 3 to 5 of card field 9."	the foundChunk	find "Hello" Put the foundChunk into msg box
*foundField	This function identifies the field number in which the text was found. For example, if the found text is in background field 1, the value returned is "background field1."	the foundField	find "Hello" put the foundField into msg box
*foundLine	This function identifies the line number and field number on which the text was found. For example, if the found text is on line 4 of card field 2, the value returned is "line 4 of card field 2."	the foundLine	find "hello" put the foundLine into msg box

Key Word	Description	Format	Examples
foundText	This function identifies the text found with the Find command. If no text was found, the value of this function is "empty."	the foundText	find "Hello" put the foundText into msg box
freeSize	This stack property tells you how much space is unused in the stack yet still taking up space on the disk. You can free this space to give you more disk storage by choosing Compact Stack from the File menu.	the freeSize	put the freeSize of this stack into msg box
functionKey	Use this message to program the function keys on a Macintosh Extended keyboard. That keyboard is the only Macintosh keyboard that includes function keys: F1 through F15. You must follow "on functionKey" with the name of a variable, but do not put this variable following "end functionKey."	functionKey	on functionKey whichKey if whichKey is 6 then go help end functionKey
get	This command puts the value of a function, container, constant, or property into the variable named It.		get short id of this card get field 1 get the visible of button 1 get the date
global	This command is used to declare variables shared by different scripts, in the same or another stack. You must declare a variable as global in each handler that uses it. By declaring variables as global, they will retain their values from one script to another instead of being emptied each time you exit a script. Global variables are emptied only when you exit HyperCard.	global <variable name>	global total global x, y, z
go	This command displays another card or stack.	go [to] <card or stack>	go to next card go to card 3 go to stack "Address" go to card 3 of stack "Address"
	Go Back takes you to the previous card shown. (Same as typing "go recent card" or pressing the tilde (~) or esc key.)	go back	
grid	This paint property turns the grid on and off. Setting the grid to true turns it on; setting it to false turns it off.		set grid to true set grid to false

Key Word	Description	Format	Examples
*height	This property applies to buttons and fields. It contains the height of an object in pixels. You can get or set this property. To change the height of field 1, for example, type set height of field 1 to 80. Field 1 will expand or contract to the new height.		set height of field 1 to 50 set height of btn 1 to height of btn 2
help	This command displays the help stack.		help go help
hide	This command renders fields and buttons invisible. (Use the Show command to make them reappear.)	hide <object name>	hide button ID 99 hide card field "Help text"
*hide picture	This command hides a card or background picture.	hide <card/background> picture hide picture of <card/ background>	hide card picture hide background picture hide picture of card ID 88
hilite	Buttons have a hilite property as well as an autoHilite property. The autoHilite property works only when the mouse button is down. The hilite property will highlight a button any time.		set hilite of me to true set hilite of btn 6 to false
home	The first card in the Home stack is the card HyperCard returns to when you type "go home."		go home
id	You can refer to an object by its ID number. Each object is automatically assigned a unique ID number. You cannot change an object's ID number.		show button ID 3425 go to card ID 4322
idle	This message tells HyperCard what to do when nothing else is happening.		on idle put the time in field end idle

if	Use this command to specify a condition that must be true before executing the instructions that follow it.
	
	You must include an "end if" statement only if "then" or"else" is followed by more than one command.
		if <condition> then
		  <command>
		
		if <condition> then
		  <command>
		  <command>
		end if
		
		if <condition> then
		  <command>
		else
		  <command>
		  <command>
		end if
			if x = 5 then go stack Home

Key Word	Description	Format	Examples
is	Use this logical operator to test if the text specified on the left is the same as text specified on the right. Same as using =.	\<container\> is "\<text\>"	if xname is "Voelkel" then put xname into fld 1
is in	Use this logical operator to test if the text specified on the left is also included in the text specified on the right.	\<"text"\> is in \<container\>	if "Ginger" is in fld 1 then print card
is not	Use this logical operator to test if the text specified on the left is not the same as the text specified on the right. Same as <> or ≠.	\<container\> is not \<"text"\>	if fld 1 is not "1001" then go next card
is not in	Use this logical operator to test if the text specified on the left is not included in the text specified on the right.	\<"text"\> is not in \<container\>	if "Ginger" is not in fld 1 then go next card
* is within * is not within	Use this logical operator to test if the pointer is or is not within a specific rectangle such as a field or button.	\<point\> is within \<rect\> \<point is not within \<rect\>	if the mouseLoc is within the rect of button 1 then beep
it	The word "It" is a variable or container. Any value obtained with the Get, Ask, Answer, Convert, or Read From File commands are automatically put into It. You can then use the Put command to empty the contents of It into another container.		ask "How many" put it into total get line 1 of card field 3 put it into field 9
*left	A field, button, and window property. It refers to the horizontal coordinate on the left edge of an object on a card. You can get or set this property. Changing this property aligns the left side of the object to the coordinate specified.		set left of btn 1 to 20 set left of tool window to x - 1
length	This function tells how many characters are in a specified group of text.	the length of \<container\> length (\<container\>)	the length of line 1 of field 2 length (line 1 of field 2)
lineFeed	This constant is used to advance the paper in the printer up one line.		print card & lineFeed
lineSize	This paint property determines the thickness of a line drawn with the line tool. You can choose a line width of 1, 2, 3, 4, 6, or 8 in pixels.		set lineSize to 4

Key Word	Description	Format	Examples
location	This property applies to buttons, fields, and windows. You can get or set this property for a specific button, field, or window.	location loc	set the loc of Tool window to 0,0 set the loc of msg box to 50,100 set the loc of card window to 0,0
	Getting the location gives you the horizontal and vertical coordinates of the center of a button, field, or window on the screen. Setting the location of an object moves it to the new location.		get the location of btn 1
*lock screen	Use this command to lock the screen while a script is running. This command works the same as setting the lockScreen to true. (See also *unlock screen*.)	lock screen	lock screen repeat with x = 1 to 10 hide card field x end repeat unlock screen
lockRecent	Set this property to true or false. Setting it to true locks the Recent card so that no more cards are added to it. Setting it to false unlocks it so cards viewed are added to the sequence in miniature form.		set lockRecent to true set lockRecent to false
lockScreen	Set this property to true or false. Setting it to true keeps one card on the screen while operations are performed "behind the scenes." Setting LockScreen to false enables you to view all cards again.		set lockScreen to true repeat with i = 1 to 10 print card i end repeat set lockScreen to false
lockText	Set this field property to true or false. Setting it to true prevents others from changing the contents of the specified field. Setting it to false unlocks the field, enabling its contents to be altered.		set lockText of field 1 to true
max	This function gets the largest number from a specified list. Separate each number or container named in the list with a comma.	max(n,n,n)	max(field 1, field 2, field 3)
me	Refers to the current object selected.		get the id of me set the hilite of me to true
*me	In version 1.2, me can also refer to the contents of a container.		

402

Key Word	Description	Format	Examples
message box	You can show or hide the message box. You can also display words, numbers, and other characters in this box. Sometimes this box is used to contain instructions to the end user.	message box msg box	show msg box put the date into msg box
min	This function gets the smallest number from a specified list. Separate each number or container named in the list with a comma.	min(n,n,n)	min(field 1, field 2, field 3)
mouse	This function tells you if the mouse button is up or down.	the mouse	if the mouse is down then hide card field 9
mouseClick	This function tells you whether the mouse button has been pressed (clicked). If it has, the value returned is true. If not, the value is false.	the mouseClick	wait until the mouseClick
mouseDown	This message tells HyperCard what to do when the mouse button is being held down.		on mouseDown set hilite of me to true end mouseDown
mouseH	This function tells you the horizontal location of the mouse (number of pixels from left side of screen).	the mouseH	get the mouseH
mouseLeave	This message tells HyperCard what to do when the cursor moves outside of a button orlocked field.		on mouseLeave set the hilite of me to false end mouseLeave
mouseLoc	This function tells you the location of the current position of the mouse on the screen. It returns the horizontal and vertical positions, in that order, for example, 512,342.	the mouseLoc	get the mouseLoc
mouseStill-Down	This message tells HyperCard what to do while the mouse button is being held down.		on mouse StillDown show card field "help txt" end mouseStillDown
mouseUp	This message tells HyperCard what to do when the mouse button is released after being held down.		on mouseUp go next card end mouseUp
mouseV	This function tells you the vertical location of the mouse (number of pixels from top of screen).	the mouseV	get the mouseV

Key Word	Description	Format	Examples
mouseWithin	This message tells HyperCard what to do when the mouse pointer is within the boundaries of a button or locked field.		on mouseWithin show card field 3 end mouseWithin
multiple .	Use this paint property within a script to set the Draw Multiple command to true or false.		set multiple to true
multiply	Multiplies numbers, putting the result in the container. The container must contain a number.	multiply <container> by <number>	multiply field 1 by 35 multiply it by field 15
multiSpace	This paint property determines how many pixels apart images are drawn when Draw Multiple is chosen or when the multiple paint property is set to true. You can choose a number between 1 and 9 for the spacing.		set multiSpace to 4

name	This property tells you the name of a stack, background, card, field, or button. Objects have a long name and a short name. The long name contains the path (name of disk and folders) as well as the object name. The short name shows the name you assigned to that object.		get the name of field 7
			put the short name of
			  card in x
			put the long name of
			  stack in y

newBackground	This message tells HyperCard what to do after creating a background card.		on new Background do Menu New Field end newBackground

newButton	This message tells HyperCard what to do after creating a button.		on newButton
			  get textStyle of
			  new button
			  set textStyle to
			  italic
			end newButton

newCard	This message tells HyperCard what to do after adding a card to the stack.		on newCard
			  add 1 to bkgnd field
			  "total"
			end newCard

newField	This message tells HyperCard what to do after adding a field.		on newField
			  get textFont of new
			  field
			  set textFont to
			  Chicago
			end newField

Key Word	Description	Format	Examples
newStack	This message tells HyperCard what to do after creating a stack.		on newStack paste card end newStack

not	Logical operator used to test an expression to see if it is true or false. If it is true, then this expression returns a value of false. If it is false, then the value is true.	\<exp\> not true/false	If field 1 > 9 is not true
			  then print card
			
			set hilite of me to not
			  hilite of me

number	This function tells you the number of backgrounds or cards in a stack, buttons or fields on a card or background, or number of lines, items, words, or characters are in a container.	the number of \<objects\>	get the number of
			  cards
			get the number of
			  fields
			repeat with i to the
			  number of cards

*number	In version 1.2, Number can refer to the number of cards in a specific background.	the number of cards of background \<name\>	repeat with i to
			  the number of cards
			  of background 1
			print card

number	Use this property to get the order number of a background, card, field, or button. This number represents the order in which the object was created on the current card. (That is, its number in the layering scheme.) You cannot change this number.		get the number of card 1 get the number of field 4

numberFormat	Use this property to determine how numbers will appear in a stack - that is, how many digits to the right of the decimal point are displayed and whether leading or trailing zeroes are shown. Enclose the format in quotation markes.
	
	Use zeroes to indicate where a zero should appear, a decimal point if you want one, and pound signs (#) to indicate how precise the number should be.
			set the numberFormat to
			  "0.##"
			set the numberFormat to
			  ".00"
			
			(The first example above will not put zeroes to the right of the decimal for whole numbers, whereas the second example will.)

on	Must be followed by a message to tell HyperCard when to execute the instructions between "on" and "end."	on \<message\>	on mouseUp go to next card end mouseUp
open	Use this command to open an application program or a specific file created with that application.		open "Doc" with "Word" open MacWrite

Key Word	Description	Format	Examples
open printing	Use this command to open the print buffer and start reading cards into it. As soon as it's read enough cards to print one page, printing begins.	open printing open printing with dialog	

open-Background	This message is sent to a background as soon as you either press Command-B or choose Background from the Edit menu to show the current background.		on openBackground
			   put the date into field
			     "date"
			end open Background

openCard	This message is sent to a card as soon as you open it.		on openCard
			   put the date into field
			     "date"
			end openCard

openField	This message is sent to an unlocked field as soon as you enter it by pressing either the Tab key or clicking the mouse into it.		on openField
			   put the date into field
			     "date"
			end openField

openStack	This message is sent to a card in this stack as soon as this stack is opened.		on openStack
			   hide menubar
			   put the time into field
			     "time"
			end openStack

optionKey	Use this function to find out whether the option key is up or down. Returns a value of either "up" or "down."	the optionKey	get the optionKey
			if the optionKey is
			   down
			   then show card field 4

or	Logical operator used to join two or more expressions. Used with the If command to return a value of true if any one of the expressions are true or a value of false if all expressions are false.	<exp> or <exp>	If x = 9 or "Yes" is in
			   field 1
			   then print card

pass	Use this command to pass a message up the hierarchy of objects so it can be used by another script.		on mouseUp
			   if the option key is
			     down
			     then pass mouseUp
			   else go next card
			end mouseUp

pattern	This paint property sets the value of a pattern to a number between 1 and 40. The numbers correspond from left to right to the patterns in the Patterns window.		set pattern to 10

Key Word	Description	Format	Examples
pattern window	Refers to the Patterns menu. Since this is a tear-off menu, you can place it anywhere on the screen. You can use the Get command to get the number of the current pattern selected.		show pattern window at 0,0 get pattern window
pi	This function returns the value of pi. The value of pi is equal to equal to 3.14159265358979323846.		multiply field 4 by pi put pi into field 3
play	Use this command to play one of the built-in sounds—beep, boing, or harpsicord—or a sound you've digitized and copied into a stack. (If the name of the sound includes a space, you must enclose that name in quotes.)	play "sound" [tempo] ["notes"]	play beep play boing play harpsicord c d e c
	Use Play stop to stop a sound before it's done playing.	play stop	play stop
polySides	Use this paint property to select the number of sides for a polygon to draw with the polygon tool. Choose any number.	set polysides to <number>	set polygon to 5 set polygon to 12
pop	Use this command to display the most recent card pushed into memory with the Push command.	pop card	pop card
powerKeys	You can set this property to true (on) or false (off). PowerKeys enables you to use single key strokes to select menu commands which is especially useful when you use the paint tools.	set powerKeys to <true/false>	set powerKeys to true set powerKeys to false

print card	Use this command to print the card currently shown on the screen.		on mouseUp
			  open printing
			  print card
			    go next
			    print card
			  close printing
			end mouseUp

push	Use this command to mark this card for later retrieval with a Pop command. Cards you push with the Push command are copied into memory in the order in which they were pushed. The last one pushed into memory is the first one popped out with the Pop command.	push card	on mouseUp push card end mouseUp
put	Use the Put command to put text, numbers, or other values into a container.	put <word> <before/after/into> <container>	put "Mary" before "Smith" in put it into temp
quit	Use this command to quit HyperCard and return to the Finder.	quit HyperCard	

Key Word	Description	Format	Examples
quote	Use this constant to put a quotation mark within a concatenated group of words.	quote	put quote &"Hello" &&"World" &quote into msg box
recent card	Refers to the previous card shown. The card before the current card as displayed on the Recent card. (Same as Back.)		go to recent card
rectangle	This property applies to buttons, fields, and windows. You can get or set this property for a specific button, field, or window. You can also resize an object with this property. Getting the location gives you the horizontal and vertical coordinates of the top-left and bottom-right corners of a button, field, or window on the screen. So, the rectangle property contains four numbers. To resize a field, button, or window, get the rectangle of that object and then drag a corner to a new location with the Drag command.	rectangle rect	get the rect of field 1

repeat	Use this command to create a loop in which the commands within it are repeated either a specific number of times or until some condition is false.	repeat <number> repeat until repeat while repeat with <exp>	repeat 10
			  go next
			  add 1 to field 1
			end repeat

reset paint	Use this command to put the paint settings back the way they were.	reset paint	
result	Use this function to find out if there was an error in the previous command. If no error is found, the value of the result is empty.	the result	if the result is empty then go Home
return	Places a carriage return in a string of text so that characters following "return" begin on the next line.		put "this is line 1"&return&"this is line 2" in field 1

*returnInField	This message tells HyperCard if the Return key is pressed while the insertion point or a selection is within a field.		on returnInfield
			  get selection
			  find it
			end returnInfield

returnKey	This message is sent to a card when the return key is pressed while the insertion point is not within a field.		on returnKey go to next card end returnKey

Key Word	Description	Format	Examples
*right	A field, button, and window property. It refers ers to the horizonal coordinate of the right edge of an object on a card. You can get or set this property. Changing this property aligns the right side of the object to the coordinate specified.		set right of btn 1 to 20 set right of msg box to 512
round	Use this function to round a number to the nearest integer. For example, 98.99 is rounded off to 99.	the round of <number> round(number)	put the round of field 1 into field 2
*screenRect	Function. Returns coordinates of the screen size of the monitor you are currently using. If you have a large screen monitor, you can use these coordinates to move the card, tool, pattern, and message box windows to various locations on the screen.	the screenRect	get the screenRect
scroll	This field property tells you how many pixels of text you've scrolled past the field.		get the scroll of field 1
*select	This command selects either a button, a field, or a chunk of text within a field or container. You cannot select hidden buttons or fields. You can also use this command to position the insertion point anywhere in a field or container. For example, Select After text of field 3 positions the insertion point after the last character in field 3. To unselect text, use Select empty.	select <name of object> select [before/after] text of <container> select [before/after] <chunk> of <container> select empty	select button 1 select field 1 select word 3 to 5 of field 7 select after text of field 1 select before line 3 of field 2
*selectedChunk	This function identifies which chunk of text is currently selected. For example, if the first five characters of a word have been selected in field 1, this function returns this value: char 1 to 5 of field 1	the selectedChunk	put the selectedChunk into field 1
*selectedField	This function identifies which field contains selected text. For example, if any text in background field 3 is selected, this function returns this value: background field 3	the selectedField	put the selectedField
*selectedLine	This function identifies the first line on which the selected text appears. For example, if the first three lines of field 1 have been selected this function returns this value: line 1 of field 1	the selectedLine	put the selectedLine

Key Word	Description	Format	Examples
*selectedText	This function gives you the currently selected text, but is not a container. Note: For selectedText, selectedLine, selectedField, and selectedChunk, if no text is selected, these functions return the constant "empty."	the selectedText	put the selectedText
selection	This container contains the text currently highlighted in a field.		get the selection put the selection into field 1
send	Use this command to send a message to an object, variable, or container.	send <message> to <target>	send mouseUp to button 1 send "delete char 1 to 5 to it
set	Use this command to change a property of an object.	set <property> of <object> to <value>	set textFont of btn 1 to Geneva set autoHilite of btn 1 to true set lockText of field 3 to true
shiftKey	Use this function to find out whether the Shift key is up or down. Returns a value of either "up" or "down."	the shiftKey	if the shiftKey is down then show card field 4
show	Use this command to display hidden objects, to display a number of cards one after the other, or to display objects at different places on the screen.	show <name of object> show <number> cards show <object> at h,v	show field 10 show all cards show tool window at 0,0 show menuBar
*show picture	Use this command to display a card or background picture previously hidden with the Hide Picture command.	show card picture show background picture show picture of <name of card or background>	
showLines	Set this field property to true or false. Setting it to true shows lines in a field. Setting it to false makes the lines invisible.		set showLines of field 1 to true
showName	Set this button property to true or false. Setting it to true displays a button's name inside the button. Setting it to false makes the name invisible.		set showName of btn 1 to true
*showPict	This property applies to cards and backgrounds. Setting it to true reveals a hidden picture. It works the same as the Show Picture command. Setting showPict to false hides the picture specified. It works the same as the Hide Picture command.		set showPict of this card to true set showPict of bkgnd 3 to false set the showPict of this card

Key Word	Description	Format	Examples
size	A stack property. Find out how large a stack is in kilobytes by typing "get the size."		get the size of this stack
sort	This command sorts all of the cards in a stack in a specified order. If no order is specified, HyperCard sorts cards by the contents of the named background field as text and in ascending order. The type can be numeric or dateTime. DateTime is used with Sort to indicate that the field to be sorted by contains a date or time.	sort by \<background field> sort /ascending/descending/ [type] by \<bkgnd field> sort dateTime by \<field>	sort by field 3 sort ascending numeric by field 1 sort dateTime by field "time" sort numeric by field "index" sort dateTime by field "time" sort dateTime by field 1
sound	This function tells you the name of the sound currently playing. If no sound is playing, this function returns "done."	the sound	on mouseUp play boing repeat until the sound is "done" set hilite of me to true end repeat end mouseUp
style	This property applies to fields and buttons. Field styles can be set to transparent, opaque, rectangle, shadow, or scrolling. Button styles can be set to transparent, opaque, rectangle, roundRect, shadow, checkBox, or radioButton.		set the style of field 1 to shadow set the style of btn 1 to checkBox
subtract	This command subtracts numbers from a container and puts the result in the container. The container must contain a number.	subtract \<number> from \<container>	subtract 12 from field 1 subtract 10 from it
tab	Places a tab character in a string of text to move the cursor to the next field in sequence.		type "this is the last line." & tab
tabKey	This message is sent to a card when the tab key is pressed. You can use it to move the insertion point to the next line in a field each time you press the Tab key.		on tabKey type return end tabKey
target	This function returns the ID number of the background, card, field, or button of the object chosen.	the target	get the target of this card
*target	In version 1.2, this function refers to the contents of a container if not preceded by the word "the."	target	put target into it

Key Word	Description	Format	Examples

textAlign	This property determines if text within a button or field or text typed with the Text tool appears aligned to the right, left, or centered within the object. Name the button or field in which the text is to be aligned. If you do not name a button or field, HyperCard assumes you mean paint text.	textAlign of \<object name\>
		textAlign
			set textAlign of field 1
			    to right
			set textAlign of btn 2
			    to left
			
			set textAlign to centere

textArrows	Set this property to true if you want the keyboard arrows keys to move the cursor within a field.		set textArrows to true

textFont	Set this property to any font in your stack. Name the object whose text font is to be changed. If you do not specify an object, HyperCard assumes you mean paint text.	textFont of \<object name\>
		textFont
			set textFont of field 1
			    to courier
			set textFont of btn 2 to
			    Monaco
			set textFont to Times

textHeight	The text height is the vertical distance between two lines of text, also known as "leading." Name the field whose text height is to be changed. If you do not specify a field, HyperCard assumes you mean paint text.	textHeight of \<field name\> textHeight	set textHeight of field 1 to 12 set textHeight to 16

textSize	Set this property to any size font in your stack. Name the object whose text size is to be changed. If you do not specify an object, HyperCard assumes you mean paint text.	textSize of \<object name\>
		textSize
			set textSize of field 1 to
			    18
			set textSize of btn 2 to
			    9
			set textSize to 24

textStyle	Set this property to one or more of these styles: plain, bold, italic, underline, outline, or shadow.
	
	Plain resets the text of a button or field to plain, which refers to the default text style, font, and size used: Plain, Geneva,14 point.
		textStyle of \<object name\>	set the textStyle of field
			    1 to bold
			set the textstyle of btn
			    1 to bold, ital
			
			set textStyle of btn 1 to
			    plain

time	This function returns the current time. The time is determined by the setting on the internal Macintosh clock. the short time hh:mm:ss the long time	the time the long time	get the time put the stime into field "time"
tool	This function tells you the name of the tool currently selected in the Tools window.	the tool	get the tool
tool window	Refers to the Tools menu. Since this is a tear-off menu, you can place it anywhere on the screen.		show tool window at 0,0

412

Key Word	Description	Format	Examples

*top	This property applies to fields, buttons, and windows. It refers to the current vertical coordinate of the top of the object. You can get or set this property. Use this property to move an object up or down on a card or to move the insertion point within a field.		get top of card field 1
			set top of btn 9 to 200
			set top of tool window
			  to 2
			click at the top of field
			  1

*topLeft	This property applies to fields, buttons, and windows. It refers to the horizontal and vertical coordinates of the top left corner of an object. You can get or set this property. Use this property to move an object to a new position on the card or to move the insertion point within a field.		get topLeft of btn 1
			set topLeft of btn 1 to
			  9,9
			
			click at the topLeft of
			  field 1

true	True is a constant. Some properties have a value of either true or false. Setting a property to true is the same as turning a feature on.
	
	You can set up conditional commands that tell HyperCard what to do when a property is true and what to do when it is false.
	
	It is also useful at times to assign a value of true or false to a variable.
			set hilite of button 1 to
			  true
			set the visible of field 1
			  to true
			set blindTyping to true
			
			if the hilite of button 1
			  is true
			  then hide card field 4
			
			set tempflag to true

type	This command types text one letter at a time, as though it were being typed on the keyboard. If the insertion point is not within a field, the letters will be typed into the message box.	type "<text to type>"	type "hello" send tabKey type "hi there"
*unlock screen	This command unlocks a screen previously locked with the Lock Screen command. Unlock Screen works the same as setting the lockScreen to false. (See also *lock screen*.)	unlock screen	
userLevel	You can set this HyperCard property to 1 for browsing, 2 for typing, 3 for painting, 4 for authoring, or 5 for scripting.		set userLevel to 1 set userLevel to 2 set userLevel to 3 set userLevel to 4 set userLevel to 5

413

Key Word	Description	Format	Examples
*userModify	This system property when set to true enables you to use the paint tools and type text into the fields of a locked stack. The changes are only temporarily saved. When you close the card, the changes you made disappear. You'll also be able to make temporary changes to stacks whose cantModify property has been set to true, or if Can't Modify Stack has been checked in the Protect Stack dialog box.		set the userModify to true set the userModify to false
version	This function tells you which version of HyperCard you are using.	the version	put the version in msg box
visible	Use this property to hide or show a button, field, or window. Setting the visible property of an object to true makes it appear if hidden; setting it to false makes it invisible.		set the visible of button 1 to true set the visible of button 1 to false
visual	This command enables you to assign a visual effect to use as a transition between two cards or two stacks. Here are the names of effects you can use: zoom <open/close/in/out> iris <open/close> barn door <open/close> checkerboard venetian blinds wipe <up/down/left/right> dissolve scroll <up/down/left/right> You can set the speed of the effect following the name of the effect: fast, very fast, slow, very slow. You can also specify one of these images to dissolve to: black, gray, white, inverse, card. In version 1.2, you can also spell "gray" as "grey."	visual [effect] <name of effect>[speed] [to [image]]	visual barn door open visual zoom close visual dissolve slowly visual dissolve slow to black

Key Word	Description	Format	Examples
wait	This command tells HyperCard to pause for a specific amount of time, or while some condition is true, or until some condition is false before executing the next command in the script.	wait <number> seconds wait <number> ticks wait while<condition> wait until <condition>	wait 2 seconds wait while the mouse is down wait until the sound is "done" wait 30 ticks
	One tick equals 1/60th of a second. If you need HyperCard to pause between commands for less than 1 second, specify the time in ticks. In version 1.2, you can also use the singular "tick."		
wideMargins	This field property when true adds white space to the left and right margins of a field so the text is not right up against the field's boundaries.		set wideMargins of field 1 to true set wideMargins of field 1 to false
*width	This property applies to buttons and fields. It contains the width of an object in pixels. You can get or set this property. To change the width of field 1, for example, type set width of field 1 to 10. Field 1 will expand or contract to the new width.		set width of field 1 to 50 set width of btn 1 to width of btn 2

Operators used in expressions:

  &   Combine two groups of characters.

 &&   Combine two groups of characters and add one space between each group.

  *   Multiply

  +   Add

  -       Subtract

  /   Divide

  <   Less than

 <=   Less than or equal to

  >   Greater than

 >=   Greater than or equal to

  ^   Exponentiation

QUICK REFERENCE COMMAND CARDS

Tear out these cards and keep them by your Macintosh for quick reference to keyboard commands that are equivalent menu choices.

Function	Equivalent Keyboard Command	Special Notes
General		
Cancel	⌘- .(period)	Cancels current action such as printing. Stops scripts from executing.
Choose Browse tool	⌘-Tab	Works only when a paint tool is not selected.
Hide/show menu bar	⌘-Spacebar	Toggles menu bar on and off.
Hide/show Tools menu	Option-Tab	Toggles Tools menu on and off when using a paint tool.
Open a stack	⌘-O	Asks for name of stack to open.
Print one card	⌘-P	Prints card shown on screen.

Function	Equivalent Keyboard Command	Special Notes
Show buttons	⌘-Option	With the Browse tool chosen, hold down these keys to outline all visible buttons. Background buttons have a thicker outline than card buttons.
		With the Button tool chosen, holding down these keys shows both visible and hidden buttons.
Show fields	⌘-Option	With Field tool chosen, hold down these keys to outline all fields—both hidden and visible.
Show hidden objects	Shift-⌘-Option	In version 1.0.1 and 1.1, holding down these keys makes hidden objects appear.
		In version 1.2, holding down these keys outlines all buttons and fields, both hidden and visible.
Quit HyperCard	⌘-Q	

Peeking at Scripts

Function	Equivalent Keyboard Command	Special Notes
Peek at button script	Double-click on shift key button.	For versions 1.0.1 or 1.1: To see a button's script, choose the Button tool, then hold down the Shift key and double-click on that button.
	⌘-Option Click on button.	For version 1.2: Press ⌘-Option and click on a button to see its script.
Peek at field script	Shift key Double-click on field.	For versions 1.0.1 and 1.1: To see a field's script, choose the Field tool, then hold down the Shift key and double-click on that field.
	Shift-⌘-Option Click on field.	For version 1.2: Press Shift-⌘-Option and click on a field to see its scrip
Peek at script of current card	Shift key Choose Card Info	For versions 1.0.1 and 1.1: Hold down the Shift key while choosing Card Info from Objects menu to see the card script.
	⌘-Option-C	For version 1.2: Press ⌘-Option-C to see its script.

Function	Equivalent Keyboard Command	Special Notes
Peek at script of current background	Shift key Choose Background Info.	For versions 1.0.1 and 1.1: Hold down the Shift key while choosing Background Info from the Objects menu to see the background script.
	⌘-Option-B	For version 1.2: Press ⌘-Option-B to see its script.
Peek at script of current stack	Shift key Choose Stack Info	For versions 1.0.1 and 1.1: Hold down the Shift key while choosing Stack Info from the Objects menu to see the stack script.
	⌘-Option-S	For version 1.2: Press ⌘-Option-S to see its script.

Editing

Background	⌘-B	Toggles background on and off.
Copy	⌘-C	Select any object first.
Cut	⌘-X	Select any object first
Delete card	⌘-Backspace	Deletes card shown.
New card	⌘-N	Adds it after the card shown.
Paste	⌘-V	Pastes object cut or copied.
Paste miniature	⌘-Shift-V	Creates a small picture of the card.
Text Style	⌘-T	Choose text tool first.
Undo	⌘-Z	Cannot undo buttons or fields. Undoes last paint or edit change.

Navigating

Find	⌘-F	Finds word typed between quotations.
Go back	tilde (~) or esc key or ↓	Goes to previous card shown.
Go Help	⌘-?	Opens Help Stack
Go Home	⌘-H	Opens Home stack
Go to next field	Tab	
Go to previous field	Shift-Tab	
Go First card	⌘-1 or ⌘-←	Shows first card in stack

Function	Equivalent Keyboard Command	Special Notes
Go Prev card	⌘-2 or ←	Shows previous card in stack.
Go Next card	⌘-3 or →	Shows next card in stack.
Go Last card	⌘-4 or ⌘-→	Shows last card in stack.
Message box	⌘-M	Toggles on and off.
Pop card	⌘-↑	Shows last card pushed.
Push card	⌘-↓	Marks card shown for later retrieval
Recent card	⌘-R	Shows Recent card

Buttons and Fields

These keys work for buttons when the Button tool is selected and fields when the Field tool is selected.

Bring Closer	⌘ +	Raises the order number of selected object by 1.
Send Farther	⌘ -	Lowers the order number of selected object by 1.
Copy buttons or fields.	Option key	Holding down the option key while dragging creates an exact copy of the selected object.
Delete button or field.	Backspace or Clear	Selected object is deleted.
New Button	⌘-drag	First choose Button tool. Hold down the ⌘ key and drag to create a transparent button.
New Field	⌘-drag	First choose Field tool. Hold down the ⌘ key and drag to create a transparent field.
Use larger font size.	⌘->	Works only with field text. Choose Field tool first.
Use smaller font size.	⌘-<	Works only with field text. Choose Field tool first.
Use next font listed in Field Info box.	⌘-Shift->	Works only with field text. Choose Field tool first.

419

Function	Equivalent Keyboard Command	Special Notes
Use previous font listed in Field Info.	⌘-Shift-<	Works only with field text. Choose Field tool first.
Increase spacing between lines by 1.	⌘-Shift-Option->	For version 1.2 only.
	⌘-Option->	For version 1.1 and before. (You don't need to hold down the Shift key.)
Decrease spacing between lines by 1.	⌘-Shift-Option-<	For version 1.2 only.
	⌘-Option-<	For version 1.1 and before. (You don't need to hold down the Shift key.)

Painting

Function	Equivalent Keyboard Command	Special Notes
Choose Grabber while in FatBits	Option	Hold down Option key while in FatBits to use the grabber. Release the Option key to use the tool you were previously using.
Constrain selection to outer limits of picture	⌘ with select tool	Hold down ⌘ key before selecting object with select tool.
Draw parallel lines	Shift-drag with Line tool selected.	
Edit Pattern	Double-click on a pattern.	Enables you to edit any pattern. Changes are saved only in the stack opened when you edited the pattern.
FatBits	Option-F	Toggles FatBits on and off.
Keep this version	⌘-K	Saves current version of card. Choosing Revert displays the last version kept with the Keep command.
Move in a straight line.	Shift-drag selection	Hold down Shift key while dragging selection either horizontally or vertically.
Select all	⌘-A	Selects entire card or background, whichever is shown.
Select paint text	⌘-S	Selects most recently typed paint text.
Select picture	⌘-click	Choose lasso tool before pressing these with keys to lasso the picture.

Function	Equivalent Keyboard Command	Special Notes
Set spacing between objects copied with Draw Multiple.	Option-*n*	*n* represents a number between 1 and 9. Small numbers draw pictures closer together; large numbers draw them farther apart.
Show opaque	Option -O	Shows all opaque objects while the Option key is held down.
Show Patterns menu	Tab	Toggles this menu on and off when a paint tool is chosen.
Show Tools menu	Option-Tab	Toggles this menu on and off when any tool is chosen.
Use pattern for border.	Option key	Hold down the Option key while drawing a line or shape to use a pattern other than black for a line or border of a shape. The pattern used is the one currently selected.

Paint Shortcuts

Tool	Double-Click	With ⌘ Key
<select>	Selects entire card or background, including white space.	Shrink or enlarge selection depending on which way you're dragging it.
<lasso>	Lassoes all pictures on card or background, excluding white space.	
<pencil>	Toggles between Fatbits and not FatBits.	Selects a location to enlarge in FatBits.
<brush>	Shows several brush sizes from which to choose.	Erases instead of paints.
<eraser>	Erases entire card or background.	Paints opaque white over objects and pictures.
<line>	Shows line widths from which to choose.	

Function	Equivalent Keyboard Command	Special Notes
<rectangle> <round rect <oval> <curve> <polygon>	Toggles Draw Filled on and off. Uses last pattern chosen.	
<regular polygon>	Shows shapes from which to choose. Each has a different number of sides.	
<bucket>	Shows Patterns from which to choose.	
<text>	Shows Text Style dialog box.	

Scripting

Align commands	Tab	All of these commands work only in the script window.
Extend command to next line	Option-Return	
Find next word	⌘-G	
Select entire script	⌘-A	

Power Keys

You can make menu selections by simply pressing one or two keys while any paint tool is chosen. To do so, you must first choose Power Keys from the Options menu or check the box next to "Power Keys" on the User Preferences card.

Paint Menu

Select	s	Selects last picture drawn. To select paint text, hold down the ⌘ key and press S immediately after typing the text.
Select All	a	Selects entire screen.
Fill	f	Fills selected area with pattern.
Invert	i	White turns black; black turns white.

Function	Equivalent Keyboard Command	Special Notes
Pick up	p	Draw a filled object on top of the picture you want to copy. Then press P to pick up a copy of that picture. Its borders will be in the shape of the filled object.
Darken	d	Darken selected object
Lighten	l	Lighten selected object
Trace Edges	e	Outlines drawing.
Rotate Left	[	Turn selection to the left
Rotate Right	]	Turn selection to the right
Flip Vertically	v	
Flip Horizontally	h	
Opaque	o	Whatever is selected turns opaque.
Transparent	t	Whatever is selected turns transparent.
Revert	r	Goes back to previously saved version.

Options Menu

Grid	g	Toggles grid on and off.
Line size	1,2,3,4,6, or 8	These numbers represent the choices of lines in the Line Size box, from left to right.
Draw Centered	c	Draws lines, rectangles, and ovals from their center.
Draw Multiple	m	Makes a copy of the selection. Holding downt the ⌘ and Option keys while dragging makes several copies of the selection.

Patterns Menu

Choose black pattern	b	
Choose white pattern	w	

APPENDIX D STACKS YOU SHOULD KNOW ABOUT

This appendix lists some of the best stacks available through most computer retail stores, software distributors, and organizations.

Commercial stacks (available through computer retail stores or directly through the publisher):

Name	Description	Publisher:
BusinessClass	Gives you quick access to information from over 65 different countries.	Mediagenics 2350 Bayshore Parkway Mountain View, California 94943-1177
FocalPoint	Helps you manage your time.	Mediagenics
DTP Advisor	A project manager, tutorial, and advisor for desktop publishing.	Broderbund Software, Inc. 17 Paul Drive San Rafael, California 94903-2101
HyperDA	Enables you to open HyperCard stacks from within other applications. You can look at stacks in Browse mode, but can't make changes to those stacks.	Symmetry Corporation 761 E. University Drive Mesa, Arizona 85203 (800) 624-2485 (outside Arizona) (602) 844-2199 (within Arizona)

Hyper BookMaker	Enables you to print cards in book form. Choose from different formats and print cards in any order. Print cards from several stacks. Prints on both sides of the paper.	IdeaForm Inc. P.O. Box 1540 612 W. Kirkwood Fairfield, Iowa 52556 (515) 472-7256
HyperTutor	Forty-one interactive lessons to help you learn how to program with HyperTalk.	Teligraphics P.O. Box 271 Ross, California 94957
HyperSound	Included with MacRecorder, a sound digitzer compatible with HyperCard.	Farallon 2150 Kittredge St. Berkeley, California 94704 415/849-2331
Clip Sounds	Contains 16 sounds. Enables users to import sounds to either VideoWorks II or HyperCard. This stack is compatible with sounds created by the MacRecorder Sound System, SoundCap, and SoundWave programs.	MacroMind Publishing 1028 W. Wolfram Chicago, Illinois 60657 312/871-0987
ScriptExpert	Enables you to create scripts for stacks without programming.	Hyperpress Publishing P.O. Box 8243 Foster City, California 94404 415/345-4620
Icon Factory	Enables you to create your own icons.	Hyperpress Publishing

Software Distributors:

N a m e	**A d d r e s s**	**Phone numbers**
EDUCOMP Computer Services	742 Genevieve, Suite D Solana Beach CA 92075	(800) 843-9497 for orders outside California. (800) 654-5181 for California orders.
	Distributes public domain and ShareWare software for Macintosh computers. Their catalog includes HyperCard stacks.	
Heizer Software	1941 Oak Park Blvd. Suite 30 Pleasant Hill, CA 94523	(415) 943-7667 for a free catalog. (800) 888-7667 to order the sample disk for $4.00 (includes free catalog).
	Distributes public domain and ShareWare software for Macintosh computers. Their catalog includes HyperCard stacks.	

The Walking Shadow Press

P.O. Box 2092
Saratoga, CA 95071

Publisher: Mike Westphal.

Distributes StackWare and HyperCard related products.
Also distributes "The Open Stack," a free newsletter about HyperCard
and HyperTalk.

Bulletin Boards:

N a m e	A d d r e s s	Phone numbers
CompuServe	5000 Arlington Centre Blvd. P.O. Box 20212 Columbus, OH 43220	
	You can buy the CompuServe Kit from any software retail store. You need the user ID and password in this kit to log on. Check out the APPHYPER forum. You can download stacks posted here.	
GEnie		800-638-9636 (voice)

Organizations:

Apple Programmer's and Developer's Association, APDA
290 SW 43rd StreetRenton, WA 98055
Phone: (206)251-6548

Apple HyperCard User Group, AHUG
10500 N. DeAnza Blvd. MS:27-AN
Cupertino, CA 95014

Bryan K. Carter
President, AHUG

AHUG Information HotLine (408)974-1707
(This number is subject to change without notice. Every attempt will be made to alert users/callers of any
changes.)

Free Stacks:

Name	Description	Created by:
Apple Glossary	A list of technical terms and their definitions. You can obtain a copy free from a Macintosh Users' Group.	The Apple Library
ResCopier	Enables you to copy resources such as sounds and icons from one stack to another easily. This stack was created by Steve Maller. You can get a copy of this stack from any Macintosh Users' Group or download it from CompuServe.	Steve Maller of Apple Computer
Groupies	Enables you to align buttons and fields.	Sioux Lacy of Apple Computer

Index

"CUT IT OUT"

That's what a lot of HyperCard merchants are telling us, because they don't want us to sell our stacks so inexpensively.

But if you want a good deal on some good stacks, just cut out the card below, enclose a check, and mail it in. If someone beat you to the card, send any readable facsimile.

Two disk are currently available (but more are arriving daily!):

Disk 1:   **The Book's Stacks** — all the stacks in this book, plus extras (like sound for the music stacks).

Disk 2:   **Learn French with Olivier** — a stack that talks back in French and teaches you how to get around in Paris or put snooty headwaiters in their place at home.

    Each disk is only $16.00 (which includes all shipping, handling, and taxes!)

    Make your check payable to: *HyperStuff*

    Mail to: *HyperStuff*
P.O. BOX 160535
Cupertino, CA   95016-0535

✂ cut   cut   ✂ cut   cut   ✂ cut   cut   ✂ cut   cut   ✂ cut   cut

Number of Disk 1 ordered: _____

Number of Disk 2 ordered: _____

Total number of disks ordered:_____

Amount Enclosed $_____

❐ **YES**, send me a free catalog of other good stacks.

Name_____

Address_____

City_____ State_____ ZIP_____

Please allow a couple of weeks for delivery